Angels and Demons:

The Personification of Communication

(Logology)

Stan A. Lindsay

Published by

Say Press
P.O. Box 691063
Orlando, FL 32869-1063

Copyright © 2020 by Stan A. Lindsay

Printed in the United States of America

All rights reserved. No part of this book shall be reproduced or transmitted in any form or by any means, electronic or mechanical, including photocopying, recording, or by any information or retrieval system, without written permission from:

Stan A. Lindsay

P.O. Box 691063

Orlando, FL 32869

ISBN: 978-0-9914793-5-1

Contents

Preface ix

Acknowledgements xxi

Chapter 1 When did the Angels Fall? 1

Chapter 2 The "Prometheus" Connection 7

Chapter 3 Where Have All the Fallen Angels Gone? 13

Chapter 4 "The Great Satan" of Iran 17

Chapter 5 What Law Did the Angels Break? 23

Chapter 6 An "Innocent" Fallen Angel Story 31

Chapter 7 Can Animals, Children, or Angels SIN? 37

Chapter 8 Sex and the Knowledge of Good and Evil 41

Chapter 9 Angels Have Only the Good Inclination 47

Chapter 10 The Fallen Angels of Jude and 2nd Peter 53

Chapter 11 Can Angels "on Earth" Sin, but Not Angels "in Heaven"? 63

Chapter 12 Angels Cannot Engage in Sex 73

Chapter 13 Who Are the "Sons of God" in Genesis?	79
Chapter 14 Can Angels Rebel against God?	91
Chapter 15 If He is NOT Satan, Who is Lucifer?	95
Chapter 16 Did Satan Disobey God by Refusing to Worship Adam and/or Jesus?	99
Chapter 17 *The Life of Adam and Eve* (Satan Refuses to Worship God's Image)	105
Chapter 18 God Commanded Angels to Worship Jesus, but Not Adam	109
Chapter 19 Satan Temporarily Laid Off (From his Second Job)	115
Chapter 20 Jacob's Ladder, with the Guardian Angels of Each Nation—Rising and Falling	125
Chapter 21 One Final (Sinless) Fallen Angel Story	131
Chapter 22 Recap of the Fallen Angel Stories	139
Chapter 23 Angels as the Personification of God's Word	149
Chapter 24 Angels as the Personification of God's Creative Fiats	153
Chapter 25 Angels as the Personification of God's Intrapersonal Communication	157
Chapter 26 The Angel of Truth (and the Spirit of Truth)	161
Chapter 27 The Spirit of Truth and God's Communication Network	165
Chapter 28 Angels as Agents of Divine "Feedback"	173
Chapter 29 Demons as the Communication of False Information	179
Chapter 30 Demons as False Entities	185
Chapter 31 Demons, Voodoo, Hypnosis, Hexes, and Psychogenic Illnesses	189

Chapter 32 The Rite, the Exorcist, and Severe Demon Possession in the Bible 195

Chapter 33 Diagnosis: Demon Possession or Illness? 203

Chapter 34 Revelation and Aggadah Concerning the Origin of Demons 213

Bibliography 217

Scripture Index 241

Index 249

To Two of my Scholarly Angels:

Beauford H. Bryant, Ph.D. (University of Edinburgh)

[My uncle, Professor of New Testament at Immanuel School of Religion in Tennessee.]

and

Henry A. Fischel, Ph.D. (University of Edinburgh)

[Holocaust survivor, my major professor in Hebrew and Rabbinic Culture at Indiana University]

Angels and Demons: The Personification of Communication (Logology)

Preface

Popular audiences have had an obsession with "angels and demons" in motion pictures, in the past three decades: Angels and Demons (2009), Michael (1996), Fallen (1998), Angels in the Outfield (1994), Angels in the Endzone (1997), City of Angels (1998), Angels in the Infield (2000), Constantine (2005), Gabriel (2007), Legion (2010), The Littlest Angel (2011), Dark Angel: The Ascent (1994), Little Nicky (2000), Ghost Rider (2007), Ghost Rider: Spirit of Vengeance (2012), Fallen (2015), and Dogma (1999), for example. Popular and scholarly audiences for books have likewise been fascinated with angels and demons. Harold Bloom, in his 2007 Yale University Press book *Fallen Angels*, sees a "present-day obsession with angels, which reached its greatest intensity as the current millennium approached." According to the world's largest bookseller, 137,175 book titles dealing with "angels" are available, along with 45,163 book titles dealing with "demons."

Nevertheless, pop culture perpetrates several myths regarding angels and demons that are alien to the literature of the Old or New Testament and early Rabbinic period. This book, however, pertains only to the angelology in that literature. Here are corrections some of the myths:

1. Lucifer is NOT the devil, Satan, or even a Fallen Angel or demon. Mentioned only in Isaiah, Lucifer (meaning "Shining One") is a nickname for the King of Babylon, who thinks he is god-like, but will die like any other man.
2. Satan is not an "evil god" who is at war with the Good God.
3. The fallen angel stories you have heard do not occur anywhere in the Bible.
4. Demons, such as the ones in the Exorcist with Linda Blair, or even in the Rite with Anthony Hopkins, are incorrectly portrayed, according the literature of the Old and New Testaments and early Rabbinic period. There is no levitation, no spinning heads, etc. in demon possession stories in the New Testament.
5. Demons, according to the Apostle Paul, do not even exist as actual entities; they are nothing: the equivalent of Idols or False Gods.
6. Angels have no capacity for having sex or for reproduction.
7. Angels cannot rebel against God. Even Satan is restricted to following the commands of God.
8. While angels can "fall," such a fall is not due to any specific "sin." Angels cannot sin.
9. Angels do not have "free will." They do not have "choice."
10. Stories about angels do not proliferate until the times of the Persian and Greek Empires, occurring between the end of the Old Testament and the beginning of the New Testament, attempting to accommodate the Persian theology about a good god vs. a bad god, and the Greek theology of multiple gods who marry human women. These Greek and Persian influences were systematically eliminated by Rabbinic Jews and New Testament authors.

Instead of these popular myths, what we find in Biblical and Early Rabbinic literature concerning Angels and Demons pertains to the Personification of Communication—one of my two scholarly disciplines! Later in his academic career, Communication legend Kenneth Burke focused increasingly on Logology, a subject he coined. The key term for Logology is "words," and the goal of Logology is to track down how "words" work. This book explores the ancient Biblical concepts of angels and demons as ways of explaining communication processes. The biblical words for angel--the Hebrew word MALAKH and the Greek word AGGELOS—both mean messenger; hence, for example, the cognate word ev*angel*ist is one who brings a good *message*. Angels have always represented communication processes. Even the Hebrew word SATAN means "prosecuting attorney" or "accuser"—i.e., other (professional) communicating positions.

Burke points to his interest in Logology in his last chapter in *Dramatism and Development*-- "Archetype and Entelechy."[1] The Greek term ARCHĒ (from which ARCHETYPE is derived) and the term TELOS (from which ENTELECHY is derived) are two of the four *causes* of Aristotle's grammar of motion/action/KINĒSIS. Briefly, Archetype is the focus of the anthropologist; Entelechy is the focus of Burke. They are looking at the same phenomenon from the two opposite ends of the spectrum. The anthropologist looks for the incunabula (the sense of beginning). What STARTED the KINĒSIS? Burke looks for the ending. What is the *final* purpose of the KINĒSIS? Of course, whenever one looks for "beginnings," one often finds oneself

---

[1] Kenneth Burke, *Dramatism and Development* [hereafter, DD] (Worcester, MA: Clark University Press, 1972), 33-55.

Angels and Demons: The Personification of Communication (Logology)

in Biblical eras. The fact that "first/ARCHĒ/beginning" and "last/TELOS/ending" can be combined into a single essence is not lost on the writer of the Book of Revelation who speaks of God and the Lamb as "the alpha and omega, the first and the last, the beginning and the end" (22:13).

To this book's title, *Angels and Demons: The Personification of Communication*, we could have added the phrase: The Incunabula of Logology. Long before Burke presented Logology as concerned "not directly with religion, but rather with the terminology of religion,"[2] biblical and Early Rabbinic texts were practicing a form of logology, similar to what Burke develops. For a detailed listing of locations where Burke uses the term logology, see the Bibliography.

Angels as the Personification of God's Creative Fiats

In Genesis 1:3, God speaks a capitalized Word ("Let there be light"). The very Word he speaks has the "omnipotence" to produce light. Isaiah 55:11 goes so far as to suggest that God's Word is infallible--it cannot fail. When introducing his concept of logology, Burke points to the Bible as a basis. The prologue to the Gospel of John in the New Testament contains a concept that appeals to Burke:

> In the beginning was the Word, and the Word was with God, and the Word was God. He [Word] was with God in the beginning. Through him [Word] were all

---

[2] See Kenneth Burke, *Rhetoric of Religion: Studies in Logology* (Berkeley and Los Angeles: University of California Press, 1970), vi.

things made; without him [Word] nothing was made that has been made. (John 1:1-3 NIV)

The Greek term translated "Word" is LOGOS. Burke considers himself a student of LOGOS; hence, instead of calling his discipline "theology," it is called "logology." Using Burkean equations: for John, Word EQUALS (or is a synonym for) God.

In the first chapter of *Rhetoric of Religion* (hereafter, RR), Burke, referring to this *Logos* hymn of John (1:1-3), draws analogies between (lower case) "words" and (capitalized) "Word" (RR 11). In addition to the prologue of John, Burke points his readers to Revelation 19:12-13, the creative fiat of Genesis 1:3 ("And God said, Let there be light"), or Psalms 33:9: "He spake, and it was done; he commanded, and it stood fast" (RR 11). Burke could have also cited Isaiah 55:10-11:

> As the rain and snow come down from heaven and do not return to it without watering the earth and making it bud and flourish, so that it yields seed for the sower and bread for the eater, so is [God's] word that goes out from [God's] mouth. It will not return to [God] empty, but will accomplish what [God] desire[s] and achieve the purpose for which [God] sent it.

Christianity and Judaism are not the only religions that refer to the creative power of Word. Burke, citing Cuthbert Simpson, also recognizes that "The representation that the divine word was the agent of creation is found in the Babylonian, Egyptian, and Indian cosmogonies" (RR 11). The notion that is put forth in these cultures is that there is a type of "Word" that has the power to control the physical universe, the "realm of motion," as Burke puts it in *Permanence and Change* (hereafter, PC).[3] If some type of "Word" controls physics, there is a different type of "word" by which humans attempt to control the "actions" of humans.

It has always seemed like an "abstraction" for humans to credit a "communication" with the power to accomplish something. To make the concept more "concrete," various personifications were attached to various Words of God. According to Judaism, when God spoke "light" into existence, He effectively created an Angel of Light. This would fit into Burke's concept of (capitalized) Word.

Angels, Humans, Free Will, and Lower-Case "word"

How, then, can God give a command (lower-case word) to Adam and Eve not to eat of the Tree of Knowledge of Good and Evil, and have that word fail to achieve its purpose? How is it possible that after the command from God was issued, Adam and Eve ate anyway? The second type of word God uses is (lower-case) "word," as with the "Thou shalt not's" of the Ten Commandments. When God implicitly "tested" man's free will by giving him a command not to eat of the Tree of the Knowledge of Good and Evil, He effectively created a "testing" angel. This is equivalent to Burke's (lower-case) "word." It also supports Burke's position that a hortatory negative introduced implicitly the "free will" or "choice" of humans. But the "testing" angel was not (itself) implicitly accorded "free will."

---

[3] Kenneth Burke, *Permanence and Change: An Anatomy of Purpose* (Indianapolis: Bobbs-Merrill, 1975), 274.

Neither the term Satan nor angel is explicitly mentioned in the testing episode in Genesis (3:1-8), but later in the Bible the episode will receive the angelic or Satanic attribution. The New Testament book of James, however, comments that an angelic or Satanic explanation is even unnecessary: "Every man is tempted, when he is drawn away of his own lust, and enticed. 15 Then when lust has conceived, it brings forth sin: and sin, when it is finished, brings forth death" (James 1:14-15).

Burke suggests that the theological distinctions between "word" and "The Word" presented above make a nice entry to discussions of the power of communication to affect humans. Burke implies his "action-motion dichotomy" in his distinction between lower-case "word" and capitalized "Word." Burke draws upon his "definition of [hu]man" in the discussion of the action-motion dichotomy:

> A duality of realm is implicit in our definition of [hu]man as the symbol-using animal. Man's animality is in the realm of sheer matter, sheer motion. [Capital Word] But his "symbolicity" adds a dimension of action not reducible to the non-symbolic--for by its very nature as symbolic [lower-case word], it cannot be identical with the non-symbolic. (RR 16)

In Burke's third analogy in RR based upon the "Word" vs. "word" distinction, he identifies the primary ground upon which such a distinction can be made--the negative. Clearly implied in any "Thou shalt not" is the element of free will or choice. Burke writes:

> But implicit in the distinction between Obedience and Disobedience there is the idea of some dividing line, some "watershed" that is itself midway between the two

> slopes. Often a word used for naming this ambiguous moment is "Will," or more fully "Free Will," which is thought of as a faculty that makes possible the choice between the yea-saying of Humble Obedience or the nay-saying of Prideful Disobedience…. Ontologically and theologically, we say that this locus of freedom makes possible the kind of personal choice we have in mind when we speak of "Action." . . . Implicit in the idea of an act is the idea of free will. (RR 187)

Angels, on the other hand, are not credited with having "free will." Neither are animals nor children. For Rabbinic theologians, adult humans have that "watershed" of which Burke writes—both the good and the evil inclinations--the YETZER HA-RA' (evil inclination) and the YETZER HA-TOV (good inclination). Adult humans (past the age of puberty) have the knowledge of both good and evil. They have a measure of free will that animals and children do not. They are capable of freely choosing to be either selfish or selfless. Once humans reach the age of puberty—12 for girls, 13 for boys—they are held responsible for their choices. Therefore, according to Jewish theology, ONLY BEINGS that POSSESS BOTH THE YETZER HA-RA' AND THE YETZER HA-TOV ARE CONSIDERED CAPABLE OF SIN. If a being (such as a child or an animal) does not have the full capability to choose freely between good and evil alternatives, that being is not held "accountable" for any sins. In present-day advertising law, we protect children from certain advertising practices because we do not consider them capable of correctly exercising free will. Jewish theologians say that, unlike animals and children, angels DO NOT possess ONLY the evil inclination: the YETZER HA-RA'. On the contrary, angels do not have the evil inclination at all! They possess ONLY the good inclination: the YETZER HA-TOV. They do not have selfish motives whatsoever. Everything they do is what is commanded by the One who created them. They are totally selfless—LIKE ROBOTS.

The Four Realms of Words

Burke, the logologist, categorizes the various "realms to which words may refer." In RR, Burke proposes "four realms to which words may refer" (RR 14ff.):

1. The first realm is "words for the natural . . . for things, for material operations, physiological conditions, animality, and the like." [These would almost always be Capitalized Words—and they have their own "angels"—Light, Death, Firmament, etc.]

2. The second realm is "words for the socio-political . . . for social relations, laws, right, wrong, rule, and the like." [Based upon the hortatory negative, these would almost always be lower-case words.]

3. The third realm is "words about words . . . dictionaries, grammar, etymology, philology, literary criticism, rhetoric, poetics, dialectics--all . . . in the discipline . . . 'Logology.'"

4. The fourth realm is "words for the 'supernatural.'" [Angels and demons have always been thought to fit into the fourth realm, but I am proposing that they actually fit into the third realm, Logology.]

Intrapersonal Communication

Free will or choice is, of course, not limited to whether to choose to obey or disobey, as in the hortatory negative context. Free will or choice, as Aristotle observes, may be applied to judicial situations—as in the internal struggles of a juror over whether or not the defendant is guilty or not guilty. Again, with Aristotle, free will pertains to deliberative or futuristic choices. What should we do in the future? Bereshit Rabbah 8.5 provides an account of an angel who was cast to earth because his conclusion regarding the wisdom of creating man conflicted with God's. It appeared to some rabbis that the Angel of Truth temporarily became a "fallen angel" because of his opposition to the creation of man. The Bereshit Rabbah account is based on Psalm 85:11-12a. A combat between Mercy and Truth, and Righteousness and Peace is presented as an argument over the creation of man. Mercy and Righteousness want him to be created, Truth and Peace do not. "*Intra*personal communication" is communication within one single individual person. This is rather abstract; therefore, angels are used by the theologians to personify the process, making it more concrete.

Demons as the Personification of False Communication

John's gospel quotes Jesus (8:44): "You have the devil for your father and you wish to practice the desires of your father; . . . he could not stay in the truth, because there is no truth in him. When he tells a lie, he speaks according to his nature; for he is a liar and the father of liars." Jesus is probably referring to Satan's role as a tempter. In a sense, all believed lies have the power of demons. The Ad Council ran a one-minute PSA from 2012 to 2019. Although the PSA was designed to combat bullying, it makes a perfect example of the point I am making regarding Demons as the personification of communication:

> "Today in school I learned a lot. In Chemistry, I learned that no one likes me. In English, I learned that I'm disgusting. And, in Physics, I learned that I am a loser. Today in school I learned that I am ugly and useless, and in Gym, I learned that I'm pathetic and a joke. In History I learned that I am trash. Today in English I learned that I make people sick. At lunch I sit alone because I smell. In Biology I learned that I am fat and stupid. And in Math I learned that I am trash. The only thing I didn't learn is why no one helps."
> https://www.youtube.com/watch?v=P18WLCoV7pY

The Spirit of Truth in I John 4:6 is contrasted with the Spirit of Error. The Spirit of Error seems to be connected with false prophets, in I John 4:1. In I Corinthians 10:18, Paul asks a rhetorical question: "What then is my suggestion--that an idol offering amounts to anything or that the idol itself is anything? No, but that what they sacrifice, they are offering to demons and not to God, and I do not want you to fellowship with demons." Paul has made "idols" equal "demons" and has stated (rhetorically) that "idols" are "not anything." Earlier, in I Corinthians 8:4, he had stated, "We know that no idol really exists; that there is no God but one."

If there is no God but one, and idols do not therefore exist, and offering to idols is the same as offering to demons, we may conclude that "DEMONS DO NOT EXIST." THEY ARE FALSE ENTITIES. One might even go so far as to suggest that the "false information" itself becomes a spiritual force that affects humans.

What do demons, voodoo, hypnosis, hexes, and psychogenic illnesses have in common? They are all physical manifestations of things that do not exist in any realm other than the symbolic. They do not actually exist in the physical realm and they are not truly divine beings. Nevertheless, they do have the power to affect human beings, because humans are by nature symbol-using animals, according to Kenneth Burke. The "false information" itself becomes a spiritual force that affects humans.

In the PSA mentioned earlier, the false communication to students that they are disgusting, losers, ugly, useless, pathetic, a joke, fat, stupid, and trash are just demons—the personification of false communication—that has, nevertheless the power to negatively affect humans.

One caveat about this book: There are numerous citations from foreign language sources (Hebrew, Greek, German, etc.). Do not let this deter you from reading. The foreign language citations are always accompanied by English translations.

Stan A. Lindsay, Ph.D.

Orlando, FL

January 1, 2020

Acknowledgements

The writing of this book began in 1971 when, as a master's student of Hebrew at Indiana University, Professor Henry A. Fischel began to open the world of Rabbinic literature to me. World War II and the Holocaust had concluded only a few decades earlier. Dr. Fischel was, himself, a Holocaust survivor, but he never mentioned the fact to me. I learned only after reading his obituary from 2008 that he had spent several months in a Nazi concentration camp. His mother, nine uncles and aunts, and three cousins perished in the Holocaust. When I asked him about his family, he quickly changed the subject.

Dr. Fischel knew that I was a Christian who had taken only two years of Classical Hebrew in my B.S. program at Lincoln Christian University when he readily accepted me into the M.A. in Hebrew program at Indiana and became much more than my major professor. He personally taught virtually all of the courses in my master's program, many of them individual study courses. Dr. Fischel was a pioneer in studying the interconnections of Rabbinic Hebrew literature and Hellenistic Greek literature. I owe Dr. Fischel for teaching me scholarly method, for introducing me to the world of (Jewish) Tannaitic and Amoraic Hebrew literature, for helping me recruit a

New Testament scholar (J. Paul Sampley) and an Islamic scholar (Wadie Jwaideh) to serve on my master's thesis committee, for pointing me in the direction of countless Rabbinic sources on the subject of "angels" in the Indiana University Bloomington library, and for directing my M.A. thesis, "Anamartetous Fallen Angels." I acknowledge Dr. Fischel, first and foremost, for his contributions to this book. I also acknowledge and thank Dr. Sampley (later, of Boston University) and Dr. Jwaideh.

Classical Greek and New Testament scholars who guided my pathways in Classical rhetoric and New Testament studies were Dr. Jack Bateman of the Department of Classics at the University of Illinois, Dr. Vernon Robbins of the University of Illinois (later, of Emory University), Dr. John T. Kirby of Purdue University (later, of the University of Miami), and Dr. Donald L. Jennermann of Indiana State University.

Burkean and contemporary rhetorical scholars who guided me were Dr. Don M. Burks of Purdue University, Dr. Donald L. Jennermann of Indiana State University, and Dr. John M. Patton of the University of Illinois (later of Tulane University). While Dr. Patton introduced me to the works of Kenneth Burke, Dr. Burks, the director of my Ph.D. dissertation ("The Burkean Entelechy and the Apocalypse of John"), mentored me in the intricacies of Burke's insights, and Dr. Jennermann assured me that my applications of Burkean methods to the New Testament were scholarly. The Burkean concept of Logology (attributable to Burke, not Burks) is a major perspective of this work.

Chapter 1
When Did the Angels Fall?

If the angels fell during creation week, why did no one mention it? The six days of creation recorded in Genesis 1 say nothing about the creation of angels. They were not explicitly mentioned as being present with God when he created the heavens and the earth. They were not mentioned in any of the six days, as God created light, firmament, seas, plant life, animal life, or man. It is necessary to explore Rabbinic Jewish literature (Hebrew writings written AFTER the New Testament) to even find speculation on when they were created.

Rabbinic Judaism (from 200 to 400 A.D.) teaches that angels were created on the second day of creation,[4] although some differing opinions vary from the first[5] to the fifth[6] day; and there is even

---
[4] For abbreviations of biblical, intertestamental, patristic, and Rabbinic sources, etc., confer the appended "Bibliography." BR 1.3, 3.8, and 11.9; Tanḥuma Bereshit I.1&12; Midrash Shir ha-Shirim Rabbah 15.22; Pirke R. Eliezer 4; Midrash Tehillim 24,204, 76,373-374, and 104,442; and Midrash Konen 25.
[5] Jubilees 2.2; II Enoch 29.3; and Apocalypse of Baruch 21.6.
[6] Louis Ginzberg, *The Legends of the Jews*, Vol. V (7 vols.; Philadelphia: The Jewish Publication Society of America, 5728-1968), 20.

the contention that some angels existed prior to creation.[7] Regarding the Fall of the Angels, this date likewise varies from the creation week[8] to later in the history of man.[9]

What is significant, however, is that the discussion of the creation of angels and the Fall of the Angels did not occur until much later than the supposed event. It was not until the Hellenistic period of Jewish history (between 300 and 50 BCE) when Jews were under the control of the Greeks (Alexander the Great and his successors) that the Fall of the Angels became a topic of much conversation.[10] The concept of fallen angels is alien to the Old Testament. Nevertheless, in those years following the completion of the Old Testament, there is a flood of literature containing information on the subject.

Interestingly enough, within the literature of the new associates of the Jewish people, the Hellenistic Greeks, there is an abundance of material that, in many ways, closely parallels the various accounts of the Fallen Angel Story. Leo Jung explains: "That divine beings, even gods,

---

[7] Zohar Hadash 11b and 12a.
[8] To invalidate the protest of the Angel of Truth against the creation of man, God cast the angel down from heaven to earth. Ginzberg, *Legends*, I, 53. See further Chapter 20 of this book. Also, the fall of the Rebel Satan can be placed within the creation week. See II Enoch 29.4&5; Targum Job 28.7.
[9] The vast majority of sources place the Fall of the Angels at the time of Genesis Chapter 6. New Testament apocalyptic places the fall of Satan and his angels in the first Christian century Luke 10:18, Revelation 12:9.
[10] For a review of the argumentation surrounding the Fallen Angel concept in the Hebrew Scriptures, see Bernard J. Bamberger, *Fallen Angels* (Philadelphia: The Jewish Publication Society of America, 5712-1952), 7-14, where Bamberger demonstrates convincingly that the concept is alien to the Hebrew Bible.

have sexual intercourse with women was a well-known view, nay, a creed of Hellenistic religion."[11] We can safely assume that Greek culture had a reasonable effect on the fallen angel theme from its very outset. To be sure, many of our sources discussing the fallen angels are even written in the Greek language.

My major professor in my Master's in Hebrew degree program at Indiana University, Henry Fischel, writes:

> It is fortunate that at this stage of scholarship no further defense has to be made for the assumption that Greco-Roman situations were well-known to the creators of the Midrash, i.e, the literature that modifies the word and world of Scripture by interpretation, explicitly or implicitly. Rather, the problem is how far this knowledge went, how much of Greco-Roman academic procedure and philosophical quest was useful in that on-going process, in which the culmination of the tannaitic culture, c. 200 A.D. (the codification of the Mishnah) and that of Palestinian amoraic culture, c. 400 [A.D.] (the Jerusalem Talmud) were important stages.[12]

In this book, I discuss what we know about Angels, Fallen Angels, and Demons. Most of what people think they know about this subject is filled with legends, myths, and errors. Pop culture perpetrates several false myths regarding angels and demons that are alien to the literature of the Old or New Testament and early Rabbinic period. These myths need to be corrected:

---

[11] Leo Jung, *Fallen Angels in Jewish, Christian, and Mohammedan Literature* (New York: KTAV Publishing House, Inc., 1974), 92.
[12] Henry A. Fischel, *Rabbinic Literature and Greco-Roman Philosophy* (Leiden: E. J. Brill, 1973), xi.

1. Lucifer, from Isaiah 14:12-14, is the devil, Satan, or a Fallen Angel. Mentioned only in Isaiah, Lucifer (meaning "Shining One") is understood to be god-like (Satan), but will die like any man.
2. Satan is an "evil god" who is at war with the Good God.
3. The fallen angel stories most have heard actually occur in the Bible.
4. Demons, such as the ones in The Exorcist with Linda Blair, or even in The Rite with Anthony Hopkins, are correctly portrayed, according the literature of the Old and New Testaments and early Rabbinic period. There is levitation, spinning heads, etc., in demon possession stories in the New Testament.
5. According to the Apostle Paul, demons do exist as actual entities; they are the equivalent of false gods.
6. Angels have the capacity for having sex, for reproduction.
7. Angels can rebel against God. Satan is not restricted to following the commands of God.
8. Angels can "fall" and such a fall is due to a specific "sin."
9. Angels have "free will." They have "choice."
10. Stories about angels proliferate before the times of the Persian and Greek Empires, occurring before the end of the Old Testament; they verify the Persian theology about a good god vs. a bad god, and the Greek theology of multiple gods who marry human women. These Greek and Persian influences were not systematically eliminated by Rabbinic Jews and New Testament authors.

The New Testament is significantly consistent with Rabbinic Jewish literature on the subject, but "interpretations" of the New Testament have been distorted and clouded by the literature that appeared between the end of the Old Testament and the beginning of the New Testament. The period between the two Testaments is the Hellenistic period. It is a time in which Jewish writers tried to please their Greek masters by suggesting that their religion was very similar to Greek religion. Unfortunately, Greek religion was polytheistic and Greek gods were very sexual. While monotheistic Judaism was unwilling to present God as sexual, it latched onto the possibility that angels (who were plural, as opposed to the one-and-only God) may have engaged in sexual activity.

The subject of angels and demons is approached, in this text, from the perspectives of New Testament Christianity and Rabbinic Judaism, twin milieus that existed in the same time period. Both milieus were being influenced, as Fischel contends, by Hellenistic culture, but both milieus were recalcitrant. They were unwilling to accept certain premises: polytheism, the capability of angels to reproduce, the capability of angels to rebel, the capability of angels to sin. Christians and Jews systematically reworked the Hellenistically-tainted angelology they had inherited.

The subject of angels and demons in the New Testament and Rabbinic Jewish milieus is also approached from the perspective of Communication theory. Kenneth Burke's concept of logology (the study of theological words--not with an emphasis upon the theological, but with an emphasis upon how theological terminology helps to explain human communication)[13] plays an important role in the understanding presented, here, of how angels and demons actually functioned

---

[13] See Burke, RR.

logologically in the two milieus. As it turns out, the Communication perspective that Burke proposes with his concept of logology produces a much more useful understanding of angels and demons, in this period, as being the personification of communication.

The next chapter looks at the Greek connection. For now, readers, take note: It is no coincidence that Jewish discussion of sexual angels surfaces at the same time Jews were trying to please Greeks.

Chapter 2
The "Prometheus" Connection

One attempt at identifying fallen angels in the Old Testament centers on the Day of Atonement as discussed in Leviticus 16. The Berkeley Version of Leviticus 16:7-10 mentions a certain "Azazel," which some have identified as a fallen angel:

> He shall take the two he-goats and set them before the Lord at the entrance of the Dwelling and Aaron shall cast lots over the two he-goats, one lot for the Lord and the other for Azazel. Aaron shall bring the goat on which the lot for the Lord fell and shall prepare it for a sin offering; but the goat on which the lot for Azazel fell shall be presented alive before the Lord to make atonement with it by sending it for a scapegoat into the desert.

Notice that this scripture passage does not contain any mention of angels or demons. A footnote in the Berkeley Version states: "The name Azazel is derived from Azalzeh (dismissed one) thus properly thought of as a scapegoat."

As I mentioned in the previous chapter, in those years following the completion of the Old Testament, there is a flood of literature containing information on the subject of fallen angels. Perhaps, the most important book on the subject from that period between the Old and New

Testaments is the book of I Enoch. The book claims that the Genesis 6 passage referring to the "sons of God" marrying the "daughters of men" should be understood to mean that "angels" married "human women." I will deal in a future chapter with the issue of who these "sons of God" in Genesis 6 actually were, but I recommend that we not leap too quickly to the interpretation found in I Enoch.

In I Enoch 15:3, Enoch preaches to the fallen angels—the spirits in prison: "Why have you given up heaven . . . and cohabited with women . . . the daughters of men, and taken wives for yourselves . . . ?" According to I Enoch 54:5, iron chains were being prepared for the host of Azazel. This host will be thrown into the abyss, with jagged stones. I Enoch 65:6-7 speaks of the angel's secrets that were passed on to humans, including sorcery, incantations, and working with melted metals such as silver, lead, and tin. In other words, the fallen angels taught mankind to make tools and use fire. They brought culture to mankind.

Much of Enoch's account of fallen angels sounds like the Greek story of Prometheus. The striking similarities to various Prometheus motifs yield evidence of Hellenistic influence in the development of the Fallen Angel theme. German Jewish scholar Martin Hengel says that the analogy to the Clash of the Titans of Greek mythology lies closer to the Fallen Angel Story than does Persian dualism. He suggests that the fallen angels, like the Prometheus of Aeschylus, bring important cultural benefits and knowledge to man:

> Die Analogie zum Titanensturz des griechischen Mythos liegt hier näher als der iranische Dualismus; zumal die gefallenen Engel wie der Prometheus des Aischylos den Menschen gewisse Kulturgüter und geheimes Wissen offenbarten.[14]

Another German Jewish scholar Paul Volz says that the fallen angels brought to man all secrets of the heavens and gave to them the magic wand of world culture: "[Sie] führten die Menschen in alle Geheimnisse des Himmel sein und gaben ihnen den Zauberstab der weltlichen Kultur."[15] Greek mythology is drawn from multiple literary contributions. These pieces of literature often contradict other pieces of literature, but some elements of the Prometheus story (drawn from different accounts) sound familiar. In his *Legends of the Jews*, Louis Ginzberg[16] mentions the fact that some Jews of the period following the writing of the New Testament knew about Prometheus and connected him with Adam. Consider the following elements, gleaned from Greek mythology:

Zeus punished several of the Titans for fighting against him in the "Clash of the Titans," but since Prometheus had not sided with his aunts, uncles, and brother, Zeus spared him. Zeus then assigned Prometheus the role of working with man. Some literary sources even suggest that Zeus gave Prometheus the job of creating man out of the earth—hence, the Adam connection. Whether or not he created man, Prometheus developed a close friendship with men. Zeus did not want men to have power, especially over fire. But, Prometheus, as a friend of man, stole fire from Zeus'

---

[14] Martin Hengel, *Judentum und Hellenismus*, (Tübingen: J. C. B. Mohr, 1969), 347-8.
[15] Paul Volz, *Die Eschatologie der Jüdischen Gemeinde im Neutestamentlichen Zeitalter*, (Hildesheim: Georg Olms Verlagsbuchhandlung, 1966) 311.
[16] Ginzberg, *Legends*, V, 112.

lightning, hid it in a giant hollow stalk of fennel, and gave it to man. Prometheus also stole warfare and blacksmithing skills from the gods and gave them to man. He brought culture to mankind. As punishment, Zeus "bound" Prometheus and tormented him.

Enter the book of I Enoch. Since the book of I Enoch was actually written in Greek, the author was, no doubt, capable of being influenced by Greek thought. It seems quite logical that his account of Azazel and the culture-bearing fallen angels borrowed its plot from the Prometheus motifs. In an attempt to show religious compatibility with Greek culture, the author of I Enoch was anxious to demonstrate that his own scriptures—specifically, Genesis and Leviticus—contained the same account, with slight variations. But did they?

Although Genesis has God creating man from the dust of the Earth, it is much more than a "slight" variation to have man created by a being of the rank of Prometheus. While the story of "rebel fallen angels" (which I will discuss in Chapter 14) is not mentioned in the I Enoch account, the story of "sexual fallen angels" (which I will discuss in Chapter 12) is featured quite prominently there. Nevertheless, this sexual nature of Greek gods does not seem to figure prominently in the Prometheus story. There is, however, the common thread: both of these stories have a lower-in-the-hierarchy divine being(s) bringing the use of fire and culture to man and being subsequently punished by being bound.

Of course, missing from the Genesis account of man's creation, the account of the "sons of God" marrying the "daughters of men," and the Leviticus account of Azazel is any mention of these events involving the bringing of fire or culture to mankind. One exception might be God's making clothes of skins for Adam and Eve (after they had made clothes of fig leaves), but God is neither faulted nor punished for such an act.

In English, the word Azazel may look like a possible angel's name. Many angels' names (such as Gabriel and Michael) end in "el" [אֵל] which is probably short for "Elohim" [אלהִים], the Hebrew word for God. However, the spelling in Hebrew requires an aleph [א] immediately before the "l" [ל]. There is no aleph in the "el" portion of Azazel [עֲזָאזֵל]. In explaining the meaning of the term "Azazel," the Talmud gives a definition that Leo Jung, in his book *Fallen Angels*, clarifies:

> עזאזל The cruel, rough Azel. This may have been the original meaning, before the fallen angels were brought into contact with it, changing the rock into a demon. Azel as a rock occurs in I Sam. 20.19. With this would agree Yoma 67b: The rabbis taught (the official view as against the individual ones which follow) Azazel: 'That is the name of a rough and rocky mountain.' . . . After the official explanation of Azazel, the one which lived as the right one in the consciousness alike of priest, teacher and layman, the Talmud in its usual broadness of mind gives access to the play of folklore.[17]

The New Testament NEVER mentions Azazel or any hint of fallen angels bringing culture to mankind. Romans 5:11 mentions "atonement," but there is no sense of anything being given to a demon or fallen angel. Instead, Jesus is mentioned in an allusion to the scapegoating that secures atonement (i.e., covering of sins) for Paul's audience.

---

[17] Jung, *Fallen Angels*, 156.

My conclusion: I Enoch is wrong. The notion of fallen angels who brought culture to mankind is not biblical. It is the invention of a Greek-speaking Jew who wanted to gain favor with his Greek masters. If I Enoch got it wrong about Azazel and the culture-bearing fallen angels, we should certainly be skeptical about his introduction of angels who marry human women—especially in a Greek culture that believed all gods had sexual relations. But, more on that in future chapters.

Chapter 3
Where Have All the Fallen Angels Gone?

Although I never met him, Bernard Bamberger is the author of the most authoritative book from the late 20th century on *Fallen Angels* written from a Jewish perspective. I have a few things in common with him:

- Bamberger was the Rabbi of Temple Israel of West Lafayette, Indiana, from 1929-1944; I was a member of the West Lafayette Christian Church that met temporarily in the Temple Israel building in West Lafayette from 1979 to 1981, when I was there.

- I had gleaned a great deal of information from Bamberger's book throughout the 1970s, as I wrote my master's thesis on *Anamartetous Fallen Angels* in partial fulfillment of my Master's in Hebrew from Indiana University.

- Bamberger reached very nearly the same conclusions with regard to official Jewish literature that I reached with regard to New Testament literature as these literatures dealt with the issue of fallen angels.

Here is Bamberger's conclusion from his book:

> The astounding thing is that, after some centuries of experimentation with this idea, the authoritative teachers of Judaism dropped it altogether. . . . The main line of Jewish thought returned to an uncompromising monotheism in which there was no room for satanic rebels.[18]

In the Old Testament, there were no fallen angels. Then, right after the Old Testament, hundreds of fallen angels emerged. Then, by the New Testament, the fallen angels have disappeared again! That's amazing. In light of the flood of literature on fallen angels from the period between the Old and New Testaments, the obvious disqualification of the bulk of the fallen angel material from the official/codified scriptures of Judaism and the literature surrounding them is striking. The Hebrew Bible is silent on the subject and the official Jewish literature from the early Christian era is virtually silent on the subject. Furthermore, with the exception of a few very brief references to the story (which I shall explain in future chapters), the New Testament is virtually silent on the subject. Where have all the fallen angels gone?

One possible explanation is as follows. Jewish society did not get along with its Roman rulers in the years following Jesus' death and resurrection, as it had gotten along with its Greek rulers in the early Greek Empire. The Jews experienced a devastating seven-year war with the Romans that included the destruction of Jerusalem in 70 A.D. Many Jews were taken into captivity; all of Israel was crushed by the Romans. It may well be that the increased tensions between the Jews and their Roman rulers provided the rationale for the abrupt discontinuation of many of these Hellenistic

---

[18] Bamberger, *Fallen Angels*, 55.

themes in Jewish angelology. In fact, it is interesting that the Church Fathers were the first to restore some of these Greek and Roman religious concepts of fallen angels. Christianity was fast becoming the new religion of the Roman Empire. There would be no real obligation on the part of the Church Fathers to divorce these western concepts from their theology. Rather, the opposite (attempts to show the reasonably close resemblance) would appear to be beneficial to the Church's cause.

However, I think that early Rabbinic Judaism and New Testament Christianity just became apprehensive about the dangers of Persian, Greek, and Roman religions and how these pagan religions had been instrumental in producing the Fallen Angel Stories during the time Jews had been under the control of these cultures. Whatever the reason, the Fallen Angel Stories are virtually gone by the time of the New Testament. We are hard-pressed to produce any material from the tannaitic-amoraic period of Judaism (the period surrounding and immediately following the New Testament) or from the New Testament itself to support the Greek, Roman, or Persian themes in the Fallen Angel Stories. Since the Roman gods are, more often than not, just renamed Greek gods, I will not spend time discussing Roman religion. In the next chapter, however, I will address Persian religion as it affected Fallen Angel Stories. As we consider Greek and Persian religion, I think readers will see how erroneous concepts of Satan and fallen angels developed, and how the New Testament and Rabbinic Judaism countered these developments.

Angels and Demons: The Personification of Communication (Logology)

Chapter 4
"The Great Satan" of Iran

The Ayatollah Khomeini, whom *Time* magazine named "Man of the Year" in 1979,[19] and who became the Supreme Leader of Iran when the Shah of Iran was deposed during the Jimmy Carter administration, is famous for labeling America: "The Great Satan." It is fitting that someone from Iran speaks of "The Great Satan." Iran is another name for Persia, and in the years prior to the Persian Empire, Persian religion developed the concept of an Evil God who was constantly at war with a Good God. In other words, Persians/Iranians are largely responsible for giving the culture its popular misconceptions about Satan. Before discussing "The Great Satan," a quick tracing of world history, as it pertains to the history of the Jews, is in order:

The BABYLONIAN Empire 627-539 B.C. (King Nebuchadnezzar of Babylon carried the Jews away into captivity in 567 B.C. The prophet Daniel and his friends—Shadrach, Meshach, and

---

[19] "Man of The Year: The Mystic Who Lit The Fires of Hatred," *Time*, January 7, 1980.

Abednego—were among the young men who were captured. Daniel predicted the eventual Fall of Babylon to the Persian King Cyrus.)

The MEDO-PERSIAN Empire 539-323 B.C. (Jewish princess Esther became the Queen of Persia from 492 to 460 B.C. Around 400 B.C., under the rule of Persia, the last two books of the Hebrew Bible were written—Ezra and Nehemiah—as these two men reestablished the Jewish religion in Jerusalem.)

The GREEK Empire 323-146 B.C. (In a period entirely between the Old and New Testaments, the Greek religious influence was strong. This is called the Hellenistic period. During this time, the Maccabees mounted a successful Jewish revolt against Greece. Greek ruler Antiochus IV (Epiphanes) defiled the Jerusalem Temple with Greek religious practices and forbade the practice of the Jewish religion.)

The ROMAN Empire (146) B.C.-476 A.D. (While the Romans conquered Greece in 146 B.C., they really did not become an "Empire" until their first "Emperor" Augustus Caesar in 27 B.C. Augustus was the Emperor during whose reign Jesus was born. Christians will certainly remember the decree that went forth from Augustus Caesar. Augustus was, most likely, the First Head of the seven-headed Beast referred to by John in Revelation 13.)

One reason the influences of the Greeks and Persians on the Fallen Angel Stories is missed by so many Christians is that these influences occurred mostly during the void of 400 years spanning the end of Old Testament history and the beginning of New Testament history. Readers may wonder why so much time is being spent debunking the mistaken notions about fallen angels. The simple answer is that it is necessary to "unlearn" all of the FALSEHOODS so that one can clearly see the TRUTHS. The New Testament and Rabbinic Judaism were largely fighting against these perceived falsehoods (as will be demonstrated in future chapters). In my book, *Revelation: The Human Drama*, I comment:

> Some interpreters of Revelation consider the informing anecdote of the book to be the conflict between God and Satan. This perceived conflict is a vestige of Judaism's contact with Persian religion. Martin Hengel discounts such "iranische Dualismus" [or Persian Dualism] in accounting for the scene which, for example, produced the "fallen angel" stories in the centuries preceding the New Testament period. In perusing John's Revelation, examples of a direct rivalry between God and Satan cannot be found. While allusions are made to "fallen angels" in Revelation, it is not clear that they are typical of the Fallen Angel Stories of the centuries preceding the Christian Era.[20]

By this comment, I mean what I stated before: "Persian religion developed the concept of an Evil God who was constantly at war with a Good God." There is no picture in the Old Testament of a Satan who could rival God. The Hebrew word "SATAN" [שָׂטָן] means "adversary" or "prosecuting attorney." That is all Satan was in the Book of Job. He certainly had not "fallen" from Heaven by then. Job 1:6 has Satan joining the angels (sons of God) in presenting themselves before God. He petitions God for permission to "test" Job. He certainly does not demand anything of God. This "testing" role is also the one he assumes in the New Testament as he "tests" Jesus in

---

[20] Stan A. Lindsay, *Revelation: The Human Drama* (Bethlehem: Lehigh University Press, 2001), 73.

the desert, following his baptism. At the end of Jesus' life (Luke 22:31), Jesus informs Simon Peter that Satan has asked permission to sift him like wheat. This sounds to me like the same Satan who was in the courts of Heaven in Job. Many of my university students view me as a professor who gives difficult tests. It's probably true. Because of that fact, some of them view me as an adversary. So, if Satan forces us to endure difficult "tests," we may easily view him as the "adversary" of MAN. Nevertheless, whether as students or simply as humans, we gain dignity by enduring and passing difficult tests. Kenneth Burke states: "People who are experts at solving puzzles will prefer hard ones."[21] I explain this comment as pertaining to a sort of Competence Stress that we actually enjoy experiencing (eustress) in my book *The Seven Cs of Stress*.[22] As explained later (in Chapter 11), Louis Ginzberg[23] summarizes the theological teaching of the rabbis at the time of the New Testament: "Although man, who is a terrestrial being, is inferior to the angels, he surpasses them by overcoming the evil inclination, which the angels do not possess at all (BR 48.11)." The conclusion of Rabbinic writings then is that the "pious are therefore greater than the angels."[24] Both Burke and the rabbis agree that solving difficult puzzles or passing difficult tests lend humans dignity.

---

[21] Kenneth Burke, *Language as Symbolic Action: Essays on Life, Literature, and Methods* (Berkeley, Los Angeles, and London: University of California Press, 1966), 298.

[22] Stan A. Lindsay, *The Seven C's of Stress: A Burkean Approach* (Orlando, FL: Say Press, 2004), 87.

[23] Ginzberg, *Legends*, V, 24.

[24] The Chapter 6 innocent fallen angel account from *Beth ha-Midrash*, though it does not mention the evil inclination specifically, allows room for the interpretation that the evil inclination may have influenced the angels. On the other hand, its exclusion from that account, whereas, other versions of the legend do mention it, may be indicative of the author's intention (in the innocent

But, where is the hint in either the Old or New Testament that Satan is the adversary of GOD? God cannot be tested, according to James 1:13, and Satan "asks permission" from Him to test us. Some readers will immediately refer us to the "Lucifer" passage in Isaiah 14:12, but be careful! Nowhere does this passage mention "Satan." There is no such "Great Satan." (I'll write more on this passage in chapters 14, 15, and 22.) If one reads "Satan" into the passage, one is READING THE PASSAGE FROM THE PERSPECTIVE OF PERSIAN RELIGION. The thirtieth Yasna, the ancient Zoroastrian worship texts from Persia, states:

> Well known are the two primeval spirits correlated but independent; one is the better and the other is the worse as to thought, as to word, as to deed, and between these two let the wise choose aright.

This scripture from Persian religion tells us where this popular concept of Satan originated. Satan and God, according to Persian dualism, would be the two INDEPENDENT, PRIMEVAL SPIRITS. One is good and one is bad. Individuals must choose between them.

Interestingly, the Apostle Paul even sees Satan as a useful agent in the salvation process. I Timothy 1:20 says that Paul surrendered Hymenaeus and Alexander to Satan, so that they might be disciplined. In a similar vein, I Corinthians 5:5 has Paul counseling the church to hand over a fornicator to Satan so that Satan can destroy the fornicator's "flesh," in order that the fornicator's "spirit" might be SAVED. Satan can apparently drive humans to repent. That is useful.

---

fallen angels account) to avoid any conflict with a well-established teaching that the angels lack that inclination.

Do not misunderstand. I am not arguing that Satan is good. I am just pointing out that he is NOT the "Evil God" some make him out to be. He tests humans. In that sense, even though the serpent in Eden was not specifically called a "satan," in Genesis, the New Testament correctly identifies him as such. When he finds that we are guilty, he is the prosecuting attorney, accusing us before God. Once God judges us, Satan is the executioner. These are all negative roles, from the human perspective. Jesus came to put Satan out of a job. Jesus told his disciples, in Luke 10:18, that he had a vision of Satan falling from Heaven, like lightning. In Revelation 12:7-12, John sees Jesus' prophecy fulfilled with Satan being cast out of Heaven (by Michael, not by God) when Jesus died on the cross. Satan was thrown out because his job as "accuser" was no longer needed. Jesus' blood had secured forgiveness. No accuser is necessary in Heaven.

Chapter 5
What Law Did the Angels Break?

Fallen Angel Stories are typically justified on the basis of some sin--some perceived Law that the angels broke. Look through the Ten Commandments. Do you see any commandment targeted at angels? I do not. The Law was given to humans, not angels. But, even so, let's consider whether angels could have been guilty of breaking one of these Laws (Exodus 20:1-17):

1. "You shall have no other gods." Angels, we would assume, know the truth . . . that there ARE NO OTHER GODS, right? I suppose that, if Persian Dualism were accepted, there would be one other god—the evil god. That's what "dualism" means: that there are TWO gods—one good and one evil. By the time Jesus was born, however, Judaism was apprehensive about the dualistic implications involved in the fallen angel theme. If Greek theology were accepted, there would be dozens of gods—all marrying each other and having sexual relations with humans and having offspring—both divine and human. After toying with these polytheistic (multiple gods) ideas for nearly 400 years, Jewish teachers were determined to fight against them. If believers today are determined to resurrect these Persian and Greek theologies, they may themselves be guilty of breaking the first

commandment (Thou shalt have no other gods), but did angels break this commandment? Rhetorical question.

2. "Do not make graven image." No angel stories tell of any angel making an idol. Although Adam was created in the image of God (something I discuss in chapters 13, 16, and 25) and Angels are actually instructed to worship Jesus (but not Adam) as the image of God (something I discuss in chapters 17 and 18), both Adam and Jesus are human (fleshly) "images" of God—not graven images.

3. "Do not take my name in vain." In a non-inspired angel story from the time period of the New Testament, angels knew the name of God and knew the power of pronouncing his name. The story suggests that pronouncing his name brings one to the very throne of God. To keep humans from taking his name "in vain" (i.e., using it in an empty way), the Jews hid the pronunciation. "Jehovah" is NOT the pronunciation of his name. The Jews "wrote" his name, but only used the consonants of his name: YHWH (יהוה). They inserted vowels, but these vowels were not the vowels from his name; they were the vowels to the word "Adonai" (אֲדֹנָי) Adonai is translated "Lord." When one takes the vowels from Adonai and inserts them among the consonants from YHWH (or JHVH), the result is the word Yahowah (or Jehovah). The English letters Y and J are interchangeable (both being transliterations of the Hebrew letter י), as are the letters W and V (both being transliterations of the Hebrew letter ו). Anyone who knows the German language, for example, knows that the German expression for yes (Ja wohl) is actually pronounced "Yah Vohl." Hence, Yahowah becomes Jehovah. Actually, the Jews never pronounced this composite word.

They pronounced only the word Adonai (Lord), so that they would not take "The Lord's name" in vain. When one reads an English version of the Old Testament, and finds the word "Lord," what is actually written in the Hebrew text is the word YHWH. It is unpronounceable, because the Jews were helping individuals avoid breaking this commandment. (Incidentally, even the popular pronunciation of this word today—Yahweh—is almost certainly incorrect. It is still very difficult for one to literally violate this commandment.) Nevertheless, there are NO angel stories that tell of an angel taking the name of the Lord in vain.

4. "Remember the Sabbath Day and keep it holy." No angel stories tell of any angel breaking the Sabbath.

5. "Honor your father and mother." Angels don't have mothers. While Jesus teaches humans to address God as "Our Father in heaven," and while God calls humans his children, angels do not seem to share in that intimacy. It is true that angels were called "sons of God" in the Book of Job, but no one seriously contends that angels are the offspring of God in any parent-child sense. Ultimately, no angel stories ever accuse angels of failing to honor their "father."

6. "Do not kill." Fallen Angel Stories do not portray the angels as murderers. John's gospel, on the other hand, quotes Jesus responding to certain Jews who were seeking a way to kill him (John 8:37-44): "You have the devil for your father and you wish to practice the desires of your father; he was a slayer of men (ἀνθρωποκτόνος) from the beginning, and he could not stay in the truth, because there is no truth in him. When he tells a lie, he

speaks according to his nature; for he is a liar and the father of liars." Jesus was probably referring to the devil's roles as tempter/tester and executioner. I John 3:8 explicitly states that the devil sins from the beginning. This is probably the sense John had in mind: the devil was a manslayer and a liar. Hebrews 2:14 speaks of Jesus as neutralizing the one who wields the power of death, namely the devil. The first time the term Satan appears in the Bible is in the Book of Job, where Satan not only tests Job but also KILLS his wife and children. God restricts his power so that he cannot KILL Job himself, because Job is righteous. For those of us who are not so righteous as Job, Satan does indeed pose the threat of death. But, is this killing of humans a sin? Is Satan breaking the Law by killing men? Not if we deserve it. Romans 6:23 says the wages of sin is death. Romans 3:23 says all have sinned. In my previous chapter, I observed: "I Timothy 1:20 says that Paul surrendered Hymenaeus and Alexander to Satan, so that they might be disciplined. In a similar vein, I Corinthians 5:5 has Paul counseling the church to hand over a fornicator to Satan so that Satan can destroy the fornicator's 'flesh,' in order that the fornicator's 'spirit' might be SAVED." Ultimately, however, Jesus came to rid mankind of the various "roles" of Satan. Revelation 12 introduces the Fall of Satan as a result of Jesus' sacrifice. Satan can no longer "accuse" the brothers in the heavenly courts, because they are forgiven. However, Revelation does not assert that "accusing the brothers" was a sin; it was Satan's job in Heaven, just as punishing and executing sinners on Earth was. Revelation 20 begins by further subjugating Satan: he is bound and thrown into the Abyss. Revelation 20 ends (at least one thousand years later) by casting the devil into the Lake of Fire, which is the

Second Death. At that point, Satan will be gone—but not because he sinned. He will be gone because there will no longer be a need for any of his roles—tempter/tester, accuser/prosecuting attorney, punisher/executioner, or raiser of world empires.

7. "Do not commit adultery." Adultery consists of having sexual relations with someone else's wife or husband. Having sex with one's own wife or husband is not a sin. Even if Genesis 6 were correctly interpreted as suggesting that angels married human women, would that be a sin? We don't know of any commandments given to angels not to marry humans, and the idea of "marriage" is definitely in the Genesis 6 passage. Whoever the "sons of God" in Genesis 6 are, they are not raping the "daughters of men" or having sex with them outside the bonds of marriage. They are "marrying" them. Since this is the most significant version of the Fallen Angel Story in the Greek period, we will return to the issue of angels having sex with humans in Chapter 12. Jesus seems to suggest that it is impossible. But, for now, we are just considering what Law angels may have broken. We do not know of any Law against marrying human women.

8. "Do not steal." If, as I discussed in Chapter 2: The "Prometheus" Connection, Azazel and the fallen angels had (like Prometheus) STOLEN fire and cultural arts from God, they might be accused of breaking this commandment. However, I Enoch 65:6-7 speaks of the angel's secrets that were passed on to humans, including sorcery, incantations, and working with melted metals such as silver, lead, and tin—but never accuses the angels of STEALING such things. Furthermore, this Fallen Angel Story of bringing culture to

humans is not found anywhere in the New Testament. I surmise, therefore, that this is ALSO NOT a Law broken by angels.

9. "Do not bear false witness." This is a tough one, but it never shows up in Fallen Angel Stories. As I mentioned when discussing "Do not kill," John's gospel quotes Jesus (8:44): "You have the devil for your father and you wish to practice the desires of your father; . . . he could not stay in the truth, because there is no truth in him. When he tells a lie, he speaks according to his nature; for he is a liar and the father of liars." As I also mentioned, Jesus is probably referring to Satan's role as a tempter. If, as the New Testament asserts, the serpent of Genesis is actually Satan, it is clear that he lies. He said, "You shall not surely die." The serpent was, as a result of his act, cursed: the offspring of woman would eventually crush his head. Is this, then, the Law broken by an angel that could result in a Fallen Angel Story? It has possibilities, but, strangely enough, the Fallen Angel Stories do not make that much out of it. Jesus mentions that Satan is a man killer and a liar, but when Satan is cast out of Heaven in Revelation 12, it seems to have happened because there was no longer any room for him in Heaven. Why wait until Jesus' sacrifice to cast him out, if he has been a liar from the beginning? Even though Revelation calls him the "deceiver of all humanity," one wonders if his deceit simply amounts to something like putting a False statement in a True-False test. Yes, it is a lie, but the student is being tested to see if s/he recognizes it as such. Am I sinning when I give my students True-False tests? Rhetorical question. Since the time of Job, Satan has been presented as a prosecuting attorney. If the

commandment not to "bear false witness" is taken in a legal sense, Satan in Job does not bear false witness against Job. He tests him, but he does not falsify any evidence in order to convict him. Similarly, in Revelation 12, where Satan is the "accuser" of the brothers, he is not guilty of falsifying evidence, *per se*.

10. "Do not covet." Unless it was connected to the commandment "Do not commit adultery," no Fallen Angel Stories seem to claim that this specific Law was broken by angels. Even if connected to the sexual angel story, there seems to be no indication that the women whom the angels married belonged to someone else. Hence, the Law against coveting does not apply.

Why did we consider whether angels broke any of the Ten Commandments? Because, some sort of justification is needed for a Fallen Angel Story. Usually, that justification is found in some perceived "sin" of the angels. In the next chapter, I will relate a story. This is a fictional story, but it was written about the time of the New Testament. It tells of fallen angels who DID NOT SIN, but fell anyway. It attempts to justify a Fallen Angel Story without claiming a sin on the part of the angels. Why might that justification be?

Angels and Demons: The Personification of Communication (Logology)

Chapter 6
An "Innocent" Fallen Angel Story

Remember that the Fallen Angel Story invented by the Greek-speaking Jewish author of I Enoch relied on his interpretation of the Genesis 6 passage referring to the "sons of God" marrying the "daughters of men." He thought the passage should be understood to mean that "angels" married "human women." These unions between angels and humans produced as children "mighty men of old who made a name." This is somewhat strange. First, to assume that angels have DNA is fairly far-fetched, since angels, according to Psalm 104:4, are "spirits" and "flames of fire." One would think DNA would be necessary in order to produce offspring. Second, if the offspring shared the DNA of angels and humans, one would suspect that some of these offspring would be men, but others would actually be angels. Why is it that the offspring of these unions produced ONLY MEN—albeit, MIGHTY men of old who made a name?

Returning to the book of Genesis, only one other passage even remotely suggests that angels could engage in sexual behavior—let alone be reproductive. Genesis 19 tells of two angels visiting Lot in Sodom before God destroyed Sodom and Gomorrah. In 19:5, the men of the city, the Sodomites, surrounded Lot's house and demanded the right to rape these angels—who, they presumably thought, were men. We will never know if such behavior would have been possible, because Lot, in an attempt to protect the angels, offered the mob his own virgin daughters, instead. The Sodomites rejected the offer and threatened to rape Lot. The angels, of course, did not really need Lot's protection. They pulled Lot inside his house and struck the Sodomites with blindness. No one has ever accused these angels of being guilty or fallen angels, even though there was a "hint" that they could have been raped. It occurs to me that the angels in the Sodom account might have provided the inspiration for the following approach to the Fallen Angel Story from Jewish culture at around the time of the New Testament. Here, we also have a "hint" that angels may have been capable of sexual encounter, but—like the angels in Sodom—such an encounter never occurred.

This seems to be a distinct attempt to reform the Fallen Angel Story into something compatible with the strongly Jewish, non-Hellenistic attitudes of the New Testament period and following. This is not the only attempt to produce a Sinless Fallen Angel Story from this period, but it demonstrates the point that Jews were trying to reshape the Fallen Angel Story into something that would be less offensive to Jewish theology.

SINLESS FALLEN ANGELS

From the medieval commentary Hadar Zekenim (in its exposition of Genesis 6:2) comes a small account of the "revised" Fallen Angel Story. It is the story of a woman who was transformed into a star (or group of stars). When the angels descended to Earth, they propositioned a certain virgin. They wanted to "marry" her. Wise young lady that she was, she tricked them. She promised to

6: An "Innocent" Fallen Angel Story

agree to their proposition on one condition: they must give her their wings. Upon receiving the wings, AND PRIOR TO THE CONSUMMATION OF THE SEXUAL UNION, she flapped her wings and flew away to God's throne. According to a slightly different version of this story, she made no deal whatsoever. She just asked them what they would give her, if she obeyed them. They offered to give her their wings and to teach her to pronounce the (unpronounceable) name of the Lord (YHWH, as discussed in the previous chapter). Without an explicit agreement, the angels did both of these things. (Perhaps, in order to maintain the argument that the young woman was still sinless, as a NA'ARAH [נערה "lass"], the author/s did not even want to suggest that the young woman was guilty of lying or breaking a promise/vow). The young woman then flew to Heaven—presumably, pronouncing God's name and flapping her wings. God rewarded her for her innocence and her resisting the transgression. Either she was made into the constellation Virgo or the constellation Virgo was named for her.[25]

Following are the text and my translation from these two Mishnaic Hebrew texts, which so far as I know, are not available elsewhere in English translation:

VERSION 1:

כי טובות הנה ובמדרש טובת כתיב נערה בתולה צרקת היתה וכשירדו בני האלהים א״ל תשמעי לנו וא״ל לא אשמע לכם אם לא תעשו את הדבר הזה שתתנו לי כנפים שלכם כד״א שש כנפים לאחד נתנו

---

[25] The text being utilized is from A. Jellinek, *Beth ha-Midrasch: Sammlung Kleiner Midraschim und vermischter Abhandlungen aus der alteren judischen Literatur,* Vol. V (6 vols.: Leipzig: C. W. Vollrath, 1853-77; reprinted, Jerusalem: Wahrmann, 1967), 156.

לה כנפיהם מיד פרחה לשמים ונמלטה מן העבירה ואחזה פני כסא וקב״ה פרש על׳ה עננו וקבלה וקבעה במזלות והיינו מזל בתולה והמלאכ׳ם נשאו בארץ ולא 'כלו לעלות עד שמצאו סולם ש׳עקב אב׳נו חלם ועלו חה״ד והנה מלאכ׳ האלהים עול׳ם ו׳ורד׳ם בו

"'For they were beautiful.' (Gen. 6:2): In the Midrash Tobath [apparently, a lost midrashic fragment on Genesis 6:2 in which the word 'TOBATH,' meaning 'beautiful,' occurs] it is written: There was once a pious virgin lass. And when the 'sons of God' (Gen. 6:2) descended, they said to her, 'Obey us!' She said to them, 'I shall not obey you unless you do this thing—that is, that you give me your wings; as it [Isaiah 6:2] says, "six wings for each one."' They gave her their wings. Immediately, she flew to Heaven and escaped from the transgression, and she touched (the surface of) the Throne. And the Holy One—Blessed be He—spread his cloud over her and received her, and he fixed her among the constellations: namely, the constellation Virgo. The angels remained on Earth and were not able to ascend until they found the ladder of which Jacob our ancestor dreamed; then, they ascended. This is of which it is written: 'the angels of God ascending and descending upon it' (Gen. 28:12)."

VERSION 2:

מלאכ׳ האלהים עול׳ם ו׳ורד׳ם בו   אותם מלאכ׳ם ש׳רדו כאשר ראו בנות האדם ה׳פות לא עלו עד עתה כ׳ כש׳רדו מצאו בתולה אחת אמרו לה שמע׳ לנו אמרה להן ומה תתנו ל׳   אמרו לה כנפ׳ם שלנו ונלמדך שם המפורש וילמדו לה שם המפוריש ויתנו לה כנפ׳ם   מיד פרחה בשמים   אמר לה וקב״ה הואיל וברחת מן העבירה אקבע לך שם במזלות והיינו מזל בתולה   והמלאכ׳ם שנתנו לה כנפ׳הם לא יכלו לעלות עד עתה שמצאו סולם לעלות

"'The angels of God ascending and descending upon it' (Gen. 28:12): Those angels who descended, when they saw the daughters of man that they were beautiful, did not ascend until this time; for [at the time] when they went down, they found a certain virgin. They said to her, 'Obey us!' She said to them, 'And what will you give to me?' They said to her, 'Our wings. And we will teach you the Explicit Name.' And they taught her the Explicit Name and they gave her the wings. Immediately, she flew into the Heavens. The Holy One—Blessed be He—said to her, 'Since you fled from the transgression, I will appoint for you a name among the constellations; namely the constellation Virgo.' And the angels that gave to her their wings were not able to ascend until this time, when they found the ladder to ascend."

These two versions of the same account present fallen angels to whom no sin is attributed. Hence, they may be termed Sinless Fallen Angels. In the next few chapters, I will elucidate the details of the relationship between this account and the prevailing doctrines concerning angels in the early Christian era. There are definite BIBLICAL doctrinal motives for reforming the Fallen Angel Story into one in which the angels DID NOT SIN. We will begin the next chapter with the very doctrine of sin and whether angels are capable of it.

Chapter 7
Can Animals, Children, or Angels SIN?

Is it possible for my little dog Bandita, a cute, tiny Havanese puppy, to sin? Not according to official Jewish teachings. Why? Bandita does not possess both the good and evil inclinations. She possesses only the "evil inclination"—what Jews call the YETZER HA-RA' (יצר הרע). Although we sometimes anthropomorphize animals—such as Lassie (the canine movie star), Trigger (Roy Rogers' horse), and Flipper (the dolphin)—to make them appear to have a good inclination, animals do things for essentially SELFISH reasons. Ask any animal trainer how one secures desired behavior on the part of an animal and you will find that selfishness prevails on the part of the animal. Whenever the desired behavior occurs, the animal is rewarded, using the pleasure principle. Continual training using this selfish reinforcement is called "operant conditioning." Eventually, animal trainers train dogs, horses, dolphins, birds, etc., to behave in ways that "can be interpreted" by anthropomorphizing humans as conforming to a "good inclination"—what Jews call the YETZER HA-TOV (יצר הטוב)—but these "good" behaviors are actually selfish behaviors, induced by reward (the pleasure principle) or punishment (the pain principle).

Is it possible for children to sin? Not according to official Jewish teachings—for the same reason animals cannot sin. Children do not possess the YETZER HA-TOV, according to the Jewish Mishnah,[26] until they reach the age of 12 or 13 (12 for girls, 13 for boys). Prior to that age, they possess only the YETZER HA-RA'. They—like animals—are essentially selfish. This is why at age 13, Jewish boys are given a BAR MITZVAH (literally: "son of the commandment"). Girls, at the age of 12, have a BAT MITZVAH ("daughter of the commandment"). They are not even expected to be able to live according to the Commandments until that age. They are considered sinless, even though they are (like animals) essentially selfish. However, the Mishnah suggests that we begin training children to keep the commandments, a few years before they reach the age of accountability. The young girl who tricked the angels in my previous chapter had just reached the age of 12. There is a specific Hebrew word that indicates the fact: NA'ARAH (נערה "lass.") She had been sinless prior to this encounter with the angels, due to her age. Since she passed her first specific test and avoided the transgression, she was rewarded by God (with eternal life).

Is it possible for adult humans to sin? To quote Sarah Palin, "You betcha!" Adult humans have both the YETZER HA-RA' and the YETZER HA-TOV. They have the knowledge of both good and evil. They have a measure of free will that animals and children do not. They are capable of freely choosing to be either selfish or selfless. Virtually all (but not actually ALL) adult humans have sinned, according to the Bible, and come short of the glory of God. Even though we, at times,

---

[26] The pertinent Hebrew and English text from the Mishnah (Yoma 8:4) is supplied in Chapter 8. See also Ginzberg, *Legends* V, 81.

act unselfishly (in accordance with the YETZER HA-TOV), every one of us has also, at times, acted selfishly (in accordance with the YETZER HA-RA'). Once humans reach the age of accountability, they are held responsible for their sins. ONLY BEINGS POSSESSING BOTH THE YETZER HA-RA' AND THE YETZER HA-TOV ARE CONSIDERED CAPABLE OF SIN. If a being (such as a child or an animal) does not have the full capability to choose freely between good and evil alternatives, that being is not held "accountable" for any sins. God does not hold a being responsible for doing something that being was incapable of doing.

So, is it possible for angels to sin? Not according to official Jewish teachings. This is not because, like animals and children, angels possess only the YETZER HA-RA'. On the contrary, angels do not have the evil inclination at all! They possess only the YETZER HA-TOV. They do not have selfish motives whatsoever. Everything they do is what is commanded by the One who created them. They are totally selfless. But, they are not considered as high in God's hierarchy as are humans. This is because SOME humans who are capable of sinning CHOOSE NOT TO SIN. Angels never even have the opportunity to prove that they would choose correctly. They have no choice. They have no free will. The reason you will find no commandments in the Bible directed at angels (as we considered two chapters ago) is that there would be no point. Angels have no commandments because they are not free moral agents. They cannot sin.

Chapter 8
Sex and the Knowledge of Good and Evil

Jesus, in Matthew 22:36-40, summarized all of the commandments with the one word "love": Love the Lord with all your heart, soul and mind and love your neighbor as yourself. On these two "love" commands, according to Jesus, hang all of the Law and the Prophets. It is fitting, then, that God waited until humans were capable of love/selflessness to give them the ability to reproduce sexually. Animals engage in sex for selfish reasons—they have urges that demand to be met. Many humans, certainly, engage in sex for selfish reasons, as well. Perhaps, virtually all humans engage in sex for selfish reasons, at times. But, at least, humans have the option of acting selfishly or unselfishly. This fact relates to the fallen angel issue.

In human beings, the two YETZARIM (יצר ים/inclinations) are closely identified with sexual or reproductive stages of life. The Babylonian Talmud (Sanhedrin 91b), Midrash Kohelet Rabbah 4:13, Midrash Ha-Gadol Bereshit 108-109, et. al., teach that the YETZER HA-RA' (evil inclination) came to man at birth. Louis Ginzberg notes: "the good inclination does not make its appearance before . . . the time of puberty."[27] The Babylonian Talmud (Yoma 82a) points out that the official age for girls is 12 years. Midrash Kohelet Rabbah 4:13, Midrash Ha-Gadol Bereshit 108-109, and Midrash Tehillim 9,82 place the official age for boys at 13. Interestingly, Adam and Eve did not notice their own sexuality/nakedness until they had eaten of the "Tree of the Knowledge of Good and Evil." And they were not commanded to "be fruitful and multiply" until after they had eaten.

It is very significant that the girl of version I of the sinless fallen angel story related earlier is described in Hebrew as a NA'ARAH (נערה "lass"). According to Marcus Jastrow,[28] NA'ARAH is a legal term specially designating a "girl between twelve and twelve and a half years of age." This incident is very possibly her first real temptation since receiving the YETZER HA-TOV (good inclination). Since she responded righteously in this single instance, it could explain her being permitted to come immediately before the Throne of God, a feat that would have been inconceivable even for angels unless they were sinless.[29]

This indicates that it was necessary for an individual to have both "inclinations" in order to be held accountable for sin (and, for that matter, to be deemed righteous for passing the test/temptation).

---

[27] Ginzberg, *Legends*, V, 81.
[28] Marcus Jastrow, *Dictionary of the Targumim, the Talmud Babli and Yerushalmi, and the Midrashic Literature*, (Brooklyn: P. Shalom Publishing, Inc., 1967), II, 921-2. Cf. also J. Levy, *Chaldäisches Wörterbuch über die Targumim und einen grossen Theil des Rabbinischen Schriftthums*, (Book on Demand, 2014).
[29] Ginzberg, *Legends*, V, 169, comments: "though the angels had entertained evil thoughts, they never carried them out, otherwise their return to Heaven would hardly have been conceivable."

8: Sex and the Knowledge of Good and Evil

The rich young ruler, with whom Jesus interacts regarding eternal life in Luke 18:18-21 and parallels, insists that he has kept the "commandments" from his youth (ἐκ νεοτητος). It is arguable that he means from the time of his bar mitzvah forward. Hebrews 4:15 asserts that Jesus himself was tempted in every respect, as we are, but was without sin. We know nothing, however, about the childhood of Jesus. After the birth narratives, there is no discussion of Jesus' actions until we near his bar mitzvah. Luke picks up the narrative again, in 2:41, when Jesus was age twelve. The same theology that allows Jewish writers to tell a story of a "lass" being righteous in one temptation following her youth and being awarded eternal life is the same theology that allows Christian writers to conclude that the sinless life of Jesus permits him to be transfigured on the mountain, and later, resurrected from the dead.

Since the "lass" possessed only the "evil inclination" prior to her twelfth birthday, any selfish behavior committed prior to this time must not have been considered "sinful." This is precisely the view (the sinlessness of children) that prevailed at this time. Even the second book of Maccabees 8:4 speaks of των ἀναμαρτήτων νηπίων ("the sinless infants"). And the Mishnah (Yoma 8:4) says, concerning the Day of Atonement (Yom Kippur):

> התינוקות אין מענין אותן ביום הכפורים אבל מחנכין אותם לפני שנה ולפני שנתים בשביל שיהיו רגילין במצות
>
> "Little children [anyone just born through 13 years for boys and 12 years for girls] are not made to fast on the Day of Atonement; however, we should be initiating them beforehand one or two years in order that they will be in the habit of [following] the commandments."

It is a simple deduction that, if little children are not required to participate in the yearly atonement exercise, they must not be held guilty of any "sins" for which they would need atonement. Albrecht Oepke, a German Christian scholar, writing in Kittel's *Theological Dictionary of the New Testament*,[30] debates the assertion that Judaism accepted "the innocence of children" because, he says, "the evil impulse is there from conception or birth." That much I readily concede. Animals, likewise, have the evil impulse from conception or birth, but no one accuses animals of sinning. Consequently, in light of the passage just quoted from the Mishnah, which we may definitely call "authoritative," little children must in some way be considered sinless, or at least not responsible for their sins. I suspect that the "Lutheran" Oepke may have his own axe to grind, since Lutherans baptize babies for the forgiveness of their sins. If babies are actually sinless, there would be no need to forgive any sins. Perhaps, the point of Jesus' comment concerning little children that "of such is the kingdom of heaven" is that children are innocent, incapable of sinning.

---

[30] Albrecht Oepke, "παῖς, παιδίον, παιδάριον, τέκνον, τεκνίον, βρέφος," in *Theological Dictionary of the New Testament* (henceforth: Kittel), ed. Gerhard Friedrich (and G. Kittel), Transl. and ed. G. W. Bromiley, (Grand Rapids, MI: Wm. B. Eerdmans, 1968), V, 646-7. Oepke rejects the view that Judaism accepted "the innocence of children," though he cites "the thesis of R. Jehoschua (c. 90) that the children of the ungodly in the land of Israel will attain to the future world." That thesis, he argues, "was contested by others." Oepke notes such statements as "The child is not yet responsible up to 1 yr. or even up to 9 yrs., and to that degree it is not sinful, Pesikt., 61b; Pesikt. R., 16 (84a); Ket., 1, 2, 4; 3, 1; bJeb., 60b; Tanch. בראשית 4b, but he warns: "one cannot systematize the individual statements." In advancing his own view, he appears to rely heavily on the doctrine that "the evil impulse is there from conception or birth."

Even if children are simply not responsible for their sin—possessing only the evil inclination—we may very easily suspect that angels who possess only the good inclination would probably be considered sinless, too. Such is the case. I will present the pertinent proof, in the next chapter.

Chapter 9
Angels Have Only the Good Inclination

Based on the Hebrew text of Genesis 18:5, Judges 19:5, and Psalms 48:14 and 104:15, various Jewish rabbis from the early Christian Era (Isaac, Aḥa, and Ḥiyya) point out that the "heart" (לבב inclination) of humans is different from the "heart" (לב inclination) of angels. They assert: "The evil inclination has no power over angels." Furthermore, "The evil inclination will not return [to humans] in the hereafter" (Bereshit Rabbah 48:11).[31] Jesus seems to agree to some extent that

---

[31] Bereshit Rabbah 48:11, Ed. Theodor-Albeck, I, 488-489:

ואקחה פת לחם אמר ר' יצחק בתורה ובנביאים ובכתובים מצינו דהיא פיתא מזונית דליבא בתורה ואקחה פת לחם וסעדו לבכם בנבאים סעד לבך פת לחם ובכתובים מנין ולחם לבב אנוש יסעד אמר ר' אחא וסעדו לבבכם אין כתי אלא לבכם ח"ה שאין יצר הרע שולט במלאכים חיא דעתיח דר' חייא דאמר ר' חייא שיתו ליבכם לחילה אין כתי שיתו ליבבכם ח"ה שאין יצר הרע חוזר לעתיד לבא

TRANSLATION: "And I will fetch a morsel of bread" (Gen. 18:5)—Rabbi Isaac said: In the Torah and in the Prophets and in the Writings we find that bread is the comfort [MSS variants have "sustenance" and "strengthening," according to Theodor-Albeck notes] of the heart. In the Torah: "And I will fetch a morsel of bread, for you [pl.] must strengthen your [pl.] heart." In the Prophets: "You [sg.] must strengthen your [sg.] heart with a morsel of bread" (Judges 19:5). In the Writings: "And bread [which] strengthens the heart of man" (Psalm 104:15). Rabbi Aḥa said: It is not written, "And you must strengthen your heart (לבב), but rather

48   Angels and Demons: The Personification of Communication (Logology)

humans in the hereafter will have characteristics similar to angels (Mark 12:25, Matthew 22:30, and Luke 20:36), but he does not specifically state that this similarity with angels centers around only possessing the good inclination. Nevertheless, it seems inconsistent with a Christian view of the hereafter to envision resurrected humans capable of sinning, once again. The view of angels as lacking the evil inclination dominated Jewish teaching on angels at the time of the New Testament. Citing the Bereshit Rabbah 48:11 passage, Art(h)ur Marmorstein, a highly respected Rabbinic scholar who taught at Jews' College, London, from 1912 to 1946 (and author of the entry

---

your heart (לב). [The shorter form (לב) not the longer spelling (לבב) is used for the word heart, and Rabbi Aḥa considers this significant.] This proves that the YETZER HA-RA' has no power over angels. This opinion is Rabbi Ḥiyya's [also], for Rabbi Ḥiyya says: "Turn your [pl.] hearts to the dance" (Ps. 48.14). [H. Freedman (and Maurice Simon, eds.), *Midrash Rabbah*, Vol. I: Bereshith, (London: Soncino Press, 1939), 413 explains that the Rabbis "read 'le-ḥolah' rather than 'le-ḥelah' (ramparts), and take this passage to refer to the life of happiness (dance) in the Hereafter.] It is not written "turn your hearts (לבבכם)," but "your hearts (ליבכם)." [Again, the shorter form for the word "hearts" is used, and Rabbi Ḥiyya considers this significant.] This proves that the YETZER HA-RA' does not return in the Hereafter.

FURTHER COMMENT FROM THE AUTHOR: The statement of Rabbi Aḥa is the key statement in this passage. Quoting from Genesis 18:5, Rabbi Aḥa notes that the men for whom Abraham was willing to fetch a morsel of bread were angels. Therefore, it is the heart (or inclination/YETZER) of the angels that we are considering. Rabbi Aḥa considers the term heart (לב) used here as a synonym for YETZER (יצר). Furthermore, since Genesis uses the shortened form (לב) rather than the more dominant biblical Hebrew form (לבב), Rabbi Aḥa concludes that the limited form must indicate that the YTTZARIM (plural of YETZER) of angels must be limited (i.e., to only one YETZER, namely, the YETZER HA-TOV). Therefore, he assumes that the YETZER HA-RA' has "no power over angels." The same type of reasoning is then applied by Rabbi Ḥiyya concerning humans in the Messianic future. Whether this "midrash" is sound exegesis or not is irrelevant. The fact is, this view of angels (as lacking the YETZER HA-RA') dominates the angelology of our period. .

on "Angels and Angelology" in the *Encyclopaedia Judaica*) makes the sweeping statement: "The angels . . . are free of the YETZER HA-RA."[32]

In the Babylonian Talmud Shabbat 88b-89a, Moses is depicted explaining to angels why the Law was not given to them. The Law, according to Moses, is not suitable for angels because they do not have the evil inclination in them. The angels agree.[33]

Midrash Shir Ha-Shirim Rabbah 8.11 quotes Rabbi Judan as offering an analogy of a boy who had lost several of his fingers—nevertheless, trying to learn the art of embroidery or silk-working. Even if an expert teacher were hired, his instruction would be in vain because the boy could not possibly learn it. The essence of the art of embroidery depends on the use of the fingers. Likewise, the angels are incapable of using the Law because they lack something essential to its use. God is quoted as saying: "לאו לית שוקא נפיק מן גביכון ו" (Certainly, no satisfaction results from [the angel's] compliance [with the Law])." Marcus Jastrow explains in his *Dictionary*: "Your compliance with the Law would afford no satisfaction to Me, because you have no temptation and trials to contend

---

[32] Art(h)ur Marmorstein, ed., "Angels and Angelology," *Encyclopaedia Judaica*, (Jerusalem: The MacMillan Company, 1971), I, 968. Cf. also J. Michl, "Engel II (jüdisch)," *Reallexikon für Antike und Christentum*, Theodor Klauser, Ed., (Stuttgart: Anton Hiersemann, 1962), V., 80.

[33] The angels actually engage in a debate concerning whether or not the Torah should be given to men. This is also an example of how angels are the personification of God's intrapersonal communication—something that is discussed again in Chapter 25. The angels do not understand why Moses is ascending to receive the Law. "What is man that thou art mindful of him?" they ask. Moses is compelled by God to answer them, so he asks them rhetorical questions concerning their use of the law. His point is that the Law is not suitable for them. Why? יצר הרע יש ביניכם (Is the YETZER HA-RA' among you?), Moses asks. They concede that it is not.

with."³⁴ It is clear that this passage also holds with the teaching that angels lack the evil inclination. They are not free moral agents.

This embroidery parable is found also in Midrash Tehillim 8:74 (to which I will return again in Chapters 12 and 21) and in Pesikta Rabbati chapter 25, page 128a. These passages underscore the sinlessness of angels and assert that they are sinless by nature. According to most official Jewish views from the New Testament period,³⁵ angels cannot sin because they do not have an evil inclination.

AFTER THE NEW TESTAMENT PERIOD, Christians did begin to teach that the Fallen Angels fell through sin. Justin Martyr, somewhere around 150 A.D., wrote in Dialogue 79 from his "Dialogue with Trypho (a Jew)" describing Trypho as becoming irate concerning the suggestion that Fallen Angels fell through sin.³⁶ Though the specific sin Trypho rejected was the sin of "rebellion" (which I will discuss in Chapter 14), Trypho appears to reject the notion that angels could sin at all as being "blasphemous!" In this present book, no defense is made for the teachings of patristic Christian writers--even those so revered as Justin Martyr. In my opinion, according to New Testament and Rabbinic angelology, Justin was mistaken and Trypho the Jew was correct in this instance. I believe the New Testament supports Trypho's view more than it does Justin's.

---

³⁴ Marcus Jastrow, *Dictionary*, II, 1541.
³⁵ Amoraic and tannaitic.
³⁶ Justin, "Dialogue with Trypho," Dialogue 79, from *Iustinus Philosophus et Martyr*, ed. Otto, 3ʳᵈ ed., Vol. I of *Corpus Apologetarum Christianorum*, (Ienae: Prostat in Libraria Hermanni Dufft., 1876), 284. This dialogue is fully cited/quoted in Greek and English in Chapter 14.

9: Angels Have Only the Good Inclination

IN THE NEW TESTAMENT, angels are mentioned 170 times—virtually all of these passages depicting sinless angels. Of these 170 times, only two times is it suggested that angels are capable of sinning: 2 Peter 2:4 and Jude 6. Certainly, it is necessary for us to examine these two passages—which are quite similar in many ways. For that discussion, please see the next chapter.

Angels and Demons: The Personification of Communication (Logology)

Chapter 10
The Fallen Angels of Jude and 2nd Peter

The Book of Jude contains only thirty verses. Of those thirty verses, more than half (sixteen, according to the Nestle-Aland Greek text of the New Testament[37]) have parallels in the Book of 2 Peter. Most scholars agree that there is a dependency relationship between these two books, but disagree on which book came first and which may have borrowed from the other. These two tiny books are the only New Testament books that explicitly refer to the Fallen Angel story of the book of I Enoch. The Nestle-Aland Greek text of the New Testament also lists four references to the book of I Enoch in the thirty verses of Jude. It seems clear that the author of Jude was familiar with Enoch material. It is not as clear that 2 Peter was as familiar with Enoch material as was Jude. Nowhere does the Nestle-Aland Greek text of the New Testament list a reference to I Enoch

---

[37] Eberhard Nestle and Kurt Aland, eds., *Novum Testamentum Graece*, (London: United Bible Societies, 1967).

in 2 Peter. Nevertheless, in discussing the angels who are being kept, awaiting "judgment," 2 Peter 2:4 is the only text that asserts that these may have been "sinning" angels, and adds that the angels were being held in "Tartarus." Surely, the author got the "sinning" angels detail from I Enoch, but did he get the "Tartarus" detail from I Enoch, as well? I do not think so. Jude 6 is the only text that supplies the information that the angels were kept in "chains." According to I Enoch 54:5, iron chains were being prepared for the host of Azazel, whom I mentioned earlier, in Chapter 2. Azazel is the fallen angel from I Enoch who brought culture to mankind, as did the god Prometheus of the Greeks. Prometheus was, according to Greek legends, bound--"chained" to a rock—for bringing culture to mankind; whereas, his brother Atlas had been confined to "Tartarus" as punishment for opposing Zeus in the Clash of the Titans. It is possible that both 2 Peter and Jude derived some of the details of their accounts, not from Enoch, but from Greek legends about Prometheus.

These are the only two verses in the entire New Testament that specifically refer to the Fallen Angel Story. Interestingly, NEITHER of these two passages goes so far as to suggest that angels married human women or that angels rebelled against God. Yet, those two proposed "sins" (marrying humans and rebellion) are the two prominent explanations for the fall of the angels in literature outside the Bible. In fact, NEITHER passage spells out ANY specific "sin" of the angels. So, what was the sin 2 Peter was referring to?

Do the authors of Jude and 2 Peter believe I Enoch was actually written by Enoch, the descendant of Adam from Genesis 5, who lived 365 years and then was translated directly to eternal life, according to Hebrews 11:5, thus avoiding death altogether? If so, why did Enoch write in the Greek language instead of some ancient Semitic language? Even more puzzling: Do the authors of Jude and 2 Peter believe there really is a place called Tartarus, where Greek gods are imprisoned? Perhaps, questions such as these actually kept the book of Jude from being fully accepted into the New Testament canon for a long time.[38] I am not persuaded that the authors of Jude and 2 Peter believed any of this. Perhaps, their lack of belief in this legend is why they refused to mention the specific sin the angels were guilty of. For that matter, Jude does not even call it a "sin." He only says that they "abandoned their proper dwelling." Both agree that angels are awaiting judgment, but so does Revelation 20:10. According to Revelation, certain angels' roles are scheduled to be terminated at the end of history, but not necessarily due to sins they have committed.[39] If the

---

[38] According to *Encyclopaedia Britannica* (online, February 9, 2019): "Origen (died *c.* 254), Clement's pupil and one of the greatest thinkers of the early church, distinguished at least three classes of writings, basing his judgment on majority usage in places that he had visited: (1) *homologoumena* or *anantirrhēta,* "undisputed in the churches of God throughout the whole world" (the four Gospels, 13 Pauline Letters, I Peter, I John, Acts, and Revelation); (2) *amphiballomena,* "disputed" (II Peter, II and III John, Hebrews, James, and Jude); and (3) *notha,* "spurious" (*Gospel of the Egyptians*, *Thomas*, and others). He used the term "scripture" (*graphē*) for the *Didachē,* the *Letter of Barnabas,* and the *Shepherd of Hermas,* but did not consider them canonical. Eusebius shows the situation in the early 4th century. Universally accepted are: the four Gospels, Acts, 14 Pauline Letters (including Hebrews), I John, and I Peter. The disputed writings are of two kinds: (1) those known and accepted by many (James, Jude, II Peter, II and III John, and (2) those called "spurious" but not "foul and impious" (*Acts of Paul, Shepherd of Hermas, Apocalypse of Peter, Letter of Barnabas, Didachē* and possibly the *Gospel of the Hebrews*); finally there are the heretically spurious (*e.g., Gospel of Peter, Acts of John*). Revelation is listed both as fully accepted ("if permissible") and as spurious but not impious." (https://www.britannica.com/topic/biblical-literature/New-Testament-canon-texts-and-versions#ref597960)

[39] Lindsay, *Revelation*, 73.

authors of Jude and 2 Peter do not believe the Fallen Angel Stories to which they refer, what is going on in these passages?

Jews call it "Homiletic Aggadah." The authors of Jude and 2 Peter both lived in a Jewish milieu in which the use of homiletic Aggadah was commonplace. *The New World Encyclopedia* defines "Aggadah" as "folklore, historical anecdotes, moral exhortations, and advice. Sometimes they refer to mythical creatures, and incredible historical events." The word "homiletic" refers to sermons. In some churches, today, instead of preaching a sermon, the church leader "delivers a homily." The word homily means sermon. Budding young preachers study "homiletics" (or the art of preparing sermons) in college or seminary. In sermons, homiletic Aggadah may be fictional or historical stories used to support certain moral or spiritual teachings. Perhaps, these public speakers were following the direction of Aristotle in his groundbreaking Greek work, *On Rhetoric*, written four centuries earlier. In my book *ArguMentor*, I explain:

> Aristotle, in *Rhetoric* II.20.ii, admits both **historically-based stories** and **fictions** as his two types of paradigms, useful for inductive reasoning. A **paradigm** is an example, in the form of a narrative or story. Aristotle is saying that the stories can either be historical or fictitious. Martin Dibelius, in *From Tradition to Gospel*, emphasizes "paradigms" as the first major type of form he sees in the gospels. He sees the various forms—paradigms, tales, legends, analogies, and the passion story—as the building blocks with which the gospel writers constructed their gospels.
>
> Aristotle's comments concerning paradigms, however, apply to *all three genres of rhetoric*, but *fictions* would be more appropriately applied in the Deliberative genre. A political advisor, for example, might, using Deliberative rhetoric, warn his

candidate not to use untruths to smear his opponent: "Remember what happened to the boy who cried 'Wolf!'" Certainly, Judicial rhetoric emphasizes narratives that are *historically-based*, and the entire point of epideictic in praising and blaming is that the narratives are presumably historically-based. Aristotle discusses the two general modes of persuasion. The "example" or "paradigm" is the basis of **inductive reasoning**. The "enthymeme" is the basis of **deductive reasoning**. Epideictic is less concerned with deductive reasoning than it is with inductive reasoning. Since there are two types of "paradigms"—historical and invented, and since both historical and invented examples serve to persuade, we may expect both epideictic oratory and literature (whether historically-based or purely fictitious) to be persuasive. What then do both epideictic oratory and literature persuade? They subconsciously persuade auditors and readers to internalize the values they represent. Also, entelechially, they supply "cow paths" to follow in similar situations.

Aristotle's emphasis on the role of the paradigm in rhetorical genres, is particularly enlightening. Since Burke suggests that **form is the arousing and fulfilling of expectations**, the realization that the gospels [and "homiletic" epistles such as 2 Peter and Jude] are . . . rhetorical *form[s]*, rather than . . . literary *form[s]*, supplies an important expectation: The gospels [and, as I argue here, 2 Peter and Jude] were not intended to be classical literature, that might touch audiences in different ways throughout the ages; they were intended to be rhetorical works that were directed towards **specific audiences, in specific cultures, at specific points in time**. To interpret the gospels [and epistles such as 2 Peter and Jude], one needs to consider: What is the psychology of the audience? What are the values of the audience? What are the specific, timely needs of the audience?[40]

---

[40] Stan A. Lindsay, *ArguMentor*, (Orlando: Say Press, 2015), 66-67.

Jesus used parables. These were homiletic Aggadah. Did the Good Samaritan actually exist, or was he just a fictional character Jesus used to illustrate his point that one's neighbor can sometimes appear to be one's enemy? Was there an actual Prodigal Son that Jesus had in mind? Were there actually five wise virgins and five foolish ones that went to a marriage feast? Does it matter? No.

Sermon illustrations may be taken from history, current events, or literature. Audiences typically know which is which. A preacher today might ask in a sermon, "Do you think Jack Bauer should be punished for torturing terrorists?" If the audience is familiar with the successful Fox TV series "24," they will know that the preacher does not actually believe a real person named Jack Bauer actually tortured real terrorists. The Jack Bauer character, played by Kiefer Sutherland, presented only a scenario—which is precisely what the fallen angel story presented for the authors of Jude and 2 Peter. Just because Jack Bauer is a fictional character, it is not necessary to exclude his scenario from discussions of how America should fight a war on terror. Historical accounts may be mentioned right alongside the Bauer reference. The preacher might ask, "Should Osama bin Laden have been granted Miranda rights, if he could have been captured, rather than killed?" He might recount facts about the Fort Hood murders, the Paris massacre and the Boston Marathon bombing. Audiences can quickly switch back and forth between fiction and history, as they listen to sermons.

So, what sermon point/s were the authors of Jude and 2 Peter making? The sermon seems to be most clearly preached in 1 Peter 3:17-20. The point of the sermon (in verse 17) is: "It is better to suffer for doing right than for doing wrong." The illustrations for this point are homiletic Aggadah:

1. Christ suffered and died, but God raised him (3:18).
2. Even spirits who were disobedient at the time of Noah were imprisoned--a possible allusion to the fallen angels of I Enoch.
3. Noah was saved, even though all around him were destroyed (3:20).

2 Peter 2:1-9 seems to make a similar point with some of the same homiletic Aggadah. The point is: "The Lord knows how to rescue the godly from temptation and to keep the wicked under chastisement" (2:9). The illustrations are:

1. God did not spare sinning angels, but committed them to Tartarus (2:4).
2. Noah was saved, even though all around him were destroyed (2:5).
3. God did not spare Sodom and Gomorrah, but rescued Lot (2:6-8).

Jude 3-7 seems to be warning (7) the audience not to be like those who will be condemned (4). The illustrations are:

1. After the Lord rescued the Jews from Egypt, he destroyed those who had no faith (5).
2. Angels who abandoned their dwelling, He reserved in chains (6).
3. God did not spare Sodom and Gomorrah, when they sinned (7).

A quick glance at these three sermons shows how sermons were written in the culture of 2 Peter and Jude. The common conclusion seems to be that God will eventually save the righteous and eventually punish the wicked, even if the wicked were originally as righteous as angels.

Since I commented that the spirits who were disobedient at the time of Noah and were imprisoned was a possible allusion to the fallen angels of I Enoch (1 Peter 3:19-20), I should explain my comment before concluding this chapter. The Nestle-Aland Greek text of the New Testament lists among its notes on verse 19 the conjecture of two textual critics that the word Enoch was originally in the text, but was somehow removed by scribes who copied the text. Such a mistake would be easily explained. The words usually translated "in which also" were pronounced in Greek: "ENHOKAI." If this were pronounced "HENOKAI," the words would be translated "Enoch also" instead of "in which also." It is possible that early scribes accidentally made a mistake—or that scribes intentionally removed this reference to Enoch and fallen angels from the book of 1 Peter (because they did not want to teach the fallen angel story). This conjecture would remove a very singular and strange teaching in the Bible--that somehow Jesus went and preached to people in Hell after his death. Such a notion does not occur anywhere else in the Bible. I Enoch, on the other hand, DOES SAY that Enoch went and preached to the spirits in prison—referring to Enoch preaching to the fallen angels who had been chained. If this is an accurate conjecture, we have three references to the I Enoch account of fallen angels in the New Testament, instead of two. Nevertheless, all three seem to be related developments of the same sermon, and the characterization of homiletic Aggadah fits all three references.

My final comment on these passages is that, of all three of them, ONLY THE 2 PETER PASSAGE actually speaks of "sinning" angels (and even that passage leaves an "out" for the author). 2 Peter

2:4 DOES NOT SAY (unconditional clause), "God did not spare sinning angels." It says (conditional clause), "IF God did not spare sinning angels." The "IF" effectively removes any clear-cut doctrine of sinning angels from the entire New Testament, by making the clause into only a conditional clause.

Angels and Demons: The Personification of Communication (Logology)

Chapter 11

Can Angels "on Earth" Sin, but Not Angels "in Heaven"?

Jesus taught his disciples to pray: "Thy will be done on earth, as it is in Heaven." Was he implying that all creatures in Heaven do His will perfectly, but that creatures on earth do not do His will perfectly? We can certainly agree that humans (on earth) do not do His will perfectly, but is it also true that angels who find themselves "on earth" do not do His will perfectly, either? I ran into this theoretical snag as I completed my Master's in Hebrew at Indiana University.

I began writing my Master's thesis on Fallen Angels in 1973, at Indiana University, but was not able to complete it until 1977. Why did it take me so long? On my Master's committee, my major professor was Dr. Henry A. Fischel, a renowned Jewish scholar from Germany. He was not the problem. Fischel had personally been confined several months in a Nazi concentration camp, and his mother and 12 other family members died in the Holocaust. He was a former president of the Society of Biblical Literature in Canada and was a pioneer in studying the relationship between

Jewish literature and the Hellenistic world. Fischel was always quite happy with the quality of my work in Jewish and Hellenistic literature. A second member of my Master's committee was a Muslim, Wadie Jwaideh, the Chair of the Department of Near Eastern Languages and Literature at Indiana University. He was not the problem. Having studied at the University of Baghdad and Syracuse University, Jwaideh served as my primary resource on the Koran. Jwaideh had no problem with the quality of my work in Islamic literature. The final member of my committee was the stickler: a Christian, J. Paul Sampley, a professor of New Testament at Indiana University, at the time. He is the author of the commentaries on First and Second Corinthians in the *New Interpreter's Bible* and is now Professor Emeritus of New Testament and Christian Origins at Boston University. Sampley insisted unyieldingly, in one matter, that I accept his view of angels in my thesis, despite my findings to the contrary. His view was that while the "angels in heaven" were incapable of sinning or reproducing or having sex, the angels "on earth" were quite a different matter. He thought the New Testament taught that angels who found themselves on earth were capable of sinning. In the final analysis, after spending four years trying to please Dr. Sampley regarding my comments on angels in the New Testament, I decided that I could not write what I did not believe to be true. I removed most references to the New Testament from my Master's thesis, so that he would have nothing to object to. I finished my thesis, and he endorsed it—along with Fischel and Jwaideh. Let us analyze Sampley's thesis—that angels on earth can sin, unlike their heavenly counterpart.

In Bereshit Rabbah 27:4, Rabbis Judah and Nehemiah disagree on the derivation of the first word in the Genesis 6:6 clause וַיִּנָּחֶם יְהוָה, כִּי-עָשָׂה אֶת-הָאָדָם בָּאָרֶץ, usually translated, "And the Lord

REPENTED that He had made man on the earth." The word translated "repented" (וַיִּנָּחֶם) is the word the two rabbis call into question. Rabbi Judah accepts the traditional translation (based on a vocalization from the Nif'al stem) and therefore understands the clause to read "the Lord REPENTED," as I presented in the translation above. Rabbi Judah explains that if God had created man in Heaven, he would have remained sinless (as the angels are sinless); therefore, there is justification in God's being sorry. Rabbi Nehemiah, on the other hand, believes that the word should have been vocalized in the Pu'al stem to say, "And the Lord WAS RELIEVED that He had made man on the earth." Rabbi Nehemiah explains that if God had made man in Heaven, he would have aroused the angels also to revolt against God. Rabbi Nehemiah's explanation seems to suggest that it is possible for angels (even those in Heaven) to sin (to REBEL, in this instance). Rabbi Judah's interpretation implies that it was not possible, because—wherever they are—angels are incapable of sin. Either way, however, both are agreed that angels did not sin. Rabbi Aibu's explanation of the text, then, follows with the idea that God repented because He had made the "evil inclination" in man; otherwise, man would have never have rebelled.[41]

In Chapter 6, I related an "Innocent" Fallen Angel Story. That specific story percolated around Judaism, during the New Testament period, because it allowed Jews to believe the thesis of the Enoch stories (that angels COULD sin) while also believing the strongly monotheistic teaching of the Old Testament and New Testament eras (that angels DID NOT sin). It served as a compromise,

---

[41] Compare also *Midrash Tanhuma*, ed. S. Buber, (Vilna, 1913), I, 30, regarding the Judah-Nehemiah discussion.

or possibly even a step toward a corrected theology of angels. According to the story, the angels were TEMPTED to marry the girl, but the girl outwitted them and the marriage was never consummated.

Other Rabbinic writings discuss the theological implications of this "Innocent" Fallen Angel Story. In Midrash Agadat Bereshit,[42] we have an extension of the fallen angel account anticipating or involving the "innocent" fallen angels. According to this version, God warned the angels who wanted to descend to earth:

אם והייתם בארץ כמו שבני אדם אלו   ותראו נשים יפות שיש בניהם מיד נכנס יצ״ר בקרבכם והיה מחטיא אתכם   "If you were on the earth, as these sons of man are on it, then you would notice the beautiful women also, who are among them; immediately, the 'evil inclination' will enter you and it will cause you to sin."

Yalkut I, p. 44, contains another version of the same legend in which God warns the angels, "I know that if you inhabit the earth, the evil inclination will overpower you, and you will be more iniquitous than ever men [were]."[43] The pious maiden concocted a scheme, similar to the one I related earlier, whereby she deceived the angels[44] and was placed among the stars. In these two additional versions of the story, however, the angels "were not deterred from entering into alliances with the daughters of men."[45]

---

[42] Buber, ed., Introduction, 38.
[43] Ginzberg, *Legends*, I, 149.
[44] Specifically, Shemḥazai. Shemḥazai and Azazel are the two angelic leaders from the apocryphal and pseudepigraphal fallen angel tradition.
[45] Ginzberg, *Legends*, I, 149.

In the Chronicles of Jerahmeel[46] (another parallel to the "Innocent" Fallen Angel Story), after the angels had descended to earth, "Forthwith He allowed the evil inclination to sway them." Our maiden-becomes-star motif appears again, followed by the angels' human marriages. In other words, these accounts were accepting BOTH the "Innocent" Fallen Angel Story AND Enoch's "Sinning" Fallen Angel Story.

In all three of the variations from the "Innocent" Fallen Angel Story, just reported, it seems clear that so long as the angels remained in Heaven, they were not subject to the evil inclination. The ANGELS' MOTIVE FOR DESCENDING (in all three accounts) was TO PROVE THAT THEY COULD LIVE ON EARTH MORE RIGHTEOUSLY THAN MAN. Perhaps, the reason these versions of the story have the angels wind up sinning, anyway, is to disprove this theological precept (that angels could live on earth more righteously than man). Louis Ginzberg[47] summarizes the theological teaching of the rabbis at the time of the New Testament: "Although man, who is a terrestrial being, is inferior to the angels, he surpasses them by overcoming the evil inclination, which the angels do not possess at all (BR 48.11)." The conclusion of Rabbinic writings then is that the "pious are therefore greater than the angels."[48]

---

[46] M. Gaster, tr., *The Chronicles of Jerahmeel*, New York: KTAV Publishing House, Inc., 1971), 53 (Reprint).
[47] Ginzberg, *Legends*, V, 24.
[48] The Chapter 6 innocent fallen angel account from *Beth ha-Midrash*, though it does not mention the evil inclination specifically, allows room for the interpretation that the evil inclination may have influenced the angels. On the other hand, its exclusion from that account, whereas, other versions of the legend do mention it, may be indicative of the author's intention (in the innocent fallen angels account) to avoid any conflict with a well-established teaching that the angels lack that inclination.

Whether or not angels COULD sin was a very real and HOTLY CONTESTED DEBATE ISSUE in the New Testament period. In the previous chapter, I discussed the only two (or three) very minor passages from the New Testament (primarily Jude and 2 Peter) that suggested that angels COULD sin, and found that both (or all three) used the Fallen Angel Story as a sermon illustration (homiletic Aggadah). The Fallen Angel Story was NOT used to prove a theological point about angels, BUT to demonstrate that NO ONE (not even an angel) is immune from punishment, if he or she does wrong. I will demonstrate in future chapters that the gospels present JESUS himself in very specifically theological language DISPUTING ALL THREE MAJOR EXPLANATIONS OF THE SINNING FALLEN ANGEL STORY. Therefore, I do not believe either Jude or 2 Peter actually believed the Fallen Angel Story that they used as a sermon illustration.

As you can see, however, there certainly were Jewish rabbis in the New Testament period who agreed with Sampley's position—that angels on earth can sin, unlike their heavenly counterpart, even though the rabbis generally did not believe the angels actually DID sin. As you can also see, there were Jewish rabbis in the New Testament period who even thought it was possible even for angels in Heaven to sin (Rabbi Nehemiah). Bottom line: There were rabbis in the New Testament period who disagreed on the nature of angels just as Sampley and I disagree on the subject. That does not mean that we are both correct. Sampley's view (and the view of a FEW Jewish rabbis in the New Testament period) gives more credit to the Book of I Enoch than I (and the vast MAJORITY of Jewish rabbis in the New Testament period) do. I feel confident that Sampley is

11: Can Angels "on Earth" Sin, but Not Angels "in Heaven"?

wrong. Sampley objected when I pointed out that Jesus is quoted in Matthew 22:30, Mark 12:25, and Luke 20:35 as saying that when the righteous are resurrected, they will be like the angels—neither marrying nor giving in marriage. This statement attributed to Jesus by all three synoptic gospels[49] seems to indicate a fairly strong theological position—THAT ANGELS CANNOT MARRY. This position is identical to the position held by the majority of Jewish rabbis in the New Testament period. I will present the evidence from the Rabbinic sources that testify to this position, in the next chapter.

Is this account of Jesus refuting the premise of the Fallen Angel Story from I Enoch? I think so. Follow the logic: If angels neither marry nor give in marriage, the "sons of God" who MARRIED the daughters of men in Genesis 6 COULD NOT HAVE BEEN ANGELS. There certainly are many times when "sons of God" refers to humans (Galatians 4:6-7, for example) and only one time when the phrase clearly refers to angels (the book of Job). The dominant Greek translation of the Old Testament during New Testament times—the Septuagint—translates the Hebrew "sons of God" as "angels" in Job, but interestingly enough, NOT IN GENESIS 6, or in other important passages. Job is somewhat different from the rest of the Old Testament, anyway, in that it is a

---

[49] Although, admittedly, Sampley was questioning my use of the gospels in a way that he thought was "uncritical," based upon established Form critical and Redaction critical research that had been published.

book written from the culture and perspective of the descendents of Esau;[50] whereas, the rest of the Old Testament pertains to the descendents of Esau's brother, Jacob (a.k.a., Israel).

So, how does Sampley object? He points out that in the Matthew and Mark accounts, it is the angels "IN HEAVEN" who neither marry nor give in marriage. Of course, neither Matthew nor Mark go on to say that angels "on earth" do marry, but Sampley feels safe in the possible inference they provide him by using the phrase "in Heaven." What is astounding, then, is that Luke—the gospel writer who we believe is writing to a more Greek-oriented audience (and who could, therefore, appreciate the Greek religious doctrine that EVEN GODS MARRY human women and other gods)—would have the audacity to state it so clearly: the resurrected do not marry; they are like the angels. No possible room is left for inferring that some angels "on the earth" might marry. For Luke, angels simply do not marry.

---

[50] In line with Kenneth Burke's views on the subject of symbol systems (**Conventional Symbol Systems:** LSA 448; OHN 141, 162, 175, 234, 275; P&C 418; PC back matter; **Symbol System**: CG 22, 29, 32; HP 220; LSA viii, 2, 4-7, 9, 17, 22, 24, 28-29, 39, 48, 57, 59-61, 63, 69-70, 79, 342, 358, 387, 407, 448, 480-481, 489; MAHC 79; OHN 140, 167, 180, 211, 252, 286, 381, 385, and throughout; OSS 41, 57-59, 61, 63, 71, 73; P&C 407, 417-418; PC back matter; RR 15, 18, 20, 22, 38, 192, 202, 208, 229, 238, 268, 287-289, 297-298, 308; T&L 152), I argue that the culture of Esau's family developed different symbol systems—with words or phrases such as "sons of God" carrying different meanings—than did Jacob's family, despite their common linguistic heritage. These Burkean citations are culled from Stan A. Lindsay, *The Expanded Kenneth Burke Concordance*, (Orlando: Say Press, 2014), 82, 402. Explanations of the abbreviations for Burke's various texts cited in the list above are found on preliminary pages immediately following the Preface in that work and also in the Bibliography of this book.

11: Can Angels "on Earth" Sin, but Not Angels "in Heaven"?

What angels of whom we are aware were not "on the earth"? Gabriel brought messages to Mary and Joseph, but he had to be "on the earth" to deliver them. The angels who sang to the shepherds on the first Christmas night were at least within the atmosphere of earth. The angel (if that's what he was) who joined Shadrach, Meshach, and Abednego in the fiery furnace was "on the earth." The angel who explained the signs of Revelation to John was "on the earth." The angels who visited Abraham and Lot were "on the earth." The angel (if that's what he was) who wrestled with Jacob was "on the earth." The angels who were involved in inspiring scripture (in 1 Peter 1:12) were "on the earth." The angel who rescued Peter from prison was "on the earth." The angels guarding the empty tomb were "on the earth." Even the archangel Michael, who apparently remained in Heaven as he cast Satan down to the earth, appears to have been "on the earth" himself in Daniel 10, fighting for Daniel. Does this mean that all of the angels of whom we have ever heard were capable of marrying human women? It's a little disconcerting to think that we can't trust any of the angels who came to earth. (They might have the evil inclination.)

Luke had it right. Angels cannot marry. With him agree the vast majority of the Jewish rabbis in the New Testament period. I contend that Sampley (and those few rabbis who agree with him) had it wrong, according to the New Testament. Matthew and Mark were not trying to hint that there was a difference between angels in Heaven and angels on earth. They were simply using respectful language (such as Christians use when, in the Lord's Prayer, they address God as "Our Father who is 'in Heaven.'" No one would suggest that when God was "on earth" walking with Adam in the cool of the evening, he was a different kind of being, would they?

The author of I Enoch had it wrong, according to New Testament and Rabbinic teaching, when he said in I Enoch 84:4, "The angels of your heaven are doing wrong."

Chapter 12
Angels Cannot Engage in Sex

By far, the most famous Fallen Angel Story in all of literature is the story of angels who married human women and had children. In his article on angels in Judaism in the *Reallexikon für Antike und Christentum*, J. Michl[51] reports that, in Judaism, the angels were created free of moral decision-making capacity ("Die Engel wurden mit der Freiheit zur sittlichen Entscheidung erschaffen"). He does however point out that they were fallible, citing Job 4:18 and 15:15. These two passages do not charge angels with sin, but they do charge angels with making mistakes—suggesting that they were not infallible. Was having sex with humans one of those areas in which angels were fallible? The literature between the Old Testament and New Testament certainly seems to make that claim. Michl lists the following texts that claim that some angels sinned ("Ein Teil der Engel hat gesündigt, und zwar, wie man im Anschluss an Genesis 6,2.4 meinte, in sexueller Vereinigung mit menschlichen Frauen")[52]--as the authors of these texts formed their opinions, based on Genesis 6, that angels had sexual unions with human wives:

---

[51] J. Michl, "Engel II, V, 80.
[52] Ibid.

Jubilees 4.22, 5.1, 7.21, and 10.5,

I Enoch 6f., 12.4, 15, 69.2-4, 84.4, and 86.1-6,

II Enoch 18.3-5, and (possibly) 7.1-3,

Testament of Ruben 5.6,

Testament of Naphtali 3.4,

Syriac Apocalypse of Baruch 56.12,

Damaskusschriften 3.4,

Philo, On the Giants 6,

Josephus, Antiquities 1.31, and

The Testament of Solomon 5:3.

As is easily seen, the story of sexual angels was a popular one, in the Hellenistic Period. There is an abundance of literature written after the Old Testament on this subject—so much, in fact, that the composer(s) of the "Innocent Fallen Angel Story" I have been citing in the prior chapters[53] was, no doubt, familiar with the theme. The composer(s) found it important enough to include the idea of sexuality in the new Fallen Angel Story. It is not quite clear in the "Innocent Fallen Angel Story" whether, if the young girl were willing to consummate the sexual union, it would have even

---

[53] Jellinek, *Beth ha-Midrasch,* V, 156.

been possible. The proceedings never reached that stage, and (so far as this account is concerned) the angels were never again accused of making such a proposal. Herein lies part of the ingenuity of the "Innocent Fallen Angel Story." Without totally disavowing the potential for angelic-human sexual intercourse, it nevertheless concludes that such an occurrence never came about. It[54] appears to be a link between the popular (legendary) Fallen Angel Story and the more-or-less official angelology of the rabbis. The Jewish rabbis of the New Testament period, on the whole, stood solidly on the contention that the "Fallen Angel Story" from I Enoch and others cited above was unacceptable, because angels had no sexual capacity. In Chapter 9, I cited Midrash Tehillim 8.74 arguing that angels are incapable of sinning by comparing their status with that of a boy lacking fingers attempting to embroider. It is simply impossible. There, to be more specific, God is quoted as explaining to the angels: אין התורה מתקיימת אצלכם לפי שאין פריה ורביה ביניכם ("The Torah is not being fulfilled with you, because there is not fruit [reproductive increase] or propagation among you.")

The Testament of Solomon, the final text listed by Michl, was actually written sometime between 100 and 400 A.D.[55] That work claims that all angels (not just fallen ones) have sexual capacity. It alludes to the Sexual Fallen Angel Story when it says: σὺ μὲν υἱὸς ἀνθρώπου εἶ, κἀγὼ ἀγγέλου, καὶ διὰ θυγατρός ἀνθρώπου ἐγεννήθην "You, on the one hand, are the son of a man, but I, of an

---

[54] The Jellinek, *Beth ha-Midrasch* account.
[55] Chester C. McCown, *The Testament of Solomon*, (Leipzig: J. C. Hinrichs, 1922), pp. 105-108.

angel, and by a daughter of man was I born."[56] Louis Ginzberg[57] comments: "The Testament of Solomon, though containing a great many Jewish elements, is on the whole of a strongly syncretistic character. The pagan element is obvious in the fact that the angels (not only the fallen ones) are made to have offspring. This is neither Jewish nor Christian, but pagan." The rabbis and the New Testament writers stayed away from this teaching.

As Bamberger points out:[58] "The Talmud NEVER speaks of fallen or rebel angels. This is no accident; nor were the rabbis ignorant of the legend. They knew and suppressed it." In other words, the Sexual Fallen Angel Story was intentionally subverted by the rabbis. Only a few brief references to the Sexual Fallen Angel tradition remain. In the New Testament, as I have indicated in prior chapters, three of the gospels quote Jesus as teaching that angels neither marry nor give in marriage. Even in the LONE New Testament passage that suggests that angels could have "sinned" (2 Peter 2:4), the idea is only presented in a CONDITIONAL clause—"IF God did not spare sinning angels." And EVEN THERE, there is no mention of the SEXUAL Fallen Angel Story. Like the rabbis, the author of 2 Peter (along with his audience) knew the legend, and the writer suppressed it. In the parallel passage in Jude 6, the angels are NOT EVEN ACCUSED OF SINNING. They are accused only of "abandon[ing] their proper dwelling." Like the rabbis, the author of Jude (and his audience) knew the legend and the writer suppressed it. So intent upon suppressing the Sexual Fallen Angel Story were the New Testament writers and early scribes that

---

[56] McCown, *Testament Solomon*, 21* (* text pagination).
[57] Ginzberg, *Legends*, VI, 293.
[58] Bamberger, *Fallen Angels*, 90.

the name Enoch may have even been intentionally expunged from 1 Peter 3:19, as I discussed in Chapter 10. Neither the rabbis nor the New Testament writers support the Sexual Fallen Angel Story. But, does the Old Testament support the Sexual Fallen Angel Story? I will discuss the Genesis 6 passage on its own merits, in the next chapter.

Angels and Demons: The Personification of Communication (Logology)

Chapter 13
Who Are the "Sons of God" in Genesis?

The word "son" (Hebrew: בֵּן/BEN) occurs 4580 times in the Hebrew Bible. In the vast majority of those occurrences, the term is used to refer to the parent-child relationship between a human father and his physically-begotten human "son." To my knowledge, no one seriously claims that the Hebrew God physically fathered any angels. Even Christians, who admit to no "physical begetting" while asserting that God "spiritually" begat Jesus, claim that Jesus was God's "ONLY begotten Son." Therefore, Christians do not hold that God (even spiritually) begat any angels. My initial conclusion, then, is that the phrase with which we are dealing in Genesis 6 is to be interpreted either figuratively or metaphorically. Those who married the daughters of men, in Genesis 6, are in some figurative or metaphorical sense "sons of God." What are our figurative/metaphorical options?

1. The Septuagint (LXX), the major Greek translation of the Hebrew Old Testament during the New Testament period, does translate the phrase "sons of God" [בְּנֵי־הָאֱלֹהִים] with the Greek words for "angels of God" [οἱ ἄγγελοι τοῦ Θεοῦ] in the book of Job, but interestingly

enough, not in Genesis 6! The Greek translators of the Hebrew Bible—even though they were probably quite familiar with the interpretation offered in I Enoch that these were angels who married human women—chose not to translate the phrase as "angels of God" in Genesis 6, but rather as simply "sons of God" [οἱ υἱοὶ τοῦ Θεοῦ].

2. H. Haag observes, in his article on "BEN" [בֵּן] in the *Theological Dictionary of the Old Testament*,[59] that the word may be used to indicate a lineage or ethnic identity, as when all offspring of the lineage of Jacob are called the "sons (children) of Israel." This is a possibility that I will revisit.

3. The word can be used to indicate a geographical origin. Various humans are referred to as sons of Bethlehem, sons of Jerusalem, sons of Zion, sons of Eden, sons of Samaria, etc. While the terms "God" and "Heaven" are sometimes used as synonyms—as in the phrases "Kingdom of Heaven" and "Kingdom of God"—the contrast with "daughters of men" in the Genesis passage makes this an unlikely option.

4. Haag also observes: "An individual is distinguished from the collective community of which he is a part or from man" by expressions translated "son of man." This option may be more pertinent to the expression "daughters of men," possibly indicating that not all human women married "sons of God," but that certain "individual" women did.

---

[59] H. Haag, "BEN in the Semitic Languages," *Theological Dictionary of the Old Testament*, Eds. G. Johannes Botterweck and Helmer Ringgren, Trans. John T. Willis (Grand Rapids, MI: William B. Eerdmans, 1975), II: 147-159.

5. The word, according to Haag, "is used as an affectionate address to younger students or hearers," much as we may use the word "son" in American discourse. I don't think this interpretation has much merit.

6. It is used figuratively to express the source from which something comes in such expressions as "son of oil" (referring to a hill or to an "anointed one"/messianic office holder), "son of dawn" (referring to the Morning Star), "sons of fire" (referring to sparks), and "sons of the bow" or "sons of the quiver" (referring to arrows).

7. BEN is also used to express membership in a social group, such as "sons of exile," "sons of nobles," "sons of the poor," and "sons of the common people." A group of musicians may be called "sons of Korah" or "sons of Asaph." Priests are called "sons of Aaron." Disciples of prophets are called "sons of the prophets." Worthless people are called "sons of Belial."

8. The term is also an idiom that is better translated "-like." Thus, "sons of strength" are strong, "sons of pride" are conceited, "sons of rebellion" are rebellious, "sons of uproar" are uproarious. In this sense, "sons of God" would be "God-like." This interpretation has a great deal of merit.

9. Lastly, the term may be used to suggest a length of time. Thus, a "son of eight days" or a "son of five hundred years" would refer to an eight day old child or a very old man. This is not how Genesis 6 is using the term.

While literature written in the Hellenistic period, before the New Testament times, embraces the interpretation "angels" for the "sons of God,"[60] the Rabbinic literature and the New Testament contain a different interpretation. According to Bereshit Rabbah 26.5, Rabbi Simeon ben Yoḥai translates the "sons of God" as "sons of judges" (קרי להון בני דייניח). Targum Onkelos on Genesis 6 translates the phrase as "sons of the nobles."[61] Siphre Zuta on Numbers, section 86, agrees with this interpretation/translation. Midrash Wayyikra Rabbah 23:9 treats the Genesis account as if it is talking about human activity. These translations would easily fit in the 7th and 8th categories, listed above. In addition to Jesus' rejection of the notion that angels can marry (discussed in the previous chapter), Jesus is quoted in John 10:33-36 as clearly implying that the term "sons of the Most High" (from Psalm 82:6—a passage we shall return to, later) refers to "human judges." Human judges are even called "gods/ELOHIM" in both Psalm 82:6 and Exodus 22:28. Jesus was making the point that it was not blasphemous for him to be called "god" or "son of God," if even humans (judges) could be called "gods" and "sons of the Most High." Even though Haag[62] argues that the passages in which "sons of God" are most prominent in the Old Testament (Job, Genesis

---

[60] That was the common interpretation in post-biblical Judaism until the tannaitic period, as J. Michl, "Engel II," *Reallexikon*, V, 80 points out (italics mine):

> Die Gen. 6,2.4 erwähnten ‚Söhne Gottes' wurden nämlich als E(ngel) gedeutet (vgl. Die Lesart ἄγγελοι Gen. 6,2 im Cod. Alex. u. bei Philo *gigant.* 6; Aug. civ. D. 15,23; L. Jung: JewQuRev 16 [1925/6] 180/205. 287/95; Bousset, Rel. 491f.; H. J. Schoeps: Biblica 26 [1945] 108; *im rabbinischen Schriftum finden sich nur sehr wenige Spuren dieser Anschauung, die doch vorhanden gewesen sein muss* . . . .)

[61] Cf. also S. Buber, ed., *Midrash Tanḥuma*, I, pp. 23f.; also Targum Neofiti *ad loc.*
[62] H. Haag, "ben," pp. 147-159.

6, and Psalm 82) presuppose some sort of heavenly council in which God seeks input from other heavenly beings (such as angels), the Septuagint is only willing to explicitly apply that interpretation to Job. The rabbis rejected the notion that Psalm 82 referred to angels, as did John 10:33-36. Furthermore, the three other (synoptic) gospels (and the rabbis) reject the notion that angels can marry. Given that premise, Genesis 6 could not refer to angels, from the perspective of the New Testament gospels. According to Haag, Dexinger (in more recent years) interprets the "sons of God" in Genesis 6 as "heroes" and Scharbert interprets the "sons of God" in Genesis 6 as the descendents of Seth. Is God actually objecting to heroes marrying common women or to Seth's descendents marrying Cain's descendents? Why would such unions produce "heroes"?

Louis Ginzberg notes that all of the Enoch legends "left no trace in the authoritative rabbinic sources,"[63] and Bamberger goes so far as to say that Enoch "is not mentioned at all" in "the two Talmuds and in the tannaitic literature."[64] Bamberger does admit, in the footnotes,[65] that "actually Enoch is mentioned (but just mentioned)" in Seder Olam Rabbah, chapter 1, beginning. Then, two or three more references in the standard midrashim round out the references to Enoch. One of those references (Bereshit Rabbah 25.1) mentions Enoch, but only to claim that he was NOT translated to Heaven.[66]   Other than the reference to Enoch in Jude 14 and the few allusions to I

---

[63] Ginzberg, *Legends*, V, 156.
[64] Bamberger, *Fallen Angels*, 92.
[65] Bamberger, *Fallen Angels*, 275.
[66] The Chapter 6 innocent fallen angel account from *Beth ha-Midrash* reflects the attitudes of the tannaitic-amoraic period in Jewish literature, in that it, at least, diminishes the importance of the reproductive factor in its development of the fallen angel story. Though the angels are presented

Enoch in Jude, the only reference to Enoch in the New Testament is Hebrews 11:5, which merely lists Enoch as an example of faith who did not die (something that could be gleaned from Genesis 5:24 and that has no bearing on the "sons of God" issue).

So, let us consider the Genesis 6:1-8 text and see what makes sense:

> When "man/אדם/ADAM" began to multiply on the face of the earth and daughters were born to them, the sons of God saw the daughters of "man" that they were beautiful and they took wives for themselves from all whom they chose. And the Lord said, "My spirit shall not always ידון/YADON with (or in/ב) 'man'; in their erring, he is flesh. And his days shall be a hundred twenty years. The giants (נפלים/NEPHILIM) were on the earth in those days and even afterwards, when the sons of God came in to the daughters of 'man' and they bore for them. They [Who are 'they'?] were the heroes who existed from ancient time, men/אנשי/ANOSH of name. And the Lord saw that the evil (הרע/HA-RA') of 'man' on the earth was great. And every inclination (יצר/YETZER) of the thoughts of his 'heart' was only evil (רע/RA') all the day. And God repented that he had made 'man' on the earth and He was grieved in His 'heart.' And the Lord said, 'I will wipe off "man" whom I have created from the face of the earth—from man to beast to creeping thing to

---

as once desirous of sexual union with human women, the midrashic account disavows ultimately any sexual involvement between angels and humans.

13: Who Are the "Sons of God" in Genesis?

the fowl of the heavens. I regret that I made them.' But Noah found grace in the eyes of the Lord."

Notice that this passage is all about "man." The word "man/ADAM" is used eight times in these eight verses:

- Man multiplies.
- His daughters are beautiful.
- God's spirit will not YADON in him; he errs; he is flesh.
- He seems to be obsessed ONLY with his "evil inclination/YETZER HA-RA'."
- God repented that He had made him.
- God plans to wipe him off the face of the earth.

Where is God's outrage toward "angels"? If this passage is supposed to report the story of "fallen angels," why is God only regretful that he made man, beast, creeping thing, and fowl? Why doesn't God regret making the angels? Why doesn't He punish the angels? To believe I Enoch, one would have to assume that having children who were heroes is punishment enough for them! This is not an account of fallen angels. Whoever these "sons of God" were, they were almost certainly human. Perhaps, they were judges or sons of the judges, in line with Psalm 82:6 and Exodus 22:28. Judges were generally pretty intelligent and, like Samson and Gideon, they were usually good warriors. They could have had children who were "heroes."

Some interpreters have tried to make something out of the term הַנְּפִלִים/the NEPHILIM (translated "giants"). The term can be associated etymologically with the root נפל/NAPHAL, which means "to fall." Hence, some say, "Aha! Fallen Angels!" But, that interpretation of NEPHILIM has its own problems. Numbers 13:33 gives the clear indication that NEPHILIM were just human giants. When the Hebrew spies went in to scope out the land of Canaan, they reported that there were NEPHILIM (giants) in the land—i.e., the sons of Anak. The spies reported that they were as grasshoppers compared to the Canaanites (a situation in which the spies clearly used hyperbole). One would have assumed that they would have been more specific, if they had actually seen fallen angels. In the Genesis 6 text recorded above, I inserted the question "Who are they?" where the text says "They were the heroes who existed from ancient time, men/אנשי /ANOSH of name." Was the text saying that giants were the heroes—men of name? Or was the text saying that the sons of God were the heroes—men of name? If Genesis were following strict grammatical rules, as set down for English journalists by Strunk and White, the sons of God would be the heroes, but we cannot hold the Hebrew author of Genesis to English rules of grammar. The third possibility is not very grammatically correct for English readers, but works in the Hebrew: that the heroes (men of name) were the offspring of the sons of God and daughters of men. Whether the heroes were the "sons of God," the giants, or the offspring of the sons of God and daughters of men, one thing is clear: they were MEN (men of name). They were not part-man/part angel.

One other Hebrew term in this text is important, the term YADON, found in the comment from God: "My spirit shall not always ידון/YADON with (or in) 'man'; in their erring, he is flesh."

Frankly, we do not know what this word means. It is what scholars of ancient writings call a *hapax legomenon*. A *hapax legomenon* is a word that occurs only once in all of literature. We were able to interpret the word NEPHILIM in Genesis 6 as "human giants" because it occurs other places in literature. Numbers 13:33 gives the clear indication that NEPHILIM were just human giants. The word YADON, however, was never used before and never used again in ancient literature. You could say that your guess is as good as mine regarding the meaning of this word.

Nevertheless, I will hazard a guess, based on the dichotomies that are developed in this text. My perspective on the meaning of this word stems from my application of the Twentieth Century communication theorist Kenneth Burke's definition of human. In my book, *Disneology: Religious Rhetoric at Walt Disney World*,[67] I develop Burke's view of humans as the symbol-using animal (p. 12). Burke sees a dichotomy in humans: they have animality and they have symbolicity (p. 65). In that book, I suggest possibilities for viewing the point at which humans existed "in God's image." While I did not discuss this point in that book, Genesis 1:26 quotes God: "Let us make man 'into' our image." The Hebrew consonant (ב) that I have translated "into" is typically translated "in." Nevertheless "into" is a perfectly legitimate translation. Another legitimate translation would be: "Let us make man 'with' our image." Due to the scientific recalcitrance of the fossil record that seems to provide evidence of the existence of a non-symbol-using version of man that predates the symbol-using variety, a translation of "into" or "with" could accommodate

---

[67] Stan A. Lindsay, *Disneology: Religious Rhetoric at Walt Disney World* (Orlando: Say Press, 2010).

such evidence. In other words, a possibility exists that God originally made a man (such as, Neanderthal?) who did not have strongly developed symbol-using capacities. He could not speak a language, make tools [?], paint pictures on cave walls, etc. Then, at some point, God made the same basic type of being—but with symbol-using capacities (i.e., with His image: He created Adam). This variety of man possessed *both* animality *and* symbolicity. Just as Genesis 6 says, God's "spirit" (=symbolicity) shall not always "prevail/ידון/YADON" in man" because man is also "flesh" (=animality). The word "prevail" (as I have translated YADON) is at least a shade of the meaning of the word "strive"—the most common translation of the word YADON. It also makes perfect sense, if one notes that this passage is discussing man's "evil inclination /YETZER יצר HA-RA׳ הרע" which was "prevailing" all day long (presumably, over man's "good inclination/YETZER יצר HA-TOV הטוב"). The sons of God, in this scenario, would be the offspring of Adam—those who were created "with" God's image, and hence, could be thought of as his "sons." The daughters of men, in this scenario, would be the female offspring of the purely "animal" man, the Neanderthals or some such. This uses the "lineage" approach (#2, above) for interpreting "sons." The fact that the latest Neanderthals lived at the same time as, and even bred with the earliest forms of Modern Man has been in the news, lately.[68] What would happen if one bred a very intelligent (symbolicity=God's spirit=son of God) man with a very physically adapted (animality= YETZER HA-RA'=daughter of man) woman? Would their offspring not have the capability of being "heroes" and "men of name?" Furthermore, such unions between "symbol-using" humans and their "animal" counterparts might be attributed to the purely sexual attraction of "sons of God" to the "daughters of men." Their "evil inclination" could be interpreted as "prevailing" over their "good inclination"—because they are also flesh. This "prevailing" of the evil inclination of men over their good inclination could be viewed as having produced an understandable "regret" on the part of God that he had made either "animal man" or even "symbol-using man."

Caveat: It is not necessary to accept this Burkean philosophically dichotomous interpretation of Genesis 6 (which certainly would not have been known to interpreters in the New Testament and Rabbinic Jewish period), however, to see that the sons of God were not angels; they were humans.

---

[68] According to Charles Q. Choi, "Why Neanderthals Likely Fathered Few Kids with Modern Humans," *Live Science* [http://www.livescience.com/54359-neanderthal-y-chromosome-caused-miscarriages.html]: "Humans today often carry around a small chunk of DNA from Neanderthals, suggesting we interbred with our closest known extinct relatives at some point in our history. So why isn't there more Neanderthal DNA in modern humans? Turns out, the Y chromosome may have been key in keeping the two lineages apart by creating conditions that might often have led to miscarriages if or when the two got together, researchers now say."

Angels and Demons: The Personification of Communication (Logology)

Chapter 14

Can Angels Rebel against God?

While some Christians are familiar with the notion of angels marrying human women, and while that Fallen Angel Story is the most prevalent one in the period preceding the New Testament, most Christians are more inclined to link the fall of the angels to some rebellion of angels. Specifically, Lucifer in Isaiah 14:12-14 (who many Christians believe is Satan) is thought to have led an angel rebellion against God:

יב אֵיךְ נָפַלְתָּ מִשָּׁמַיִם, הֵילֵל בֶּן-שָׁחַר; נִגְדַּעְתָּ לָאָרֶץ, חוֹלֵשׁ עַל-גּוֹיִם.

יג וְאַתָּה אָמַרְתָּ בִלְבָבְךָ, הַשָּׁמַיִם אֶעֱלֶה--מִמַּעַל לְכוֹכְבֵי-אֵל, אָרִים כִּסְאִי; וְאֵשֵׁב בְּהַר-מוֹעֵד, בְּיַרְכְּתֵי צָפוֹן.

יד אֶעֱלֶה, עַל-בָּמֳתֵי עָב; אֶדַּמֶּה, לְעֶלְיוֹן.

12 How art thou fallen from heaven, O day-star [Lucifer/הֵילֵל], son of the morning! How art thou cut down to the ground, that didst cast lots over the nations!

13 And thou saidst in thy heart: 'I will ascend into heaven, above the stars of God will I exalt my throne, and I will sit upon the mount of meeting, in the uttermost parts of the north;

14 I will ascend above the heights of the clouds; I will be like the Most High.' (KJV)

The motif of lesser gods rebelling against Zeus is the basis for the "Clash of the Titans" in Greek mythology. Therefore, the motif of angels rebelling against God made a good deal of sense to Jews who were living in the Greek Empire of Alexander the Great and his successors (between the Old and New Testaments). Furthermore, although the Isaiah 14 account has Lucifer "die like men" and be, thus, shown to be far inferior to God, many Christians view this Lucifer/Satan who led the supposed angelic rebellion against God to be almost equal to God in his strength and power. They believe that God and Lucifer/Satan are currently at war with one another, and some even believe it is possible that Lucifer/Satan will win. This motif of a Good God who is locked in struggle with an Evil God is neither Greek nor Jewish/Hebrew; it is Persian. (See Chapter 4: The "Great Satan" of Iran.) Both the New Testament and Rabbinic Judaism from the New Testament period reject the view that angels can rebel against God.

Bereshit Rabbah 27:4, a passage cited in Chapter 11: Can Angels "on Earth" Sin, but Not Angels "in Heaven"?, presents evidence that angels were incapable of rebellion against God. There, in his exposition of Genesis 6:6 (in which God repented that He had made man), Rabbi Judah, from the second century A.D., quotes God as saying regarding MAN: שאלו בראתי אותו מלמעלה לא היה מורד בי Translation: "For behold, (if) I had created him from above, he would not have rebelled against Me." The point of Rabbi Judah's remark is that, if man had been created out of the same substance as heavenly beings, he would have been incapable of rebellion against God. Even if one accepts the view of Rabbi Nehemiah, also from the second century A.D., in the same Bereshit Rabbah passage, that if God had made man in Heaven, he would have caused the heavenly beings to rebel against God [היה ממריד בי את העליונים], one still finds the same basic conclusion: that heavenly beings have never rebelled against God. Otherwise, Rabbi Nehemiah would not have presented God as "relieved" that he had made man "on the earth."

In Tanḥuma Book I, page 30 (an account that parallels Bereshit Rabbah 27:4), the common term for "angels" is used instead of the term "heavenly beings." Rabbi Judah (c. 150 A.D.) is quoted as saying that angels do not sin: שאין המלאכים חוטאין. Rabbi Nehemiah (c. 150 A.D.) says that God was consoled that He had not made man in heaven, because he [man] would have caused the angels to rebel: המלאכים היה ממרידן . Here, then, as in Bereshit Rabbah 27:4, angels remain non-rebellious.

The authoritative Judaic teaching of the period under consideration is in line with this Bereshit Rabbah passage. Angels did not rebel against God. However, we should hasten to add that this was not the position of the Church Fathers—those Christians who wrote, noncanonically, in the centuries following the New Testament period. As I mentioned in Chapter 9: Angels Have Only the Good Inclination, in Justin's *Dialogue with Trypho a Jew*, Dialogue 79, Trypho accuses Justin of blasphemy, because Justin says that angels sin and rebel against God [ἀγγέλους γάρ πονηρευσαμένους καὶ ἀποστάντας τοῦ θεοῦ λέγεις]. Here, it is clear that the Church Father taught that angels rebel, and it is equally clear that Judaism rejected that teaching.[69]

---

[69] Following is the text and translation of this passage from Justin, "Trypho," p. 284. :

Jews in this Post-New Testament Period even REWROTE the Book of Enoch. *The Hebrew Book of Enoch*, written by various authors of this time,[70] contains NO FALLEN REBEL ANGEL STORIES. It contains no account of rebellious fallen angels, such as the versions of the Book of Enoch written BETWEEN the Old and New Testaments do.[71] According to Bamberger (p. 94), "nowhere in Talmudic sources is Satan depicted as a rebel against God." Neither is any account of Satan rebelling against God to be found in the New Testament. According to the New Testament, the account of Lucifer in Isaiah 14:12-14 is NOT TALKING ABOUT THE FALL OF SATAN. Lucifer is NOT SATAN. I will discuss Lucifer and who he is in the next chapter.

Καί ὁ Τρύφων, ὑπαγανακτῶν μὲν, αἰδούμενος δὲ τὰς γραφάς, ὡς ἐδηλοῦτο ἀπὸ τοῦ προσώπου αὐτοῦ, εἶπε πρός με• Τὰ μὲν τοῦ θεοῦ ἁγιά ἐστιν, αἱ δὲ ὑμέτεραι ἐξηγήσεις τετεχνασμέναι εἰσίν, ὡς φαίνεται καὶ ἐκ τῶν ἐξηγημένων ὑπὸ σοῦ, μᾶλλον δὲ καὶ βλάσφημοι• ἀγγέλους γὰρ πονηρευσαμένους καὶ ἀποστάντας τοῦ θεοῦ λέγεις.

And Trypho, who was irritated, but reverenced the Scriptures, as was made visible from his countenance, said to me, "The words of God are holy, but your interpretations are contrived as is shown even by your explanations (themselves); moreover, they are blasphemous. For you say that angels sinned and rebelled against God.

[70] Hugo Odeberg, *3 Enoch (or) The Hebrew Book of Enoch*, a volume of *The Library of Biblical Studies*, ed. Harry M. Orlinsky (New York: KTAV Publishing House, Inc., 1973), pages 42 and 31 (Reprint) states that this book is "no homogeneous unity, or a work by a definite author in the modern sense of the words," but nevertheless contains passages that "compel the conclusion that the Hebrew Book of Enoch cannot have been written later than the time of the Babylonian Talmud."

[71] Cf. I Enoch 6-8 & 18.15-16, and II Enoch 18. This is, of course, an argument from silence, and the definite quotations in the sources previously cited are of much more value in establishing the view of the non-rebellious nature of angels, during this period.

Chapter 15

If He is NOT Satan, Who is Lucifer?

Presidents Barack Obama and Bill Clinton (and former-First-Lady-and-Secretary-of-State Hillary Clinton) are fans of Saul Alinsky, the author of the book *Rules for Radicals*. The book—which is also recommended by the NEA (National Association of Educators)--contains a quote about Lucifer: "Lest we forget at least an over-the-shoulder acknowledgment to the very first radical: from all our legends, mythology, and history (and who is to know where mythology leaves off and history begins -- or which is which), the first radical known to man who rebelled against the establishment and did it so effectively that he at least won his own kingdom -- Lucifer."[72]

Who is this Lucifer whom Alinsky acknowledges as the first radical, the first rebel against the establishment? Surely, Alinsky—in citing "legends, mythology, and history"—was intending to refer to Satan, thinking that Satan / Lucifer was a Fallen Angel who rebelled against the

---

[72] Saul D. Alinsky, *Rules for Radicals: A Pragmatic Primer for Realistic Radicals* (New York: Random House, 1971), preliminary materials.

establishment imposed by God. This view of Lucifer is based on an interpretation of Isaiah 14:12-15 (KJV):[73]

> "How art thou fallen from heaven, O Lucifer, son of the morning! [how] art thou cut down to the ground, which didst weaken the nations! For thou hast said in thine heart, I will ascend into heaven, I will exalt my throne above the stars of God: I will sit also upon the mount of the congregation, in the sides of the north: I will ascend above the heights of the clouds; I will be like the most High. Yet thou shalt be brought down to hell, to the sides of the pit."

Granted, if we begin reading in the middle of this chapter, at verse 12, Lucifer can appear to be a powerful angel who has fallen because of his attempt to rebel against "the Most High." That is, until we reach verse 16 (where it is clear that Lucifer is a man): "They that see thee shall narrowly look upon thee, [and] consider thee, [saying, Is] this the MAN that made the earth to tremble, that did shake kingdoms?" Verses 18-20 (KJV), furthermore, point out that Lucifer is a "king":

> All the kings of the nations, [even] all of them, lie in glory, every one in his own house. But thou art cast out of thy grave like an abominable branch, [and as] the raiment of those that are slain, thrust through with a sword, that go down to the stones of the pit; as a carcase trodden under feet. Thou shalt not be joined with them in burial, because thou hast destroyed thy land, [and] slain thy people.

---

[73] The Hebrew text of this passage is printed in Chapter 14: Can Angels Rebel against God?

We confirm this identification of Lucifer as the "king of Babylon" in the 4th verse of chapter 14: "That thou shalt take up this proverb against the king of Babylon." What follows, including the Lucifer passage in the middle of this chapter, is all a proverb denouncing the king of Babylon. Nowhere else in the entire Bible do we find an account of Satan being "buried"; yet we find burial concerns for Lucifer throughout verses 18-20, and in the verse immediately preceding verse twelve's Lucifer reference, Isaiah states concerning Lucifer: "Thy pomp is brought down to the grave, [and] the noise of thy viols: the worm is spread under thee, and the worms cover thee."

Politicians, especially those as powerful as the Clintons and Obamas, should be very hesitant to endorse Alinsky as he acknowledges Lucifer. This is true not because Lucifer is a "fallen angel" (he is NOT), but because Lucifer was a deluded human "POLITICAL ENTITY!" As the king of Babylon, Lucifer relished his power. Lucifer, the king of Babylon, as a powerful king "oppressed" the people of Israel, God's people (14:1-6). He did not hesitate to "persecute" (verse 6) the religious followers of the God of Abraham. Perhaps, in his freely oppressing God's people, he thought he was, thus, equal to the Most High (verse 14). Isaiah 14 is a condemnation of a political entity that thought he was so important that he could oppress and persecute followers of the Most High God.

Only two passages in the New Testament allude to the Lucifer passage in Isaiah:

Matthew 11:23 quotes Jesus: "And you Capernaum, were you not exalted to heaven? Brought down to Hades you will be." Jesus explains (in 11:20-25) that Chorazin, Bethsaida, and

Capernaum were cities (political entities) that did not repent from their conceited rejection of Jesus, and that other political entities such as Tyre and Sidon and Sodom would receive more grace on the day of judgment than they.

Luke 10:8-15 reports the same account, but in a somewhat more abbreviated form: "Capernaum, will you be lifted up to heaven? No, you will sink to Hades." Here, Jesus suggests that these towns would be treated less leniently than Sodom, Tyre, and Sidon, but not just because of their treatment of him. It will be so because of their treatment of his followers.

Notice that neither of these passages make any reference to Satan. Clearly, they understand the Isaiah passage to represent a condemnation of HUMAN political entities—those who mistreat the followers of the Most High God. The Lucifer of the Bible is not a fallen angel. Although there are some indications that Isaiah may have drawn upon some Babylonian mythology in his condemnation of the king of Babylon, he is not introducing a Fallen Angel Story. If any conclusions may be drawn from the Lucifer passage in Isaiah 14, it is that political entities who exercise power over God's people should be extremely careful not to mistreat God's followers.

Chapter 16

Did Satan Disobey God by Refusing to Worship Adam and/or Jesus?

Since I Enoch "claims" to be written by the man Enoch who lived before the Flood of Noah, we are pretty certain that the "claimed" authorship of the book is false. Enoch certainly would have lived long before the Greek language even came into existence, yet he wrote in Greek! We call such a book (whose authorship is falsified): "pseudepigrapha." Another book that is termed "pseudepigrapha" is the Latin book, *The Life of Adam and Eve* (*Vita Adae et Evae*, sometimes shortened to *Vita Adae*). This book is written in Latin, but Adam and Eve would have lived long before the Latin language even came into existence.

This book about Adam and Eve, however, presents another possible Fallen Angel Story.[74] The Devil is presented as an angel who was cast out of Heaven because of his refusal to bow down and

---

[74] Wells's translation of the Latin text may be found in: Wells, *The Books of Adam and Eve*. From *The Apocrypha and Pseudepigrapha of the Old Testament*, Ed. R. H. Charles, Volume II: Pseudepigrapha, (Oxford: At the Clarendon Press, 1913), 137.

worship Adam. He was expected to worship Adam because Adam was the "image of God" (Genesis 1:26). Later human cultures would make "graven images" of their gods and worship those images, so the author of *The Life of Adam and Eve* thought it logical that angels would have been expected to worship the (living) image of the one true God—Adam. According to this source, when the Devil's angels, over whom he was placed, heard of the Devil's refusal to honor Adam by bowing down, they also refused. Michael, who had been the first angel to worship Adam, then warned the Devil of the wrath of God should he persist in his refusal to pay homage to Adam. Whereupon the Devil was quoted as saying that he would set his seat above the stars of Heaven and would be like the Highest. I agree with Ginzberg[75] that this last statement is a reference to Isaiah 14:12-14 (the Lucifer passage), a reference which Ginzberg says R. H. Charles (the editor of the *Pseudipigrapha* text in which the *Life of Adam and Eve* is published) failed to recognize. I will present the full text of this *Life of Adam and Eve* Fallen Angel Story in the next chapter.

In this excerpt from the *Life of Adam and Eve*, however, we have parallels to Revelation 12:7-13.[76] In both accounts, it is Michael who leads in opposing the Devil. In both accounts, the serpent of

---

[75] Ginzberg, *Legends*, V, 35.
[76] Καὶ ἐγένετο πόλεμος ἐν τῷ οὐρανῷ, ὁ Μιχαὴλ καὶ οἱ ἄγγελοι αὐτοῦ τοῦ πολεμῆσαι μετὰ τοῦ δράκοντος. καὶ ὁ δράκων ἐπολέμησεν καὶ οἱ ἄγγελοι αὐτοῦ, καὶ οὐκ ἴσχυσαν, οὐδὲ τόπος εὑρέθη αὐτῶν ἔτι ἐν τῷ οὐρανῷ. καὶ ἐβλήθη ὁ δράκων ὁ μέγας, ὁ ὄφις ὁ ἀρχαῖος, ὁ καλούμενος Διάβολος καὶ Ὁ Σατανᾶς, ὁ πλανῶν τὴν οἰκουμένην ὅλην, ἐβλήθη εἰς τὴν γῆν, καὶ οἱ ἄγγελοι αὐτοῦ μετ' αὐτοῦ ἐβλήθησαν. καὶ ἤκουσα φωνὴν μεγάλην ἐν τῷ οὐρανῷ λέγουσαν Ἄρτι ἐγένετο ἡ σωτηρία καὶ ἡ δύναμις καὶ ἡ βασιλεία τοῦ Θεοῦ ἡμῶν καὶ ἡ ἐξουσία τοῦ Χριστοῦ αὐτοῦ, ὅτι ἐβλήθη ὁ κατήγωρ τῶν ἀδελφῶν ἡμῶν, ὁ κατηγορῶν αὐτοὺς ἐνώπιον τοῦ Θεοῦ ἡμῶν ἡμέρας καὶ νυκτός. καὶ αὐτοὶ ἐνίκησαν αὐτὸν διὰ τὸ αἷμα τοῦ Ἀρνίου καὶ διὰ τὸν λόγον τῆς μαρτυρίας αὐτῶν, καὶ οὐκ ἠγάπησαν τὴν ψυχὴν αὐτῶν ἄχρι θανάτου. διὰ τοῦτο εὐφραίνεσθε, οὐρανοὶ καὶ οἱ ἐν αὐτοῖς

Genesis is understood to be the Devil. In both accounts, the angels of the Devil are also indicted, along with the Devil himself. In both accounts, the Devil is cast down from Heaven to earth. Both accounts also refer to the "anger" of the Devil and his "pursuit" of mankind (*Life of Adam and Eve* 12 and Revelation 12:12-13).

Missing from the Revelation account, however, is any allusion to the Isaiah 14 passage. Missing from the *Life of Adam and Eve* account is the strong "dragon" imagery of the Revelation account. There is no mention in Revelation 12 of the Devil's refusal to worship Adam, though the Devil/Dragon has an apparent feeling of enmity towards the new-born child. He stands in the presence of the woman who was about to give birth in order to devour her child when he is born (καὶ ὁ δράκων ἕστηκεν ἐνώπιον τῆς γυναικὸς τῆς μελλούσης τεκεῖν, ἵνα ὅταν τέκῃ τὸ τέκνον αὐτῆς

σκηνοῦντες· οὐαὶ τὴν γῆν καὶ τὴν θάλασσαν, ὅτι κατέβη ὁ διάβολος πρὸς ὑμᾶς ἔχων θυμὸν μέγαν, εἰδὼς ὅτι ὀλίγον καιρὸν ἔχει. Καὶ ὅτε εἶδεν ὁ δράκων ὅτι ἐβλήθη εἰς τὴν γῆν, ἐδίωξεν τὴν γυναῖκα ἥτις ἔτεκεν τὸν ἄρσενα. (Nestle Greek text, 1904)
TRANSLATION (KJV): **7** And there was war in heaven: Michael and his angels fought against the dragon; and the dragon fought and his angels, **8** And prevailed not; neither was their place found any more in heaven. **9** And the great dragon was cast out, that old serpent, called the Devil, and Satan, which deceiveth the whole world: he was cast out into the earth, and his angels were cast out with him. **10** And I heard a loud voice saying in heaven, Now is come salvation, and strength, and the kingdom of our God, and the power of his Christ: for the accuser of our brethren is cast down, which accused them before our God day and night. **11** And they overcame him by the blood of the Lamb, and by the word of their testimony; and they loved not their lives unto the death. **12** Therefore rejoice, ye heavens, and ye that dwell in them. Woe to the inhabiters of the earth and of the sea! for the devil is come down unto you, having great wrath, because he knoweth that he hath but a short time. **13** And when the dragon saw that he was cast unto the earth, he persecuted the woman which brought forth the man child.

καταφάγῃ). I agree with R. H. Charles's[77] and Martin Kiddle's[78] commentaries on Revelation when they say that the "child" of Revelation 12 is a messianic reference. Jesus is the child. I Corinthians 15:45-47, in stating that the first Adam became a living soul, while the last Adam became a life-giving spirit, strongly implies that Jesus should be understood to be a second Adam. In this same vein, Ginzberg[79] comments: "It is quite possible that Hebrews 1:6 goes back to [*The Life of Adam and Eve*] . . . and[80] . . . makes the angels worship the second Adam (=Jesus), instead of the first." Hebrews 1:6 states:

> ὅταν δὲ πάλιν εἰσαγάγῃ τὸν πρωτότοκον εἰς τὴν οἰκουμένην, λέγει Καὶ προσκυνησάτωσαν αὐτῷ πάντες ἄγγελοι Θεοῦ.
>
> TRANSLATION: And again, when He leads the first-born into the inhabited world, He says, "And let all of the angels of God prostrate themselves before him!"

A parallel indictment of the Devil in both accounts is that he "misleads." In the *Life of Adam and Eve* account, Eve was misled; in Revelation, the Devil/Dragon misled the whole world. There is no indication, however, in Revelation that the Devil/Dragon is an angel like the Devil of the *Life of Adam and Eve* account, nor is it clear whether "his angels" in Revelation 12 are, like the Devil's angels in the *Life of Adam and Eve* account, actually "angels of God under the Devil's authority."

---

[77] R. H. Charles, *The Revelation of St. John*, Vol. 44 of *The International Critical Commentary*, (44 vols.; New York: Charles Scribner's Sons, 1920), I, 320.
[78] Martin Kiddle, *The Revelation of St. John*, from *The Moffat New Testament Commentary*, (multi-volume; New York & London: Harper and Brothers), 213.
[79] Ginzberg, *Legends*, V, 85.
[80] "in midrashic fashion"

16: Did Satan Disobey God by Refusing to Worship Adam and/or Jesus?

I have already discussed the Devil's "misleading/lying/deceiving" in Chapter 5: What Law Did the Angels Break? I do not find it necessarily to be a sin.

The parallels between Revelation and the *Life of Adam and Eve* account do seem to indicate that John, the author of Revelation, was familiar with the pseudepigraphal book, *The Life of Adam and Eve*. Frankly, John is familiar with a tremendous amount of literature and he draws profusely on images from that literature as he writes the book of Revelation. This, of course, does not mean that John believes *The Life of Adam and Eve* is inspired. He does seem to think there is merit in the belief that the second Adam is worthy of worship, however. He shows how the transition from worshiping only God (in Revelation 4) to worshiping BOTH God AND the Lamb (in Revelation 5) was accomplished. And, he asserts that both God and the Lamb are "worthy" of worship by every creature in Heaven and on earth, in the seas, and under the earth (Revelation 5:13-14).

So, Revelation seeks to establish that Jesus, the second Adam, is worthy of worship. It does not present the Devil and/or his angels, however, as refusing to worship him. The Devil is, indeed, cast out of Heaven in Revelation 12:7-9, but not because of any refusal to worship Jesus. He was cast out because "there was no room (τόπος) found for him in Heaven." His job as accuser had been downsized. Jesus' blood had paid the price for the sins of all those he was accusing.

As an aside, and along the same line, in my book *Revelation: The Human Drama* (80), I comment:

> Wellhausen claims, "The [image of the Beast] is the alter ego of the empire just as Jesus was called the [image] of God" (cf. II Corinthians 4:4 and Colossians 1:15), then a living human being serves as the "image" of the beast, just as the human,

Jesus, serves as the "image" of God. Where exactly Wellhausen derives his information that Jesus is the [image] of God, Charles does not indicate; and the explicit statement is found nowhere in Revelation. However, the [*Life of Adam and Eve*] 13-14 passage clearly calls Adam the "image" of God, and Ginzberg sees in . . . Heb. 1:6 the link which makes Jesus a second Adam in the fashion of [*The Life of Adam and Eve*], hence making him worthy of worship. Thus, intertestamental literature with which John could easily be familiar has a human serving as an "image," and therefore receiving "worship."

If John is making the "image" of God (Jesus) in Revelation 5 "worthy of praise," then, in antithetical fashion, he could be making the "image" of the beast (the high priest) in Revelation 13 the object of (unworthy) antichristian worship. In this way, John could be saying that ironically the abomination which the Jews had felt that they had avoided in the assassination of Caligula happened anyway! Instead of an image of stone, the Jews had in the middle of their temple an amazing sign--an image that could "speak" (13:15)! He was the voice of the Empire in the midst of the temple.

Chapter 17

The Life of Adam and Eve- (Satan Refuses to Worship God's Image)

In the previous chapter, I promised to supply the excerpt from the pseudepigraphal work in which the Devil is cast out of Heaven for refusing to worship Adam. The following is Wells' translation of the Latin text, *The Books of Adam and Eve* 12-17, taken from *The Apocrypha and Pseudepigrapha of the Old Testament*, edited by R. H. Charles, Volume II: Pseudepigrapha (Oxford: Clarendon Press, 1913), p. 137:

XII 1) And with a heavy sigh, the devil spake: "O Adam! All my hostility, envy, and sorrow is for thee, since it is for thee that I have been expelled from my glory, which I possessed in the heavens in the midst of the angels and for thee was I cast out in the earth."

2) Adam answered, "What dost thou tell me? What have I done to thee or what is my fault against thee?

3) Seeing that thou hast received no harm or injury from us, why dost thou pursue us?"

XIII 1) The devil replied, "Adam, what dost thou tell me? It is for thy sake that I have been hurled from that place.

2) When thou wast formed, I was hurled out of the presence of God and banished from the company of the angels. When God blew into thee the breath of life and thy face and likeness was made in the image of God, Michael also brought thee and made (us) worship thee in the sight of God; and God the Lord spake: 'Here is Adam. I have made thee in our image and likeness.'

XIV 1) And Michael went out and called all the angels saying: 'Worship the image of God as the Lord God hath commanded.'

2) And Michael himself worshipped first; then he called me and said: 'Worship the image of God the Lord.'

3) And I answered, 'I have no (need) to worship Adam.' And since Michael kept urging me to worship, I said to him, 'Why dost thou urge me? I will not worship an inferior and younger being (than I). I am his senior in the creation, before he was made was I already made. It is his duty to worship me.

XV 1) When the angels, who were under me, heard this, they refused to worship him.

2) And Michael saith, 'Worship the image of God, but if thou wilt not worship him, the Lord God will be wrath with thee.'

3) And I said, 'If He be wrath with me, I will set my seat above the stars of heaven and will be like the Highest.'

XVI 1) And God the Lord was wrath with me and banished me and my angels from our glory; and on thy account were we expelled from our abodes into this world and hurled on the earth.

2) And straightway we were overcome with grief, since we had been spoiled of so great glory.

3) And we were grieved when we saw thee in such joy and luxury.

4) And with guile I cheated thy wife and caused thee to be expelled through her (doing) from thy joy and luxury, as I have been driven out of my glory."

17: The Life of Adam and Eve *(Satan Refuses to Worship God's Image)*

XVII 1) When Adam heard the devil say this, he cried out and wept and spake: "O Lord my God, my life is in thy hands. Banish this Adversary far from me, who seeketh to destroy my soul, and give me his glory which he himself hath lost."

2) And at that moment, the devil vanished before him.

3) But Adam endured in his penance, standing for forty days (on end) in the water of Jordan.

For purposes of comparison, I supply my translation of Revelation 12:7-13. I drew the comparison and contrast in the previous chapter.

> And war came to pass in heaven; Michael and his angels had to war with the dragon. And the dragon waged war, also his angels, but they did not prevail, nor was there found a place for them in heaven, any longer. And the great dragon was cast out, the ancient serpent, who is called Devil and Satan, who misleads the whole inhabitable (world). He was cast to the earth and his angels were cast with him. And I heard a great voice in heaven, saying: "Now has come the salvation and the power and the kingdom of our God and of His Christ, because the accuser of our brothers, who accuses them before our God day and night, is cast out. And they overcame him by reason of the blood of the Lamb and through the word of their testimony, and they loved not their life unto death. Because of this, Rejoice! Heavens, and you who dwell in them. Woe! (upon) the earth and the sea, for the Devil came down to you, having great fury, knowing that he has a short time." And when the dragon saw that he was cast to the earth, he pursued the woman who brought forth the male.

Chapter 18
God Commanded Angels to Worship Jesus, but Not Adam

In the two prior chapters, I considered the pseudepigraphal *Book of Adam and Eve*, in which angels were expected to worship Adam, because he was the "image of God." Satan and his angels supposedly "sinned" because they refused to worship Adam, thus rebelling against the will of God. There was never, however, any "law" or "command" given to angels that they must worship Adam. The New Testament is consistent with the writings of the Jewish rabbis in the period following the New Testament, in this regard. Although Satan is certainly considered the adversary of mankind in the New Testament, nowhere is he presented as the adversary of God. 1 Peter 5:8 warns the readers: "Be on guard! Your adversary, the Devil, prowls around like a roaring lion, seeking someone to devour." Nevertheless, 1 Peter calls him YOUR adversary, not the adversary of God. Revelation 12:10 calls him the "accuser" of the "brothers," but does not paint him as a challenger to God. Instead, he seems to be doing exactly what God allows him to do: He "accuses them before our God, day and night." That is, until God has a justification for ending the accusing and casting "Satan out of his presence." Revelation 12 claims that Jesus' blood secured forgiveness for those whom Satan was accusing: "And they overcame him by reason of the blood of the Lamb and through the word of their testimony, and they loved not their life unto death." Unlike Adam, who disbelieved God's warning, rebelled against God, and thus lost his life, Jesus and his followers (the martyrs) believed God, voluntarily gave up their lives, and defeated Satan, their accuser. Adam, although he was made in the "image of God," never fulfilled the role. It remained for one of Adam's offspring or "seed" (Genesis 3:15) to perfect the role of the true "image of God."

Here is what the Jewish rabbis[81] had to say about Adam-worship. Kohelet Rabbah 6.10 offers a parable of a king and a governor who were riding together. The people wanted to address the king with respect, but did not know which of the two men was king. The king therefore pushed the governor out of the chariot. Therefore, the people knew they should pay respect to him, rather than to the governor. Kohelet Rabbah was offering this as a parable pertaining to the question of whether angels should worship God or God's image (Adam):

בשעה שברא הקב"ה אדם הראשון מעו בו מלאכי השרת ובקשו לומר לפניו קדוש מה עשה הקב"ה הפיל עליו שינה וידעו שהוא אדם. ואמר לו כי עפר אתה ואל עפר תשוב.

TRANSLATION: At the time when the Holy One—Blessed be He—created the first man, the ministering angels were mistaken in him and they wanted to pronounce before him, "Holy!" What did the Holy One—Blessed be He—do? He caused a sleep to fall upon him. And [the angels] recognized that he was man. And

---

[81] In the tannaitic-amoraic period.

> [God] said to [Adam], "For dust thou art and to dust thou shalt return" [Genesis 3:19].

This story also occurs in Bereshit Rabbah 8.10, where it is attributed to Rabbi Hoshaya. Bernard Bamberger[82] says that this account "seems to be directed against this [Adam-worshipping] . . . legend." Bamberger states: "This tale rules out the notion that the angels had to worship Adam."

Of course, one will not find anywhere in the writings of the Jewish rabbis a suggestion that God commanded angels to worship Jesus! Jewish rabbis did not believe Jesus was the Christ. But, even Moslems (who DO believe that Jesus was the Christ) are unwilling to make him the object of worship. Both Jews and Moslems reject the doctrine of Trinity. My Jewish major professor of Hebrew at Indiana University, Henry Fischel, pointed out to me that nowhere in the New Testament does the word "Trinity" occur. What both Jews and Moslems may find interesting, however, is that the Book of Revelation does not rely on any doctrine of Trinity to make Jesus worthy of worship. Revelation chapter 4 describes the scene in Heaven in which all the universe (including angels) worshipped the ONE Lord God Almighty, pronouncing the very word Kohelet Rabbah and Bereshit Rabbah employ in worship: "Holy!" Then, in chapter 5 of Revelation, the Lamb is also deemed worthy of worship (but not by using the word "Holy!"). This is a stunning development. Now, in a sense similar to the (incorrect) pseudepigraphal *Book of Adam and Eve*, someone besides God is declared worthy of worship by the angels. Yet, the Lamb is not presented there as a divine being. He is seated "at the right hand" of the One seated on the throne (5:1). He

---

[82] Bamberger, *Fallen Angels*, 94.

is presented as the "conqueror" (5:5). His conquest is associated with the shedding of his "blood" (5:9). Like God, he is "worthy" to receive praise (5:13). But, throughout the book of Revelation, although the word "almighty" is used several times to refer to the One God, it is never applied to Jesus. I comment in *Revelation: The Human Drama*:[83]

> Jesus is "known as 'the first and the last, the beginning and the end,' in 3:14; he is called 'the [beginning] of the creation of God.' (Similarly, 1:5 calls him the 'first-born . . . from the dead.') In 22:13, John provides another formula describing Jesus as [beginning and end]: 'I am the alpha and the omega.' Jesus, as 'the Lamb who was slain' (5:6,12) would serve as the archetype for John's concept of human . . . perfection. . . . Jesus as the . . . 'Lamb who was slain' can stand . . . for all perfect conquerors (martyrs). Hence, . . . he represents the proper response to Rome for every Christian. Jesus is never referred to as *pantokratôr* (the Almighty) or as the one 'who was and who is and who is coming.' However, John connects the phrase ' [the first and the last]' with Jesus in language about his being 'dead' and now being 'alive' (a similar notion) in 1:17-18 and 2:8.
>
> . . . Not unexpectedly, 'God' is also linked with such perfectionist language. In 21:6, apparently God is the self-designated 'alpha and the omega, the [beginning] and the [end].' And in 1:8, the phrase just quoted is applied to God along with another equal phrase: 'who was and who is and who is coming,' plus 'the Almighty.' Likewise, 1:4 identifies God as the one 'who was and who is and who is coming.' 4:8 and 11:17 repeat this identification of God and include [Almighty.] Other verses which identify God as [Almighty] include 15.3, 16:7,14, 19:6,15, and 21:22."

---

[83] Lindsay, *Revelation*, p. 120.

While these parallels indicate a close resemblance between God and Jesus, so does the terminology "the image of God" as it is applied to Adam. If John were trying to advance a picture of the Trinity, it seems strange that he does not include an extra chapter dedicated to worshipping the Holy Spirit. There are only TWO in Revelation who are worthy of worship--not three. I am reminded of the fact that Revelation does not promote the doctrine of Trinity every time I sing the song "Holy! Holy! Holy!" The lyrics of the song surely come from Revelation 4 and 5, and yet they offer the conclusion: "God in three persons, Blessed Trinity." This is not found in Revelation. Any Jew or Moslem who objects to the Doctrine of Trinity need not be offended by the approach of the Book of Revelation. Certainly, Jesus is worshipped by angels (and all other creatures), as is God. But the logic of why Jesus is so worshipped seems not to be related to a doctrine of Jesus' divinity. It seems closer to the view that the "image of God" should be worshipped. Adam did not fully fit the bill for deserving worship, because Adam sinned and brought death upon mankind. Jesus—Adam's seed—more clearly fits the bill, because he did not sin and yet shed his blood to nullify the role of Satan in heaven. Satan was cast out because his job as accuser had been outmoded. Jesus' blood defeated the Satan/accuser.

114 *Angels and Demons: The Personification of Communication (Logology)*

Chapter 19

Satan Temporarily Laid Off (From his Second Job)

According to Revelation, Satan lost his first job—that of "accuser of the brothers"—due to the "blood" of Jesus. Revelation, therefore, places the Fall of Satan somewhere around 30 A.D. The Hebrew word "SATAN" [שָׂטָן] means "prosecuting attorney." Prosecuting attorney was Satan's FIRST job. There is no need for a prosecutor, if all of the accused have been "pardoned." While John the writer of Revelation is familiar with virtually all of the Fallen Angel Stories I have been discussing—angels sin, angels marry human women, angels bring culture to mankind, angels rebel against God, angels refuse to worship Adam, etc.—he seems to reject them all in favor of a progressive "outmoding of Satan's jobs" approach. Satan (sometimes considered an angel in both

New Testament and Rabbinic sources) is presented as an opponent of man, though "nowhere in Talmudic sources is Satan depicted as a rebel against God."[84] According to Bamberger:

> Satan's functions are clearly described in a tannaitic statement: He descends to earth and leads men astray. Then he ascends and inflames God's wrath by reporting their sins. Having received permission, he deprives them of life.[85]

The first job of Satan to be eliminated was that of accuser/prosecuting attorney. The loss of this job resulted in Satan being cast to earth because there was no longer a job for him "in Heaven." No longer did Satan's job(s) require him to be in the presence of God. Before whom else would Satan have accused and prosecuted the brothers? God is the ultimate Judge. Satan needed to be in His presence to present the prosecution's case against the brothers. There is no sin in this task, but it is certainly a task God and "the brothers" would have been happy to see ended. Yet, Satan has other jobs: tempter, executioner, and raiser of world empires. To our knowledge, there has never been a time in human history in which Satan's jobs as tempter and executioner were put on hold. The end of those two jobs will eventually occur, according to Revelation, when Death and Hades are cast into the Lake of Fire. There was a time, however, in which Satan's second job--as the raiser of world empires--was temporarily curtailed.

John predicted the temporary elimination of Satan's second job in Revelation 20:1-3:

---

[84] Bamberger, *Fallen Angels*, 94. Concerning the Satan=angel thought, cf. J. Michl, "Engel IV (christlich)," *Reallexikon*, V, 112 (for New Testament usage; Bamberger, *Fallen Angels*, 82ff. (for Church Father usage); and Bamberger, *Fallen Angels*, 94ff. (for usage in the Talmud and Midrash).
[85] Bamberger, *Fallen Angels*, 94.

19: Satan Temporarily Laid Off (From his Second Job)

και ειδον αγγελον καταβαινοντα εκ του ουρανου εχοντα την κλειν της αβυσσου και αλυσιν μεγαλην επι την χειρα αυτου

² και εκρατησεν τον δρακοντα ο οφις ο αρχαιος ος εστιν διαβολος και ο σατανας και εδησεν αυτον χιλια ετη

³ και εβαλεν αυτον εις την αβυσσον και εκλεισεν και εσφραγισεν επανω αυτου ινα μη πλανηση ετι τα εθνη αχρι τελεσθη τα χιλια ετη μετα ταυτα δει λυθηναι αυτον μικρον χρονον

TRANSLATION: And I saw an angel descending from Heaven, holding in his hand the key to the Abyss and a gigantic chain. He overpowered the Dragon—the ancient serpent who is the devil and Satan—and bound him for one thousand years. He hurled him into the Abyss, which he closed and sealed above him, so that HE MIGHT NO LONGER LEAD THE NATIONS ASTRAY until the thousand years are ended. After that, he must be released for a little while.

We know that the point of Satan's being bound for one thousand years is to see that the NATIONS are no longer led astray, because John repeats the rationale in 20:7-8:

⁷ και οταν τελεσθη τα χιλια ετη λυθησεται ο σατανας εκ της φυλακης αυτου

⁸ και εξελευσεται πλανησαι τα εθνη τα εν ταις τεσσαρσιν γωνιαις της γης τον γωγ και μαγωγ συναγαγειν αυτους εις τον πολεμον ων ο αριθμος αυτων ως η αμμος της θαλασσης

When the thousand years have ended, Satan will be released from his prison and will go out TO LEAD ASTRAY THE NATIONS in the four corners of the Land/Earth—Gog and Magog—to muster them FOR BATTLE. Their number is as the sands of the sea.

Going along with John's concept of a temporary end to the world empires who affect God's people is the concept that each NATION/world-empire has its own guardian angel who rises, then falls. This teaching is strong in Rabbinic literature. I will discuss the Rabbinic sources of this teaching in the next chapter.

I mentioned in Chapter 4 the great world empires that had affected the Jewish nation:

> The BABYLONIAN Empire 627-539 B.C. (King Nebuchadnezzar of Babylon carried the Jews away into captivity in 567 B.C. The prophet Daniel and his friends—Shadrach, Meshach, and Abednego—were among the young men who were captured. Daniel predicted the eventual Fall of Babylon to the Persian King Cyrus.)

> The MEDO-PERSIAN Empire 539-323 B.C. (Jewish princess Esther becomes the Queen of Persia from 492 to 460 B.C. Around 400 B.C., under the rule of Persia, the last two books of the Bible were written—Ezra and Nehemiah—as these two men reestablished the Jewish religion in Jerusalem.)

> The GREEK Empire 323-146 B.C. (In a period entirely between the Old and New Testaments, the Greek religious influence was strong. This is called the Hellenistic period. During this time, the Maccabees mounted a successful Jewish revolt against Greece and, then, Greek ruler Antiochus IV Epiphanes defiled the Jerusalem Temple with Greek religious practices and forbade the practice of the Jewish religion.)

> The ROMAN Empire (146 or 27) B.C.-476 A.D. (While the Romans conquered Greece in 146 B.C., they really did not become an "Empire" until their first "Emperor" Augustus Caesar in 27 B.C. Augustus was the Emperor during whose reign Jesus was born. Christians will certainly remember the decree that went forth

from Augustus Caesar. Augustus was most likely the First Head of the seven-headed Beast of Revelation.)

John seems to be predicting that (with the Fall of the Roman Empire) there would be a one-thousand-year period during which time there would be a (relative) absence of world empires affecting the people of God. I write in *Revelation: The Human Drama*:

> The frustration with reading amillennialists (those who hold that the thousand-year period is completely figurative) is that there is definite evidence of Jewish teachings in the First Century which predicted a literal thousand or two-thousand-year reign of the Messiah.[86]

What is this evidence from First Century Jewish teachings? In *Revelation*,[87] I explain:

> At about the time John wrote the Book of Revelation, a respected school of Rabbinic (Jewish) thought, the school of Elias, was teaching a peculiar interpretation of history that attempted to sum up all of human history--past, present, and future. In some respects, this interpretation of history resembles Greek drama. The German scholar, Paul Billerbeck, observes that, according to the school of Elias, humankind would exist on earth for a total of six thousand years. Two thousand years would be spent without the Law; two thousand years with the Law; and two thousand years would be spent under the rule of the messiah.
>
> The school based its interpretation of history partly upon the Biblical formula found in Psalm 90:4 that "a thousand years in [God's] sight are like a day that has just gone by." According to the various calculations of the school, the Jewish people had been punished by God (*i.e.*, had been under the domination of foreign powers)

---

[86] Lindsay, *Revelation*, 17.
[87] Lindsay, *Revelation*, 24-25.

for a total of one thousand years, beginning with the 400 years spent in Egypt from the time of Joseph to the time of Moses. Because Israel had been punished for one thousand years, Rabbi Yehoschua, from the late first century A.D., reasons that the messianic period (the earthly reign of the Christ) should last for two thousand years. Along with other rabbis, he observes that Psalm 90:15 petitions God: "Make us glad for as many days as you have afflicted us, for as many years as we have seen trouble." Yehoschua finds it striking that, according to his calculations, the Jewish people had been "afflicted" or had "seen trouble" for one thousand years--the formulaic "day" of the Lord from the earlier passage in the same Psalm. Hence, he anticipates at least a "thousand years" messianic reign. However, Yehoschua also observes that the word "day" in 90:15 is plural, whereas in 90:4 it is singular. Therefore, Yehoschua opines that there should be "two" day_s_ of messianic reign, rather than just one. Thus, the reign of the Christ, he thought, should last for two thousand years.[88]

. . .

At least two New Testament writers (John and the author of II Peter) connect a "thousand year" formula to speculation concerning future divine activity. II Peter warns, "But do not forget this one thing, dear friends: With the Lord a day is like a thousand years, and a thousand years are like a day. . . . But the day of the Lord will come like a thief. The heavens will disappear with a roar; the elements will be destroyed by fire" (II Peter 3:8 & 10).

Billerbeck acknowledges that John may be aware of Yehoschua's interpretation of history. Yet, John does not explicitly paint himself into a corner regarding time

---

[88] Paul Billerbeck, *Die Briefe des Neuen Testaments und die Offenbarung Johannis*, Vol. III of *Kommentar zum Neuen Testament aus Talmud und Midrasch* (Munich: C. H. Beck'sche, 1961), 826-827.

frames, as do Yehoschua and the school of Elias. John does indicate that there would be at least one "thousand years" period. During these thousand years, "the dragon, that ancient serpent, who is the devil, or Satan," would be "bound" and thrown "into the Abyss . . . to keep him from deceiving the nations anymore until the thousand years were ended" (Revelation 20:2-3). Following these "thousand years," however, John does not appear to promise an immediate end to human history. Instead, "After that, [the dragon] must be set free for a short time" (Revelation 20:3). John predicts: "When the thousand years are over, Satan will be released from his prison and will go out to deceive the nations in the four corners of the earth [or 'land']" (Revelation 20:7-8). An indeterminate amount of time follows the "thousand years" of the book of Revelation. John's Revelation does not preclude the claim of Yehoschua and it is at least possible that John's vision partially corroborates the view of Yehoschua and/or the school of Elias.

I mentioned in Chapter 1 that Henry A. Fischel contends that both New Testament Christianity and Rabbinic Judaism were being influenced by Hellenistic culture, but both milieus were recalcitrant. I conclude, then, the following:

> Both Greek drama and the "weltwochenschema" (cosmic week cosmology) of the school of Elias were possibly well-known to John. There are indications that John is writing some important episodes of the "Human Drama" based upon an implicit dramatic pattern quite similar to the pattern taught by the school of Elias.[89]

John is not alone in predicting this period of freedom from the domination of world empires. As Daniel had predicted the Fall of Babylon to Persia, he can be understood to be predicting the

---

[89] Lindsay, *Revelation*, 26

succeeding empires and their falls. The conclusion of Daniel's prophecies is invariably a period dominated by God and his servants. Daniel 7:13-18 speaks of "One coming with the clouds . . . like a son of man" to whom was given" a universal "kingdom for ever and ever." Isaiah 11 describes this period of peace in such terminology as lambs lying down with lions, leopards, wolves, cattle, bears, and oxen. Isaiah 2:2-5 describes the period:

וְהָיָה בְּאַחֲרִית הַיָּמִים נָכוֹן יִהְיֶה הַר בֵּית־ יְהוָה בְּרֹאשׁ הֶהָרִים וְנִשָּׂא מִגְּבָעוֹת וְנָהֲרוּ אֵלָיו כָּל־ הַגּוֹיִם:

וְהָלְכוּ עַמִּים רַבִּים וְאָמְרוּ לְכוּ וְנַעֲלֶה אֶל־ הַר־ יְהוָה אֶל־ בֵּית אֱלֹהֵי יַעֲקֹב וְיֹרֵנוּ מִדְּרָכָיו וְנֵלְכָה בְּאֹרְחֹתָיו כִּי מִצִּיּוֹן תֵּצֵא תוֹרָה וּדְבַר־ יְהוָה מִירוּשָׁלִָם:

וְשָׁפַט בֵּין הַגּוֹיִם וְהוֹכִיחַ לְעַמִּים רַבִּים וְכִתְּתוּ חַרְבוֹתָם לְאִתִּים וַחֲנִיתוֹתֵיהֶם לְמַזְמֵרוֹת לֹא־ יִשָּׂא גוֹי אֶל־ גּוֹי חֶרֶב וְלֹא־ יִלְמְדוּ עוֹד מִלְחָמָה:

בֵּית יַעֲקֹב לְכוּ וְנֵלְכָה בְּאוֹר יְהוָה:

TRANSLATION: "Now it shall come to pass in the latter days that the mountain of the Lord's house shall be established on the top of the mountains, and shall be exalted above the hills; and all NATIONS [הַגּוֹיִם] shall flow to it. Many people shall come and say, 'Come, and let us go up to the mountain of the Lord, To the house of the God of Jacob; He will teach us His ways, And we shall walk in His paths.' For out of Zion shall go forth the Law, and the word of the Lord from Jerusalem. He shall judge between the NATIONS, and rebuke many people; they shall beat their swords into plowshares, and their spears into pruning hooks; NATION shall not lift up sword against NATION, neither shall they learn war anymore" (NIV).

19: Satan Temporarily Laid Off (From his Second Job)

The prediction from Isaiah "Nation shall not lift up sword against nation" may well be what John had in mind when he wrote of Satan "no longer lead[ing] the nations astray." I see in John's interpretation of the messianic reign as presented by Isaiah and Daniel the following elements:

- The temporary period will last one thousand years.
- It will be a time of relative peace in the sense that major "national" conflicts will not occur (nation will not rise against nation).
- A universal kingdom shall be led by a "son of man," a representative of the Lord.
- Instead of studying war, many people will study the ways of the God of Jacob.

You can imagine how I was impressed, then, when my professor of Greek Lyric Poetry at Indiana University, Willis Barnstone, made a comment in class, roughly fifty years ago, to the effect that for a thousand years, secular Greek and Roman literature was systematically destroyed and that Christian literature was the only thing that was preserved. If one desired to study anything, the only thing available to him/her was Christian literature. Barnstone was referring to the Dark Ages—the period from the Fall of the Roman Empire to the Renaissance. His comments were in line with a quotation attributed to him on Wikiquote concerning Sappho, a Greek poet from the sixth and seventh centuries BC. The Barnestone/Wikiquote calls her a "prolific and much acclaimed writer, [who] is credited with either seven or nine long books of poetry, but over a thousand years of neglect and hostility destroyed most of her work" (http://en.wikiquote.org/wiki/Sappho). Barnstone appeared to me to be unhappy that Christians had destroyed so much of Greco-Roman civilization during this thousand-year period. Yet, it occurred to me that Barnstone had also identified a one-thousand-year period in which there was a time of relative peace—in the sense that major "national" conflicts did not occur—during which time many people studied the ways of the God of Jacob. Christianity, Judaism, and Islam were all Abrahamic religions that flourished during this period and became three of the largest religions in the world.

One could actually say that the Satanic job of raising world empires was temporarily eliminated for a thousand years. Nevertheless, with the Renaissance came a rebirth in interest in Greco-Roman culture. With the Renaissance came a rebirth in NATIONALISTIC spirit, and as John predicted, THE NATIONS in the four corners of the Land (of Israel) once again mustered FOR BATTLE.

Chapter 20

Jacob's Ladder, with the Guardian Angels of Each Nation—Rising and Falling

Jacob's Ladder figures into the Sinless Fallen Angel Story I mentioned in Chapter 6—in which the righteous young maiden tricked the angels into giving her their wings and teaching her to pronounce the unpronounceable name of God. She flew away to Heaven and they were left on the earth—UNTIL they found Jacob's Ladder and climbed back into Heaven. Jacob's Ladder now, once again, figures into a Fallen Angel Story. This story is related to my previous chapter in which Satan (as the Raiser of World Empires) is chained in the Abyss for one thousand years, "so that HE MIGHT NO LONGER LEAD THE NATIONS ASTRAY until the one thousand years are ended." Here, however, the angels do not actually "fall;" instead, they just "descend." John 1:51 contains another (very difficult) account of angels who ascend and descend upon Jesus (the ladder?).[90] Beauford H. Bryant (my uncle) observes: "The saying surely has Jacob's dream in

---

[90] For a discussion of this text, cf. Raymond E. Brown, *The Gospel According to John (i-xii)*, (Garden City, NY: Doubleday & Company, Inc., 1966), 88-91.

Genesis 28:12 in mind with the angels' ascending and descending," but Bryant comments further about the order of these angelic actions.[91] The ascending-and-descending order would seem to be backward, if this were a case of fallen angels as described in previous chapters—including the Sinless Fallen Angel story of Chapter 6. Both Genesis and John use this order. This order, however, is easily justified in the ascending and descending angels of the fallen angel story considered in this chapter.

John the author of Revelation is, of course, familiar with the Jewish concept of the guardian angels of each nation—ascending and descending on Jacob's ladder—and he even agrees with the end of the Jewish story. The story ends with the angel of a certain nation ascending the ladder, but never descending. This is the story of the ascending and descending national guardian angels (also called "princes") of history's world empires. Piska 23.2 of Pesikta de-Rab Kahana [PRK] provides the following interpretation of the Jacob's Ladder account from Genesis 28:12:

(יז)אמר ר׳ ברכיה ור׳ חלבו

(יח)בן ר׳ שמעון בן יוסינא בש״ר מאיר

(יט)מלמר שרראה הקב״ה ליעקב אבינו,

שרה של בבל עולה ויורד, ושל מדי עולה ויורד, ושל יון עולה ויורד, ושל אדום עולה ויורד,

א״ל הקב״ה יעקב אף אתה עולה, באותה שעה נתיירא יעקב אבינו,

ואמר תאמר שכשם שיש לאלו ירידה,

---

[91] Beauford H. Bryant & Mark S. Krause, *The College Press NIV Commentary: John*, (Joplin, MO: The College Press Publishing Company, 1998), 68.

20: Jacob's Ladder, with the Guardian Angels of Each Nation—Rising and Falling

אף אני יש לי ירידה, א״ל הקב״ה אל תחת ישראל,

אם אתה עולה אין לך ירידה לעולם, ולא האמין ולא עלה.

TRANSLATION: Rabbi Berechiah, with Rabbi Ḥelbo, the son of Rabbi Simeon, the son of Yosina, in the name of Rabbi Meir, said: "It teaches that the Holy One—Blessed be He—caused Jacob, our Father, to see the prince of Babel (Babylon) ascending and descending, (then the prince) of Media ascending and descending, then (the prince) of Yavan (Greece) ascending and descending, then (the prince) of Edom (Rome) ascending and descending. The Holy One—Blessed be He—said to him (Jacob), 'Jacob, you are ascending, too.' In that hour, Jacob, our Father, was afraid, and he said, 'Would you say that just like what happened to these—a descending—will also happen to me—a descending?' The Holy One—Blessed be He—said to him, 'You will not come down,[92] Israel (Jeremiah 30:10). If you go up, there will never be a descent for you.' But he did not believe, and he did not ascend."

Clearly, this passage hints at an eternal kingdom by Israel, following upon the fall of Rome. John, in Revelation, paints virtually the same picture. In John's account, however, the Lion from the Tribe of Judah does, indeed, "conquer" (5:5), ascend to reign over the earth (5:10), stand on Mount Zion (14:1), with his 144,000 from the twelve tribes of Israel (7:4-8), leading the New Jerusalem (21:2) to power. And, he shall reign forever and ever (22:5), John predicts.

---

[92] Or, "you will not be disappointed."

A parallel of the PRK account is Leviticus Rabbah[93] 29:2. This version attributes the story again to Rabbi Berechiah (5th generation Amora) and Rabbi Ḥelbo (4th generation Amora) and ultimately to R. Meir (3rd generation Tanna), in agreement with the PRK passage. It identifies Rabbi Simeon ben Menasya (4th generation Tanna) as the secondary source of the story, thus varying from PRK which mentions a Simeon ben Yosina as the father of Rabbi Ḥelbo.

The word "Amora," incidentally, refers to a Jewish academy leader/scholar who lived and wrote from 219-500 AD. The word "Tanna" refers to a Jewish academy leader/scholar who lived and wrote from 10-220 AD. Therefore, the Tannaim (plural of Tanna) lived closer in time to the New Testament period than did the Amoraim (plural of Amora). Rabbi Meir, for example, lived between 120 and 165 AD. Nevertheless, the rabbis claim that they are simply passing on information that they received from their teachers, so the teachings are understood to have been generated earlier in history than the recording of the teachings.

The Leviticus Rabbah passage is a more abbreviated form of the story. It omits the directive from God for Jacob to ascend and also Jacob's resulting fright. This time, Jacob addresses God as רבון העולמים (Lord of the Worlds), and proceeds to express his concern about a similar descent for himself. The language used agrees (nearly verbatim) with PRK. God, in reply, again quotes

---

[93] *MIDRASH WAYYIKRA RABBAH A Critical Edition based on Manuscripts and Genizah Fragments with Variants and Notes Part Three, Chapters XXI-XXIX,* Mordecai Margulies, ed. (Jerusalem: The Louis M. And Minnie Epstein Fund of The American Academy For Jewish Research, 1956).

20: Jacob's Ladder, with the Guardian Angels of Each Nation—Rising and Falling

Jeremiah 30:10, but drops the (vocative) direct address ("Israel"). The conclusion is phrased as follows:

עלה שאת עולה ואין את יורד. ואעפ״ב נתירא ולא עלה

TRANSLATION: "Once you ascend, there will be no descent for you!" Nevertheless, he was fearful, and did not ascend.

In another parallel, Midrash Tehillim 78,347, supplies the number of rungs each of the princes climbed, and attributes these details also to Rabbi Meir,[94] as quoted by Rabbi Berechiah, Rabbi Levi (3rd generation Amora), and still another Simeon—Simeon ben Jose (4th generation Tanna). PRK 23.2a provides those same details, but in a midrash belonging to Rabbi Samuel bar Naḥman (3rd generation Amora), paralleled also in Leviticus Rabbah 29:2.[95]

---

[94] According to Herman L. Strack, *Introduction to the Talmud and Midrash*, (Atheneum, NY: A Temple Book, 1969), 211, we should consider the details regarding the number of rungs ascended (as recorded in Midrash Tehillim) to be erroneously linked to Rabbi Meir. Strack writes: "Theodor, in my judgement, has proved that the Midrashim Levit. R., and Lamentations are rather dependent upon the Pesiḳta." Indeed, the variations between PRK and Leviticus Rabbah are insignificant to the meaning of the story. Furthermore, in light of the PRK 23.2a passage, it seems unlikely that the details concerning the number of rungs ascended would have been segregated from the Meir story, if they were actually his.

[95] In terms of the variants, there appears to be a real question as to which Simeon (or all or none of them) had anything to do with the chain of this tradition. Rabbi Levi is mentioned in only one source (Tehillim), and may or may not have taught this midrash. The key figures in the chain, however, seem to be firmly fixed. Rabbi Meir is the original source of the quote. Meir, a third generation Tanna, was one of the most respected authorities, having served as Hakam (Speaker) in the academy of Rabban Simeon ben Gamaliel II. [Strack, *Introduction*, 117.] The dominant Amoraic teachers of this midrash were Rabbi Berechiah and his teacher, Rabbi Ḥelbo.

In a similar vein, Bereshit Rabbah 68end refers to the princes of the four empires who ascended and descended and relates this Ladder vision to Nebuchadnezzar's "image" vision (Daniel 2:31-45). According to the Nebuchadnezzar's "image" vision, after the fifth kingdom (beginning with the Babylonian Empire) falls, God will establish an eternal kingdom that will never fall.

It is striking that Jewish scholars of the First to Fifth Centuries after the birth of Jesus who continued a tradition that suggests a plan of God to establish an eternal kingdom with a Jewish leader at the helm following the fall of the Roman Empire, failed to recognize that such a kingdom was developing. With the Roman Empire effectively "Christianized" by Constantine, shortly after 300 A.D., this tiny sect, led by a Jewish teacher (Jesus)—a child of Israel—was finally catapulted to a position of international repute. It was not until the Renaissance of a thousand years later that Greco-Roman literature would begin to rebound from a situation in which Judeo-Christian literature and thought dominated much of the world. One can almost envision the scene of Jacob's Ladder:

> "The Holy One—Blessed be He—said to him (Jacob), 'Jacob, you are ascending, too.' In that hour, Jacob, our Father, was afraid, and he said, 'Would you say that just like what happened to these—a descending—will also happen to me—a descending?' The Holy One—Blessed be He—said to him, 'You will not come down, Israel' (Jeremiah 30:10). If you go up, there will never be a descent for you.'"

Chapter 21

One Final (Sinless) Fallen Angel Story

The two previous chapters discuss the fall of angels who were involved in the rise and fall of world empires. According to Revelation, Satan (a.k.a., the Dragon) is the one who raises the world empires. After his Fall from Heaven, he fought (and lost) a few earthly battles, culminating with the Fall of the Roman Empire. Then, he was chained for one thousand years and thrown into the Abyss. During this time (The Dark Ages?), he was not permitted to raise up world empires. According to Rabbinic sources, (the angels of) the empires who ASCENDED (Jacob's Ladder) and were in power also DESCENDED (or FELL) from power as, for example, Rome fell. This perspective on angels may, therefore, be considered a Fallen Angel Story. The primary source for this Fallen Angel Story appears to be Rabbi Meir, a third generation Tanna, who served as Hakam (speaker) of the academy of Rabban Simeon ben Gamaliel II.

What is clear is that the Fallen Angels (or Descended Angels) of this account were SINLESS, just as were virtually all other fallen angels of the New Testament period. The question of sin does not even enter the account of the descending princes/guardian angels (except for the behavior of the human cultures the angels represented). The vision is to be interpreted as a prophetic account of world history. The descent of the princes is not understood to be related to any moral impropriety on the part of the angels. Even if the nations which the various guardian angels represented did themselves (the nations) behave immorally, their princes were not considered sinful by association. Otherwise, Israel's own prince would have been indicted often.

On the contrary, Midrash Shir ha-Shirim Rabbah 2.1, in an account attributed to Rabbi Eleazar the Modiite (2nd generation Tanna), the guardian angels are very much part of the divine economy (though playing a near-satanic role), and are accusing and defending men, not cognizant of any need to defend themselves. A translation of that text follows:

עתידים שרי אומות העולם לעתיד לבא

שיבואו לקטרג את ישראל לפני הקב"ה

ואומרים רבש"ע

אלו עבדו עבודת כוכבים ואלו עבדו עבודת כוכבים אלו גלו עריות ואלו גלו עריות

אלו שפכו דמים ואלו שפכו דמים

מפני מה אלו יורדין לגיהנם ואלו אין יורדין

TRANSLATION: The time will come regarding the princes of the nations of the world, in the future to come, that they will enter to accuse Israel before the Holy One—blessed be He. And they say, "Lord of the World, these (the heathen) certainly worshipped idols and these (the Israelites) certainly worshipped idols; these (the heathen) uncovered genitals and these (the Israelites) uncovered genitals; these (the heathen) shed blood and these (the Israelites) shed blood. For what

21: One Final (Sinless) Fallen Angel Story

reason do these (the heathen) go to hell (Gehinnom), but these (the Israelites) do not go down?"

These national guardian angels are often hostile to Israel, a trait that makes them similar to the angels of Truth and Peace in the final Fallen Angel Story of this period, which is now considered. Bereshit Rabbah 8.5 provides an account of an angel who was cast to earth because his conclusion regarding the wisdom of creating man conflicted with God's. The account of groups of angels being "consumed" because of their opposition to the creation of man can be found in other locations.[96] Here, however, the Angel of Truth temporarily became a "fallen angel" because of his opposition to the creation of man. The biblical text that serves as the basis for the Bereshit Rabbah 8.5 account is Psalm 85:11-12a (or 10-11a):

חֶסֶד־וֶאֱמֶת נִפְגָּשׁוּ צֶדֶק וְשָׁלוֹם נָשָׁקוּ׃

אֱמֶת מֵאֶרֶץ תִּצְמָח

TRANSLATION: Mercy and Truth met each other; Righteousness and Peace kissed each other. Truth will arise from the Earth.

According to H. Freedman, however, the Rabbinic account "interprets 'met' in the sense of 'fought,' and derives נָשָׁקוּ /'NASHAKU [kissed]' from 'NESHEK [arms]', rendering: 'have taken arms against each other.'"[97] This combat between Mercy and Truth, and Righteousness and Peace, is then presented as an argument over the creation of man:

---

[96] Ginsberg, *Legends*, V, 69.
[97] H. Freedman, *Midrash Rabbah*, I: Bereshith, 58.

חסד אומר יברא שהוא גומל חסדים

ואמת אומר אל יברא שכולו שקרים

צדק אומר יברא שהוא עושה צדקות5

שלום אומר אל יברא דכוליה קטטה

מה עשה הקב״ה

נטל אמת והשליכו לארץ

הה״ד ותשלך אמת ארצה

אמרו מלאכי השרת לפני הקב״ה רבון העולמים מה אתה מבזה תכסיס אלטיכסייה[98] שלך תעלה אמת מן הארץ

הדא הוא דכתיב אמת מארץ תצמח

TRANSLATION: Mercy says, "Let him be created; for he does merciful things." Truth says, "Let him not be created; for he is all lies." Righteousness says, "Let him be created; for he does righteous things." Peace says, "Do not let him be created; he is all quarrel." What did the Holy One—blessed be He—do? He took Truth and cast him down to the Earth.[99] This is that which is written: "And it cast Truth down to the Earth" (Daniel 8.12). The angels who attend before the Holy One—blessed be He—said, "Lord of the worlds, why are you spurning [the rank

---

[98] Jacob Levy translates, assuming that the Hebrew תכסיס אלטיכסייה is a transliteration (from the Greek words τάξις and ἀλήθεια-plus-ἀξία). תכסיס is missing in the parallels [Wörterbuch...s.v.] and is probably a dittography. Jastrow: "your chief of court ceremonies." Rashi: "seal." More variants with Theodor Albeck, *Midrash Rabbah*, *ad loc*.

[99] A second (but, non-fallen-angel) interpretive possibility is that Truth was merely cast to the ground (ארצה).

of] your worthy Truth?[100] Let Truth rise up from the Earth." This is that which is written: "Truth will arise from the earth" (Psalm 85.12a).

The ambivalent character of mankind provides the material for this angelic debate (which becomes the logological equivalent of God's own intrapersonal communication). Obviously, each contestant in the matter could easily produce evidence to substantiate his claim. Mankind is, of course, merciful-yet-false, righteous-yet-quarrelsome. The Angel of Truth was not lying here; he was being truthful. He has not broken any of the biblical commandments. Neither is he presented as a "rebel" against God. He is not even arguing with God (even though his conclusion is in disagreement with God's)—he is arguing (battling?) with other angels. His ultimate opponent, however, is neither God nor angels; he is opposed to "man." He does not favor the creation of man.

The concept of angelic-human rivalry is not at all uncommon in the New Testament/Rabbinic period. I have already mentioned Babylonian Talmud Shabbat 88b-89a, Midrash Shir ha-Shirim Rabbah 8.11, Midrash Tehillim 8.74, and Pesikta Rabbati ch. 25, p. 128a,[101] which all have some concern with the angels' opposition to mankind's receiving the Law/Torah. In Midrash Agadat Bereshit (Buber edition, Introduction, p. 38), Yalkut (I, p. 44), and *Chronicles of Jerahmeel* (p. 53)[102]— parallels of the innocent fallen angels [BHM] account from Chapter 6, in which the young girl tricked the angels into giving her their wings—the angels' motive for descending to earth was

---

[100] See the footnote on the previous page regarding (this) Jacob Levy translation.
[101] See Chapter 9.
[102] See Chapter 11.

to prove their superiority to man (their rival). Additionally, the Babylonian Talmud Sanhedrin 38b speaks of hosts of angels who were "consumed" because of their opposition to the creation of Adam. Peter Schäfer wrote a book on the rivalry between angels and humans.[103] I commented in Chapter 18 that Satan also has a rivalry with man:

> Although Satan is certainly considered the adversary of mankind in the New Testament, nowhere is he presented as the adversary of God. I Peter 5:8 warns the readers: "Be on guard! Your adversary, the Devil, prowls around like a roaring lion, seeking someone to devour." Nevertheless, I Peter calls him YOUR adversary, not the adversary of God. Revelation 12:10 calls him the "accuser" of the "brothers," but does not paint him as a challenger to God. Instead, he seems to be doing exactly what God allows him to do: He "accuses them before our God, day and night."

In addition to Revelation's presentation of Satan's Fall as linked to his enmity toward man, Rabbinic literature presents the Fall of Satan (also known as Sammael) as the result of his enmity toward man. In Midrash Pirke de Rabbi Eliezer, chapters 13-14, Sammael fell because of his conspiracy against Adam in which he misled Adam to sin. Jewish scholar Louis Ginzberg[104] believes this "corresponds to Revelation 12:9," as do I. The Koran also agrees, to a certain extent. In Abdullah Yusuf Ali's translation of *The Holy Qur-an* (Volume I, pp. 24ff.), there is an angelic

---

[103] Peter Schäfer, *Rivalität zwischen Engeln und Menschen*, (Gruyter, 1975).
[104] Ginzberg, *Legends*, V, 85.

debate concerning the advisability of creating man, Iblīs's (the Devil's) refusal to bow down to Adam, and Satan's causing the couple to slip from the Garden.[105]

Returning to the "Angel of Truth" story, however, I conclude that "opposition to man" was not necessarily considered a sin. It is evidently quite unsatisfactory to God, since the Angel of Truth was cast down to earth for his opinion. But, if this is a Fallen Angel Story, we find that in the resolution of the story, Truth "arises from the Earth." Apparently, then, this angel—like the angels who gave up their wings to the young girl—was not guilty of any sins. Otherwise, it would have been impossible for him to return to God's Throne.[106]

---

[105] Abdullah Yusuf Ali, *The Holy Qur-an* (3 vols.; Lahore: Shaikh Muhammad Ashraf), I, 24ff.
[106] Ginzberg, *Legends*, V, 169, comments: "though the angels had entertained evil thoughts, they never carried them out, otherwise their return to Heaven would hardly have been conceivable." See Chapter 8, supra. It is by no means certain, however, that this story is a fallen angel story at all. The common interpretation understands Truth as having been cast to the "ground," rather than the "Earth." (See earlier footnote in this Chapter: "A second (but, non-fallen-angel) interpretive possibility is that Truth was merely cast to the ground [ארצה].") Thus, Soncino translation. On the other hand, Ginzberg, *Legends*, I, 53, evidently took the passage to mean "Earth," for he states: "God cast the Angel of Truth down from heaven to earth…"

Angels and Demons: The Personification of Communication (Logology)

Chapter 22
Recap of the Fallen Angel Stories

The twenty-one previous chapters have been discussing Fallen Angel Stories. Some readers may have become lost in all the variations of these stories, so this internal summary of the various Fallen Angel Stories is offered. In the Old Testament, there were no fallen angels. Right after the Old Testament, hundreds of Fallen Angel Stories emerged. Then, by the New Testament, the fallen angels have almost completely disappeared again! In light of the flood of literature on fallen angels from the period between the Old and New Testaments, the obvious disqualification of the bulk of the fallen angel material from the official/codified scriptures of Christianity, Judaism, and the literature surrounding them is striking. If readers have not encountered some of these stories, prior to now, they may take that as evidence that the stories were rejected for one reason or another. Here is a recap of the various fallen angel stories that developed between the Old Testament and New Testament periods:

1. FALLEN ANGELS WHO SINNED BY BRINGING CULTURE TO MANKIND. According to I Enoch 54:5, iron chains were being prepared for the host of Azazel. This host will be thrown into the abyss, with jagged stones. I Enoch 65:6-7 speaks of the angel's secrets that were passed on to humans, including sorcery, incantations, and working with melted metals such as silver, lead, and tin. In other words, the fallen angels taught mankind to make tools and use fire. They brought culture to mankind. This story developed from Greek legends of Prometheus who was punished by Zeus for the same behavior. This story is rejected by the New Testament period.

2. AN EVIL GOD WHO IS EQUAL TO AND WHO WARS AGAINST A GOOD GOD. Persian religion developed the concept of an Evil God who was constantly at war with a Good God. There is no picture in the Old Testament of a Satan who could rival God. The Hebrew word "SATAN" means "adversary" or "prosecuting attorney." Satan was an adversary of man, not of God. That's all Satan was in the Book of Job. He certainly had not "fallen" from Heaven by then. Job 1:6 has Satan joining the angels in presenting themselves before God. He petitions God for permission to "test" Job. He certainly does not demand anything of God. This story is rejected by the New Testament period.

3. ANGELS WHO SINNED BY MARRYING HUMAN WOMEN. Whoever the "sons of God" in Genesis 6 are, they are not raping the "daughters of men" or having sex with them outside the bonds of marriage. They are "marrying" them. Since this is the most significant version of the Fallen Angel Story in the Greek period, the possibility of angels having sex with humans is at issue. Jesus and the rabbis seem to suggest that it is impossible. Leo

Jung explains: "That divine beings, even gods, have sexual intercourse with women was a well-known view, nay, a creed of Hellenistic religion."[107] We can safely assume that Greek culture had a reasonable effect on the fallen angel theme from its very outset. To be sure, many of our sources discussing the fallen angels are even written in the Greek language. This story is rejected by the New Testament period.

4. LUCIFER (AND HIS ANGELS) WHO REBELLED BY TRYING TO BE EQUAL TO GOD AND WAS CAST TO EARTH. It is clear that Lucifer (from Isaiah 14:12) is a man: "They that see thee shall narrowly look upon thee, [and] consider thee, [saying, Is] this the MAN that made the earth to tremble, that did shake kingdoms?" Verses 18-20, furthermore, point out that Lucifer is a "king": "All the kings of the nations, [even] all of them, lie in glory, every one in his own house. But thou . . . shalt not be joined with them in burial, because thou hast destroyed thy land, [and] slain thy people." We confirm this identification of Lucifer as the "king of Babylon" in the 4th verse of chapter 14: "That thou shalt take up this proverb against the king of Babylon." What follows, including the Lucifer passage in the middle of this chapter, is all a proverb denouncing the king of Babylon. This fallen angel story is rejected by the New Testament period.

5. ANGELS (OTHER THAN LUCIFER) WHO REBELLED AGAINST GOD. After the New Testament period, (the Christian) Justin Martyr, somewhere around 150 A.D., described Trypho (a Jew) as becoming irate concerning the suggestion that Fallen Angels fell through the sin of "rebellion." Trypho appears to reject the notion that angels could

---

[107] Leo Jung, *Fallen Angels,* 92.

sin at all as being "blasphemous!"[108] I believe Justin was mistaken and that Trypho the Jew was correct in this instance. The New Testament supports Trypho more than it does Justin. Martin says that the analogy to the Clash of the Titans of Greek mythology lies close to the Fallen Angel Story.[109] The motif of lesser gods rebelling against Zeus is the basis for the "Clash of the Titans" in Greek mythology. Therefore, the motif of angels rebelling against God made a good deal of sense to Jews who were living in the Greek Empire of Alexander the Great and his successors (between the Old and New Testaments). This story is rejected by the New Testament period.

6. ANGELS WHO SINNED BY JUDGING UNFAIRLY. In Psalm 82, God speaks to certain judges (calling them "gods" and "sons of the Most High"). He accuses them of judging unjustly and favoring the wicked. He tells them that they shall all "die as men and fall as one of the princes." Jesus, however, is quoted in John 10:33-36 as clearly implying that the term "sons of the Most High" (from Psalm 82:6) refers to "human judges." These human judges are called "gods/ELOHIM" in both Psalm 82:6 and Exodus 22:28. Jesus was making the point that it was not blasphemous for him to be called "god" or "son of God," if even human judges could be called "gods" and "sons of the Most High." Even though Haag[110] argues that the passages in which "sons of God" are most prominent in the Old Testament (Job, Genesis 6, and Psalm 82) presuppose some sort of heavenly council

---

[108] Justin, "Trypho," 284.
[109] Hengel, *Judentum und Hellenismus*, 347-8.
[110] H. Haag, "ben," 147-159.

in which God seeks input from other heavenly beings (such as angels), the Septuagint is only willing to explicitly apply that interpretation to Job. The rabbis rejected the notion that Psalm 82 referred to angels, as did John 10:33-36.

7. ANGELS WHO SINNED BY REFUSING TO WORSHIP ADAM. In the book *The Lives of Adam and Eve*,[111] The Devil is presented as an angel who was cast out of Heaven because of his refusal to bow down and worship Adam. He was expected to worship Adam because Adam was the "image of God" (Genesis 1:26). Later human cultures would make "graven images" of their gods and worship those images, so the author of The Life of Adam and Eve thought it logical that angels would have been expected to worship the (living) image of the one true God—Adam. According to this source, when the Devil's angels, over whom he was placed, heard of the Devil's refusal to honor Adam by bowing down, they also refused. While the authors of the books of Revelation and Hebrews in the New Testament appear to be familiar with this story, they use only its logic for demonstrating that angels should bow down and worship Jesus—the Second Adam.

8. THE DEVIL WHO SINNED BY MURDERING AND LYING (AS A FALLEN ANGEL). I John 3:8 explicitly states that the devil sins from the beginning. Very well, what exactly was that "sin" in the beginning? Jesus, in John 8:37-44, says: "You have the devil for your father and you wish to practice the desires of your father; he was a slayer of men from the beginning, and he could not stay in the truth, because there is no truth in him. When he tells a lie, he speaks according to his nature; for he is a liar and the father of liars." Jesus

---

[111] Ed. R. H. Charles, *Apocrypha.* Vol. II: Pseudepigrapha, 137.

was probably referring to the devil's roles as tempter/tester and executioner. Hebrews 2:14 speaks of Jesus as neutralizing the one who wields the power of death, namely the devil. The first time the term Satan explicitly appears in the Bible is in the Book of Job, where Satan not only tests Job but also KILLS his wife and children. God restricts his power so that he cannot KILL Job himself, because Job is righteous. For those who are not as righteous as Job, Satan does indeed pose the threat of death. But, is this killing of humans a sin? Is Satan breaking the Law by killing men? Not if the humans deserve it. Romans 6:23 says the wages of sin is death. Romans 3:23 says all have sinned. Even though Revelation calls the devil the "deceiver of all humanity," one wonders if his deceit simply amounts to something like putting a False statement in a True-False test. Yes, it is a lie, but the student is being TESTED to see if s/he recognizes it as such.

9. (SINLESS) ANGELS WHO ATTEMPTED TO MARRY A HUMAN GIRL, BUT WERE OUTWITTED BY THE GIRL. According to this story, when the angels descended to Earth, they propositioned a certain virgin. They wanted to "marry" her. Wise young lady that she was, she tricked them. She promised to agree to their proposition on one condition: they must give her their wings. Upon receiving the wings, and prior to the consummation of the sexual union, she flapped her wings and flew away to God's throne. Either she was

made into the constellation Virgo or the constellation Virgo was named for her.[112] While the rabbis allowed this story to be taught, the New Testament makes no reference to it.

10. (SINLESS) GUARDIAN ANGELS (PRINCES) WHO ASCENDED, THEN DESCENDED, JACOB'S LADDER. The Jewish concept of the guardian angels of various nations ascending and descending on Jacob's ladder ends with the angel of the nation of Israel ascending the ladder, but never descending. This is the story of the ascending and descending national guardian angels (also called "princes") of history's world empires. The rabbis allowed this story to be taught.[113] The New Testament comes close to accepting this story in Revelation Chapter 12, with Michael (traditionally understood to be the national guardian angel of Israel) defeating Satan (with the blood of the Lamb) and casting him to earth. Perhaps, this story also figures into the curious comment attributed to Jesus by John (in John 1:51): "Truly, I assure you all, you shall see heaven opened and the angels of God ascending and descending on the Son of Man."

11. A (SINLESS) ANGEL OF TRUTH WHO DISAGREED WITH THE CREATION OF MAN AND WAS CAST TO THE EARTH. The Angel of Truth temporarily became a "fallen angel" because of his opposition to the creation of man. The biblical text that serves as the basis for the Bereshit Rabbah 8.5 account is Psalm 85:11-12a: "Mercy and Truth met each other; Righteousness and Peace kissed each other. Truth will arise from the Earth."

---

[112] Jellinek, *Beth ha-Midrasch,* V, 156.
[113] Piska 23.2 of Pesikta de-Rab Kahana, *et. al.* See Chapter 12 of this book.

According to H. Freedman,[114] however, the Rabbinic account "interprets 'met' in the sense of 'fought,' and derives 'NASHAKU [kissed]' from 'NESHEK [arms]', rendering: 'have taken arms against each other.'" This combat between Mercy and Truth, and Righteousness and Peace, is then presented as an argument over the creation of man: "Mercy says, 'Let him be created; for he does merciful things.' Truth says, 'Let him not be created; for he is all lies.' Righteousness says, 'Let him be created; for he does righteous things.' Peace says, 'Do not let him be created; he is all quarrel.' What did the Holy One—blessed be He—do? He took Truth and cast him down to the Earth. This is that which is written: 'And it cast Truth down to the Earth' (Daniel 8.12). The angels who attend before the Holy One—blessed be He—said, 'Lord of the worlds, why are you spurning [the rank of] your worthy Truth? Let Truth rise up from the Earth.' This is that which is written: 'Truth will arise from the earth' (Psalm 85.12a)." I conclude, however, that "opposition to man" was not necessarily considered a sin. Otherwise, it would have been impossible for him to return to God's Throne.

12. SATAN (AND HIS ANGELS) WHO FELL BECAUSE SATAN'S JOB WAS ELIMINATED. According to Revelation, Satan lost his first job—that of "accuser of the brothers"—due to the "Blood" of Jesus. Revelation, therefore, places the Fall of Satan somewhere around 30 AD. The Hebrew word "SATAN" means "prosecuting attorney." Prosecuting attorney was Satan's FIRST job. There is no need for a prosecutor, if all of

---

[114] H. Freedman, *Midrash Rabbah*, Vol I: Bereshith, p. 58.

22: Recap of the Fallen Angel Stories

the accused have been "pardoned." While John the writer of Revelation is familiar with virtually all of the Fallen Angel Stories, he seems to reject them all in favor of a progressive "outmoding of Satan's jobs" approach. The first job to go was that of accuser/prosecuting attorney. The loss of this job resulted in Satan being cast to earth because there was no longer a job for him "in Heaven." No longer did Satan's job(s) require him to be in the presence of God. Before whom else would Satan have accused and prosecuted the brothers? God is the ultimate Judge. Satan needed to be in His presence to present the prosecution's case against the brothers. There is no sin in this task, but it is certainly a task God and "the brothers" were happy to see ended.

Chapter 23
Angels as the Personification of God's Word

The best way to understand the concept of angels, for the most part, is to view them as "the personification of God's words." For those who wonder why a professor of "Communication" is writing a work on angels and demons, here is the connection. Angels and demons are religious ways of discussing "communication." When God spoke "light" into existence, He effectively created an Angel of Light. When He implicitly "tested" man's free will by giving him a command not to eat of the Tree of the Knowledge of Good and Evil, He effectively created a "testing" angel. Once man sinned and God "cursed" him with "death," He effectively created a Death Angel, etc. G. B. Caird[115] seems to suggest that there is confusion in the book of Revelation over whether the "seven stars" of Revelation chapters 2 and 3 are "angels" or "spirits":

> It is important . . . to notice that the seven stars do not mean in this letter [to Sardis] what they meant in the letter to Ephesus. There they were the angels of the

---

[115] G. B. Caird, *Commentary on the Revelation of St. John the Divine*. 2nd ed. (London: A & C Black, 1966), 47.

churches, here they are the sevenfold Spirit of God; and since the Spirit, in speaking to the churches, addresses the angels of the churches, the two are clearly not to be identified. The one symbol does double service.

Keep in mind: Caird's terminology of the "sevenfold Spirit of God" is his own interpretation (an attempt, I think, to find evidence of the doctrine of Trinity in Revelation). John defines the seven stars as the seven spirits of God in the letter to Sardis, whereas they were "angels" of the seven churches, earlier. Furthermore, also present in the letters to the seven churches is John's recurring comment about the "spirit . . . say[ing]" things "to the churches." John is not confused; he is a master craftsman. John is using synecdoche—figurative language employing the use of the whole for a part or a part for the whole, the container for the thing contained, and various parts of a whole that can stand for each other. For John, angel, spirit, and word are all "parts" of the same "whole"—the communication of God. In a sense, an "angel" is the same thing as a "spirit," which is the same thing as a "word."

Jewish scholar G. F. Moore links the three terms (of Caird's "seven stars" confusion) together quite easily. In his chapter entitled, "The Word of God: The Spirit," Moore states, "God's will is made known or effectuated in the world not only through personal agents (*ANGELS*), but directly by his *WORD* or by his *SPIRIT*" (emphases mine).[116] Here all three terms of Caird's puzzle fit neatly together. If the seven stars represent "angels," then "angels" are a part of the whole. If the stars

---

[116] G. F. Moore, *Judaism: In the First Centuries of the Christian Era the Age of the Tannaim*, (Cambridge: Harvard University Press, 1932), I, 414.

"represent" "spirits of God," then spirits are a part of the whole. If "the spirit" is "say[ing]" things to the churches, then what "the spirit says" (*i.e.,* the "word") is a part of the whole.

For John, as for other Jews of his generation, a concept of a whole from which parts spring up and to which they return is the concept of the Nehar di-Nur (the "stream of fire"). Louis Ginzberg states: "Thus there are angels who spring up daily out of the stream Dinur (='stream of fire'; comp. Dan. 7.10); they praise God, and then disappear. Out of every word uttered by God angels are created."[117] Ginzberg also says that the Rabbis further connected this stream with at least one STAR: "The stream of fire in which the SUN bathes, is identical with the Nehar di-Nur."[118] An easy connection would be to see other heavenly lights, such as "stars," bathing in and arising out of the stream of fire, as well.

John is familiar with the "stream of fire." He does not mention this stream, but he describes a "lake of fire" into which the Devil and his angels are thrown. Not only is John familiar with the "stream of fire," he even adds a twist to the concept: A "stream" keeps on flowing, but a "lake" is the end of the line. Water flows into a lake, but does not flow out. According to Ginzberg, later Jewish writers speak of souls passing through the river of fire where "the wicked" are "judged."[119] Whether these Jewish writers originated the idea of a river of fiery judgment or picked up on John's "lake of fire" is uncertain, but their concept does seem to demonstrate the ease with which fiery judgment and the stream of fire may be connected.

---

[117] Ginzberg, *Legends*, V, 21.
[118] Ginzberg, *Legends*, V, 37.
[119] Ginzberg, *Legends*, V, 125.

Having discussed the various Fallen Angel Stories in previous chapters, I am now shifting my focus to a discussion of the nature of angels, in general, rather than just the "fallen" variety. In future chapters, I will discuss the ways in which angels are the personification of God's word.

Chapter 24

Angels as the Personification of God's Creative Fiats

In my book, *Disneology: Religious Rhetoric at Walt Disney World*,[120] I describe the difference between the two types of "words/Words" used by God, according to Kenneth Burke:

> Even though, theoretically, God, like humans, uses symbols or words, he uses two types of words. Burke calls the first type--words he uses in creating the world (capitalized) "Word." If God speaks a "Word," that Word has "*omnipotence*" (or, at least, the total power necessary to complete its task). In Genesis 1:3, God speaks a Word ("And God said, 'Let there be light'"). The very Word he speaks has the "omnipotence" to produce light. Psalms 33:9 confirms the power of this (capitalized) Word: "He spoke, and it was done; he commanded, and [the universe] stood fast." The Word of God has tremendous power. Isaiah 55:11 goes so far as to suggest that God's Word is *infallible*--it cannot fail: "So is my word that goes out from my mouth; it will not return to me empty, but will accomplish what I desire and achieve the purpose for which I sent it."

---

[120] Lindsay, *Disneology*, 74-75.

How, then, can God give a command (word) to Adam and Eve not to eat of the Tree of Knowledge of Good and Evil, and have that word *fail* to achieve its purpose? How is it possible that after the command from God was issued, Adam and Eve ate anyway? The second type of word God uses is (lower-case) "word." Burke offers theological distinctions between "word" and "Word." This (lower-case) "word" has much less power to affect humans. Burke identifies the *basis upon which he distinguishes between the two types of words*--the negative. . . . Burke, however, is most interested in what he calls the *hortatory* negative, the negative of command, as with the "Thou shalt not's" of the Ten Commandments.

Clearly implied in any "Thou shalt not" is the element of free will or choice. We do *not* tell anyone "Thou shalt not" do something it is *impossible* to not do. It does no good to tell a baby not to cry. We do not tell people not to digest the food in their intestines. We do not tell someone not to let his or her heart beat, hair or fingernails grow, or kidneys work. We do not use such hortatory negatives because people have no choice in such matters. On the other hand, if we tell people, "Thou shalt not kill, lie, steal, rape, commit adultery, or slander," it is clear that humans have free will or choice in such matters. They may choose either to kill or to not kill. They may choose to lie or to tell the truth. They may choose to steal or to refrain from stealing, to rape or refrain from raping, to commit adultery or to refrain from committing adultery, to slander or not to slander. Having this distinction in mind, I should point out that, although God's utterance is presented as "Word" in the case of the creative fiat ("Let there be light!"), God's utterance might be understood as "word" in the case of the Ten Commandments. In the first instance, there is no implicit free will attributed to that which is created. In the second instance, humans to whom the Ten Commandments are directed are implicitly credited with free will.

24: Angels as the Personification of God's Creative Fiats

One of the reasons angels were considered by Jewish teachers to be incapable of sinning is that they were considered to be generated by God's use of "Word" (capitalized). When Ginzberg states, "Out of every word uttered by God angels are created,"[121] he is picturing angels as the personification of God's creative fiats. He presents these angels, not as the free moral agents humans are, but as the commissioned forces that are charged with making certain that God's Words are infallibly fulfilled. One might view such angels as more like robots than humans. They do not have the (human free-will) options of deciding NOT to fulfill God's commands. When God says, "Let there be light," an Angel of Light (Gabriel?) is created who infallibly produces light. When God says, "Let there be a firmament (or separation) dividing the waters above the earth from the waters on the earth," an Angel of the Firmament (*Hlm Hml/Hhml Haml* http://www.hafapea.com/angelpages/angels3.html) is created who infallibly produces that separation. When God says, "Let the earth bring forth vegetation," an Angel of Plants (*Sachluph* http://www.angelfire.com/biz3/danielkudra/AngelReference_S_to_U_index.html) is created to fulfill God's command. There are angels of the Sun, the Moon, the Planets, and the Stars. There are angels of the fish, the fowl, the tame beasts, and the wild beasts.

In his *Dictionary of Angels*, Gustav Davidson writes:

> There were 7 [angels of Creation] in the beginning (i.e., at the time of Creation) . . . who set down the events of the "first days." The 7 angels of creation usually given

---

[121] Ginzberg, *Legends*, V, 21.

are Orifiel, Anael, Zachariel, Samael (before this angel rebelled, and fell), Raphael, Gabriel, and Michael. The Book of Enoch reports that the angels of Creation reside in the 6th Heaven.[122]

Although Davidson reports that Samael rebelled and fell (in the Book of Enoch), Jewish angelology could not ultimately accept the premise that an angel could do anything counter to his explicit instructions from God. Angels were nothing more than personified spirit forces that were charged with carrying out the terms of God's creative fiats. As Isaiah 55:11 reports: "So is my word that goes out from my mouth; it will not return to me empty, but will accomplish what I desire and achieve the purpose for which I sent it." To put this in Burkean terms, God has a (capitalized) Word, that may be personified as an angel, whose sole task and capability is to effect the result commanded in God's creative fiat.

---

[122] Gustav Davidson, *Dictionary of Angels: Including the Fallen Angels*, (New York: The Free Press, 1967), p. 25

Chapter 25
Angels as the Personification of God's Intrapersonal Communication

Four chapters ago, I discussed my final Sinless Fallen Angel Story. Bereshit Rabbah 8.5 provides an account of an angel who was cast to earth because his conclusion regarding the wisdom of creating man conflicted with God's. It appeared to some rabbis that the Angel of Truth temporarily became a "fallen angel" because of his opposition to the creation of man. The Bereshit Rabbah account is based on Psalm 85:11-12a. Combats between Mercy and Truth, and Righteousness and Peace is presented as an argument over the creation of man:[123] "Mercy says, 'Let him be created; for he does merciful things.' Truth says, 'Let him not be created; for he is all lies.' Righteousness says, 'Let him be created; for he does righteous things.' Peace says, 'Do not let him be created; he is all quarrel.'" Each contestant in the matter could easily produce evidence to substantiate his

---

[123] Freedman, *Midrash Rabbah*, I, 58.

claim. Mankind is, of course, merciful-yet-false, righteous-yet-quarrelsome. The Angel of Truth was not lying here; he was being truthful.

Not all rabbis agree, by the way, that this is a Fallen Angel Story. The common interpretation understands Truth as having been cast to the "ground," rather than to the "Earth." The Hebrew word may be translated either way. On the other hand, Ginzberg apparently took the passage to mean "Earth," for he states (in I.53): "God cast the Angel of Truth down from heaven to earth . . . ."[124] It is, nevertheless, likely that Rabbi Simon was as intent to give meaning to the difficult Daniel 8:12 and Psalm 85:12a passages in an ethics-centered homily (recall my discussion of "homiletic Aggadah" in Chapter 10: The Fallen Angels of Jude and 2nd Peter) as he was to create a "new" theology. The term translated "will arise" is generally used with reference to plants, which sprout or spring up or grow up from the earth (ground), according to major Hebrew dictionaries. The term translated "from the earth" offers no help in deciding the issue. It can be translated either "from the Earth" or "from the ground."

In my next chapter, I shall offer an extended critique of the issue of whether the fall of the Angel of Truth was indeed a Fallen Angel Story. For now, I suggest that this story affords an excellent perspective to see how Jewish angelology depicts angels as the personification of God's intrapersonal communication.

---

[124] Ginzberg, *Legends*, I, 53.

25: Angels as the Personification of God's Intrapersonal Communication

For those not familiar with the term "intrapersonal communication," it is the equivalent of talking to (even arguing with) oneself. The Jewish psychologist Sigmund Freud believed that a constant conflict is occurring in the human psyche between a pleasure principle Freud calls the Id and a morality principle Freud calls the Super-ego. A third force in the psyche—the Ego—mediates between the other two frequently opposing forces. This is bedrock "intrapersonal communication." If "INTERpersonal communication" is communication between two persons, then "INTRApersonal communication" is communication within one individual person.

As I discuss in my book *Disneology: Religious Rhetoric at Walt Disney World*,[125] humans may be said to be the image of God in the sense that they have free will, as God does. For a human, this free will stems from having the option to listen to his or her two inclinations: the good inclination and the evil inclination. These two inclinations are not far removed from Freud's notions of the Id and the Super-ego. Humans (by exercising their Ego) are free to choose between and moderate alternatives. Similarly, God, as he decided to make man into His image, may be pictured as listening to the arguments of an (inner) Angel of Truth, an Angel of Mercy, an Angel of Righteousness, and an Angel of Peace. All of these angels had legitimate arguments, but despite the contrary arguments of Truth and Peace, God chose to create man. Angels, of course, were unnecessary in order for God to have gone through His decision-making process. One might just as easily depict God as considering in His own mind the pros and cons of creating man. Yet, this concept of angels—as personifying the various considerations that may have occurred

---

[125] Lindsay, *Disneology*, 75-76.

INTRAPERSONALLY in God's own mind—allows humans to understand all sides of an issue God resolved using his own free will.

If we envision every "word" God utters as creating an angel, what is to prohibit us from envisioning every "thought" God thinks (or speaks to Himself) as being personified by an angel?

Chapter 26

The Angel of Truth (and the Spirit of Truth)

There is no "Angel of Truth" mentioned in the Old Testament. In the Old Testament, neither "truth" in Psalm 85 nor "truth" in Daniel 8 is called an angel. Rabbi Simon, however, possibly interpreted Daniel 8:12 and Psalm 85:10-13 as referring to a Fallen Angel Story, featuring the Angel of Truth. When Psalm 85:11 reports "Truth springs forth from the earth," Rabbi Simon suspects/assumes that (the Angel of) Truth had previously been cast to the earth. In Daniel 8:12, he finds corroboration of his suspicion/assumption. Daniel had seen a vision of a male goat (interpreted as the Greek Empire of Alexander the Great) who grew great and powerful. This male goat had one prominent horn (Alexander the Great) that eventually broke off (indicating Alexander's death) and was replaced with four horns (the four divisions of the Greek Empire after Alexander—the horns of Seleucus (Asia), Ptolemy (Egypt), Lysimachus (Thrace), and Cassander (Macedonia, including Greece). From one of these four horns (Seleucus), a small horn (Antiochus IV Epiphanes) emerged, that attacked Jerusalem, abolished the daily sacrifice and profaned the temple. It is this small horn (not God) who, as Daniel reports in 8:12, cast truth to the earth." This is clearly not a Fallen Angel Story in the Old Testament; it is socio-political commentary. However, it may well be a Fallen Angel Story in Rabbi Simon's interpretation. One indication that it is a Fallen Angel Story is the severity of the punishment of other angels who opposed man's creation. The account of groups of angels being "burnt" because of their opposition to the creation of man can be found in Sanhedrin 38b. By comparison, having Truth "cast to the Earth" (or thrown out of Heaven) would be closer to the severity of the punishment of the other angels who opposed man's creation. The exception to this severe punishment, however, is the other angel in this story who opposed man's creation on the basis of his quarrelsome nature—the Angel of Peace. He apparently receives no punishment at all.

The idea of "casting" an angel down is immediately reminiscent of the fallen angel theme. The exact term for "casting down" (שלך/SHALAK) used by the rabbi in the account (as borrowed from Daniel 8:12) is employed in the Fallen Angel Stories in the Hebrew "version" of I Enoch.[126] In 10.4, regarding the punishment of Azazel, the angel Raphael is instructed to "CAST him DOWN to darkness, and make an opening to the desert which is in Dudael, and CAST him DOWN thither." In verse 6, we continue: "On the day of the great judgment, he will be CAST DOWN to the midst of the fire. Chapter 21 relates Enoch's journey to a place of chaos where he saw the fallen angels (stars) in bonds. Enoch asks in verse 4: "And for what reason were they CAST DOWN here?" This chapter may be the basis for 1 Peter's homiletic Aggadah, if the Enoch-related Nestle-Aland textual suggestion on 1 Peter 3:19 is accepted. Chapter 88 (verses 1 and 3) of the Hebrew Enoch

---

[126] PRK I.29-91.

also relates the casting of the fallen angels (stars) into the abyss. As verse 3 puts it, "He caused them to be CAST DOWN to the abyss of the Earth."

In trying to accumulate evidence regarding the usage of the form אַרְצָה/ERTZAH (to the earth/ground), as it relates to Fallen Angel Stories, we face two major complications. First, in all likelihood, the form as used in Daniel 8:12 denoted a casting "to the ground." To illustrate, I cite the "Hebrew text" of *Apocalypsis Mosis*[127] chapter 27, verse 5: "And the angels fell TO THE GROUND (אַרְצָה) and prostrated themselves to the Lord." This refers to the worship of God by his angels, and therefore, demands the translation "to the ground."

While I think it is clear that the original meaning of the Daniel 8:12 passage is "(אַרְצָה) to the ground," the purpose of the Jewish practice of "midrash" is often to give a new twist to the meaning of a given text. In the Rabbinic midrash, Rabbi Simon chooses a different term to express where his "Angel of Truth" was cast. The term לארץ/LA-ARETZ (to the earth) can more easily accommodate a fallen angel interpretation.

The second complication in this "to the earth/to the ground" discussion is that the two accounts of fallen angels that seem to parallel most closely the terminology in this midrash are not available in the Hebrew text. The (Latin) *Books of Adam and Eve* 12.1 and 16.1 relate that the devil and the devil and his angels were respectively "cast out in the earth" and "hurled on the earth."

---

[127] PRK I.1-18.

Unfortunately, this is a Latin text for which we lack any Hebrew parallel/original. This passage in the *Books of Adam and Eve* also lacks any close parallels in the *Apocalypsis Mosis*. The other account which seems to parallel the terminology of the Angel of Truth midrash is the fall of the devil and his angels in Revelation 12:9b: "He was cast TO THE EARTH and his angels were cast out with him." In both the Angel of Truth midrash and the Fall of the Devil in Revelation, we have angels who were cast TO THE EARTH. Nevertheless, there is no Hebrew text of the Revelation passage with which to compare the Angel of Truth story.

There is no "Angel of Truth" mentioned in the Old Testament, nor is there an Angel of Truth in the New Testament. There is, however, a Spirit of Truth in the New Testament—in John 16:13--also known as the Comforter. We will consider the terminology "Spirit of Truth" in the next chapter.

Chapter 27

The Spirit of Truth and God's Communication Network

While the New Testament makes no comment on the existence of an Angel of Truth, as presented in Rabbinic writings, John (14:17, 15:26, and 16:13) speaks of the Spirit of Truth, whom John also identifies as the Comforter (14:16, 15:26, and 16:7), and whom John, in turn, equates with the Holy Spirit (14.26). Old Testament writers equate various terms for truth with God, some fifty times. Besides the three references to the Spirit of Truth, John connects truth with the Spirit at least one more time, with God at least four times, and with Jesus at least nine times. The Spirit of Truth shows up again in I John 4:6 where he is contrasted with the Spirit of Error. The Spirit of Error seems to be connected with false prophets, in I John 4:1. (We will return to a discussion of the Spirit of Error in future discussions of demons.) It is clear that the biblical authors would have real problems with those postmodernists who proclaim that there is no truth. They believed that God communicated truth, but that there is also the communication of error in the world.

The role of the Spirit of Truth seems to be a mediating communication role. I point out the following in Chapter 23:

> Jewish scholar G. F. Moore . . . [i]n his chapter entitled, "The Word of God: The Spirit," . . . states, "God's will is made known or effectuated in the world not only through personal agents (*ANGELS*), but directly by his *WORD* or by his *SPIRIT*" (emphases mine). Here all three terms of Caird's puzzle fit neatly together. If the seven stars represent "angels," then "angels" are a part of the whole. If the stars "represent" "spirits of God," then spirits are a part of the whole. If "the spirit" is "say[ing]" things to the churches, then what "the spirit says" (*i.e.*, the "word") is a part of the whole.

To demonstrate a further equation between the Spirit and Word, Ephesians 6:17 may be cited. Paul lists among the various pieces of the armor of God "the sword of the Spirit, which is the Word of God." The English translation is confusing and seems to indicate that the "sword" is the Word of God. The Greek word for "which," however is either a MASCULINE or NEUTER pronoun. It cannot refer to "sword" because "sword" is a FEMININE noun. "Spirit" is, however, a NEUTER noun and serves easily as the antecedent to "which." Paul clearly states that the Spirit is the Word of God.

So, what is the difference between the various methods God uses to communicate with men? Sometimes, God speaks directly to a specific human. Sometimes, God places His Holy Spirit inside a prophet, a priest, or a king and that prophet, priest, or king delivers God's message to other humans. Sometimes, God sends a message to an individual through a dream or vision. Sometimes, God sends a personal agent (or angel) to convey his message. Sometimes, His Word is written down and read to or by others. Sometimes, the message is merely audible. Once one person receives the message, he passes it on via interpersonal communication to others. It all sounds very much like the communication networks studied by organizational communication specialists. On pages 95-98 of my book, *Psychotic Entelechy: The Dangers of Spiritual Gifts Theology*, I explain the processes:

> Certainly, the Jewish Bible (the Christian Old Testament) accepts the premise that God spoke to and through certain individuals. That God spoke directly to Moses is the fundamental premise upon which Jewish Law is founded. . . . According to tradition, Moses is the essential author of all five books.
>
> Genesis provides a rapid-fire account of more than two thousand years of human history prior to Israel's four-hundred-year sojourn in Egypt. Prior to the account of human history, Genesis offers a one-chapter account of the creation of heaven, earth, and the plant and animal kingdoms. Presumably, if Moses authored the creation and human history accounts, he would need some inspiration from God to certify that his account was accurate. Moses' account has God speaking directly to Adam and Eve, warning them not to eat of the Tree of the Knowledge of Good and Evil. Following their Fall, God interrogates them and communicates to them their respective punishments. To their children, God signifies his preference for the animal sacrifices (of Abel) to the vegetable sacrifices (of Cain). Then, God warns Cain not to kill his brother. After Cain murders Abel, God personally interrogates Cain and tells Cain of his punishment. Later, God speaks to Noah, instructing him to build an Ark. After the Flood, God provides Noah and his family a brief list of laws. Then, God does not appear to communicate with humans until he begins to communicate with Abram, whom God renames Abraham.

In the final three-fourths of Genesis, God communicates frequently with Abraham and his family. God makes covenants with Abraham, his son Isaac, and Isaac's son Jacob, whom God renames Israel. In addition to his son Isaac, Abraham has another son through surrogate marriage with Hagar, the handmaid of his wife Sarah. . . . Israel has twelve sons who become the patriarchs of the twelve tribes. One of those sons, Joseph, God takes special interest in, communicating with him through dreams. God has a special purpose in mind for Joseph, which takes Joseph to Egypt. His brothers sell him into slavery, but God causes him to rise to leadership in that land. Eventually, God uses Joseph's position of influence to rescue his father and his brothers' families from famine in the land of Canaan as they emigrate to Egypt. The entire account of Genesis, if authored by Moses, would require that Moses be inspired by God to be certified historically accurate. Moses' perspective was four hundred years removed from the most recent historical circumstances he reports on. The suggestion that Joseph may have written some accounts that Moses found in the Egyptian archives would argue for some historiographical accuracy, but none of the first five books make such an assertion.

Exodus begins with the Israelites still in Egypt four hundred years later. Now, the name of Joseph is long-forgotten by the Egyptians and the Israelites have become an enslaved people. God raises up an Israelite named Moses, educates him in Pharaoh's palace, and eventually speaks to him through a burning bush, commanding him to lead the Israelites out of Egypt and back to the Promised Land (of Canaan). God infuses Moses with miraculous powers and, upon his successful campaign to lead the children of Israel out of Egypt, God gives Moses the Law on Mount Sinai. The various laws and instructions God gives to Moses are detailed in Exodus, Leviticus, Numbers, and Deuteronomy. These four books pertain to historical issues occurring during the lifetime of Moses. The exception to this observation is the final chapter of Deuteronomy, which discusses the death of

Moses. The primary purpose of spiritual gifts theology in the final four books (of Moses) is to certify the accuracy of Moses' messages concerning the Law. The Law (Torah) comes from God.

After Moses, there is a lesser profusion of spiritual giftedness throughout Jewish history. God speaks to Moses' successor Joshua throughout his leadership career in retaking the Land of Canaan. He perform[s] miracles through Joshua—such as causing the Walls of Jericho to fall. After Joshua's death, God inspires and speaks to various judges—Othniel, Deborah, Gideon, Samson, and others. These judges receive miraculous abilities and counsel from God as they defend and protect Israelites in battle.

Although Moses, following God's Law, institutes the priesthood, it is not until later that the High Priest becomes the primary vehicle for God to communicate with humans. After the time of the Judges, God speaks to Samuel, as a child, and calls him into the priesthood. God continues to communicate messages to Samuel throughout his career. Samuel, with God's direction, anoints the first Israelite king, Saul. Then, Samuel, with God's direction anoints King David to replace Saul. The anointing of Samuel as priest (and the sense in which Samuel's anointing also made him a prophet) combined with the anointing of David as King (and the sense in which David's anointing also made him a prophet) introduces a new era in God's communication with humans. The three anointed (messianic) offices—prophet, priest, and king—become God's primary mouthpieces for Israel. The Hebrew word meaning "anointed one" is "messiah." (The Greek word meaning "anointed one," incidentally, is "christ.")

King David, under inspiration from God, writes many psalms. His son King Solomon, with similar inspiration, writes many proverbs. Later kings and priests are not considered to have equal inspiration. Later prophets, however, become the voice of God to Israel. The prophet Nathan was a contemporary of David. Elijah, Elisha, Micaiah, Isaiah, Jeremiah, Ezekiel, and Daniel are the most famous prophets.

Other prophets whose writings are included in the Bible are: Hosea, Joel, Amos, Obadiah, Jonah, Micah, Nahum, Habakkuk, Zephaniah, Haggai, Zechariah, and Malachi. Pharisaic and Rabbinic Judaism and Christianity accept the premise that God spoke through these prophets. Other early Jewish groups such as Sadducees and Samaritans accepted only the inspiration of the Torah. Pharisaic and Rabbinic Judaism believes that God's activity of speaking through prophets, however, ended with the canonical prophets of the Jewish Bible. Ezra the scribe instituted a new way for God to speak to Israel—through reading the Torah aloud to the people. Even though the age of the prophets ended with the canonical Tanach (or Old Testament) for the Jews, Pharisaic and Rabbinic Judaism still allowed for the possibility that God might speak through infants and fools.

Pharisaic and Rabbinic Judaism also taught that God could speak through a Bat Qol (or "mysterious voice"). This type of communication is claimed by the early Christians on a few occasions. When Jesus was baptized, a voice from Heaven said: "This is my son, whom I love; with him I am well pleased" (Matthew 3:17 NIV). When Jesus was transfigured, his disciples were startled by a bright cloud. A voice from the cloud said: "This is my son, whom I love; with him I am well pleased. Listen to him" (Matthew 17:5 NIV). When Saul of Tarsus (who later became the Apostle Paul) was confronted on the road to Damascus, he was blinded by a light from heaven and heard a voice saying: "Saul, Saul, why do you persecute me?" Saul asks who is speaking and the voice responds: "I am Jesus, whom you are persecuting . . . . Now get up and go into the city, and you will be told what you must do" (Acts 9:5-6 NIV).

Christianity also believes that God continued to speak through the visitation of angels (as when Gabriel announced John's and Jesus' births) and through prophets and prophetesses such as Simeon and Anna (Luke 2:25-38) and especially through John the Baptist who lived at the time of Jesus. Christianity also teaches that God spoke through those (such as apostles and prophets) who had received spiritual gifts in the first generation of the church.

Angels and Demons: The Personification of Communication (Logology)

Chapter 28

Angels as Agents of Divine "Feedback"

In my scholarly capacity, I frequently serve as a referee for articles submitted for publication to scholarly journals. Recently, an article I was refereeing identified a perplexing problem for many prayerful Believers: unanswered prayer. The article analyzed the issue from the standpoint of contemporary evangelical rhetorical strategies used to defend God for His failure to answer. Although the article neither compared prayer to nor contrasted prayer with advertising in the mass media, a case could be made that there are definite similarities. Mass communication tends to be more unidirectional, as compared with intrapersonal communication, interpersonal communication, small group communication, and online communication (which are all much more interactive than mass communication). Even public communication (in which one speaker addresses an audience) has a more easily obtained feedback than does mass communication. In public communication, the speaker can, at least, see the nonverbal facial expressions and body language of his or her audience. S/he can hear the applause, gasps, or heckling. In mass communication, on the other hand, the communicator is separated from his or her audience by some "medium"—radio, television, newspaper, magazine, billboard, etc. The communicator cannot "see" how his or her messages are being received. Advertisements in the mass media are impersonal and there are problems associated with discovering whether members of the intended (target) audiences even paid attention to the advertisements, let alone whether they decoded the messages in the same sense in which the advertisers encoded them. Nor do advertisers know whether the persuasion strategies used in the advertisements were successful. Hence, advertisers seek some sort of "feedback" from their target audiences (which those audiences do not typically offer without additional prodding). I submit that to the extent advertisers are unable to secure the desired feedback, they are in much the same boat (in terms of communication feedback) as are Believers who do not sense that their prayers are being answered.

Prayer, for many Believers, is a fairly unidirectional form of communication. As is the case with the target audiences of advertisers, the intended audience (God, in this case) cannot be "seen." He may be paying attention and may be decoding the messages in the same sense in which those offering the prayers encoded them. Whether the persuasion strategies used in the prayers were successful may sometimes be adduced by whether specific requests were granted, but even then—absent some accompanying message from God--skeptics may easily question whether the granting of requests was accomplished by God or was simply a matter of happy coincidence. Believers, like advertisers, are desirous for some form of feedback. Unfortunately, while advertisers have developed quantitative and qualitative methods of acquiring feedback, Believers face a far more daunting task.

The very words for "angel" in Greek and Hebrew denote a "messenger." The Hebrew word MALACH (from which we also derive the name of the last book of the Old Testament: Malachi/מַלְאָכִי) means "messenger." A MALACH/מַלְאָךְ may be either an angel or a human messenger. The same holds true for the Greek word AGGELOS/ἄγγελος. One can easily see, for example, the word "angel" in the word "evangelist/εὐαγγελιστής"—one who is a human messenger of good news. In prior commentaries, I have demonstrated that angels are the personification of God's creative fiats, His intrapersonal communication, and His own unidirectional messages. I have indicated the role they play in God's communication network. So, here I offer a few examples of angels representing God's tangible "feedback."

Although Mary and Joseph never requested a miraculous birth, according to Luke 1:26-38, the Angel Gabriel appears to Mary to announce her pending pregnancy. Matthew 1:20-23 reports that an unnamed angel also visited Joseph in a dream to verify that Mary's pregnancy was divine. Since these two angelic visitations, however, were not prompted by a prayer request, they are not to be classified as "feedback." They are, instead, in the category of God's own unidirectional messages. Joseph's angelic message was presented as entirely unidirectional; Mary's encounter with Gabriel included interaction between Mary and Gabriel, as Mary questioned how the virgin birth would be possible. This is interpersonal communication, or dialogue.

While the angelic encounters of Mary and Joseph were classed as God's own unidirectional (or interpersonal, dialogic) messages, the similar encounter between Zachariah (the father of John the Baptist) and an unnamed angel, in Luke 1:11-20, fits the category of "feedback." In Luke 1:13, the angel says to Zachariah, "Your prayer has been heard." The old man Zachariah and his old, barren wife, Elizabeth, are to have a child. This is angelic/divine feedback.

In Acts 10:31, the gentile Cornelius reports being visited by a man in bright clothing (no doubt, an angel) who says, "Cornelius, your prayer was heard and your alms were remembered before God." The angel directs Cornelius to the house where Simon Peter was staying and Cornelius becomes the first gentile Christian.

Acts Chapter 12 relates an account of Herod persecuting the church. He has the Apostle James executed and, since that act appears to please some Jews, he next proceeds to arrest the Apostle Peter (with a similar end goal or result in mind). The church meeting in the house of Mary the mother of John Mark, fearing an impending murder of Peter, prays fervently. The night before Herod planned to bring Peter to judgment, Peter is sleeping, bound with two chains, between two soldiers, with more soldiers guarding the door to the prison. An angel comes to Peter, breaks his chains, tells him to get dressed, escorts him past the guards at the prison door, and takes him to the gate in the wall of the city, which opens for them automatically. Once on the street to John Mark's mother's house, the angel leaves Peter. Peter proceeds to the house and knocks on the door. He explains what has happened and then flees to another place.

These New Testament accounts of angelic encounters exemplify God's angelic feedback. Old Testament examples include angels responding to the cry of Abraham's son Ishmael to preserve him from dying in the wilderness (Genesis 21:17), responding to Abraham's willingness to sacrifice Isaac--telling him not to do so (Genesis 22:11-12), answering the prayer of Manoah, the father of Samson--confirming that he had indeed visited Manoah's wife with instructions about Samson (Judges 13:8 ff.), answering the prayer of Elijah concerning the threat to his life (1 Kings 19:7), answering the prayers of Isaiah and King Hezekiah to defend Jerusalem (Isaiah 37 and 2 Chronicles 32:21), and of course, answering the prayers of Daniel by protecting him in the lions' den. Perhaps, the account of the angel confronting Balaam and his donkey, in Numbers 22, is also an example of divine feedback.

Angels are not the only means of feedback used by God in the Bible. Gideon's fleece, the Urim and Thummim of the high priest, and fire sent from heaven to consume sacrifices are other representative examples of feedback. The point here, however, is that angels are the personification of God's communication. Feedback is but one aspect of communication.

Angels and Demons: The Personification of Communication (Logology)

Chapter 29

Demons as the Communication of False Information

In I John 4:6, the Spirit of Truth is contrasted with the Spirit of Error. The Spirit of Error seems to be connected with false prophets, in I John 4:1. It is clear that the biblical authors believed that God communicated truth, but that there is also the communication of error in the world. I have already equated the terms Spirit, Angel, and Word, in my commentaries. For Kenneth Burke, the relationship between terms that mean roughly the same thing in a certain symbol system is indicated by the use of the equals sign (=). Although Burke correctly teaches that each INDIVIDUAL has his or her own individual symbol system, I think that LANGUAGES WITHIN THE SAME SPECIFIC MILIEUS approximate Burke's application in some respects. Therefore, I assert that in the First Century A.D., the Hebrew/Judeo-Christian symbol system contains the following equation: Spirit=Angel=Word. All three terms represent the communication of God, as the Jews and Jewish Christians used the terms. In the New Testament Period, we could also add to this list of equations the following terms: =Bat Qol=prophecy=spiritual gifts (and all of the terms that equal [=] spiritual gifts).

While Burke teaches that an equals sign is operative in symbol systems, he teaches that a "vs." sign is also operative. In other words, while Angel, Spirit, and Word all equal each other, they all also stand in opposition to certain other terms, such as Spirit of Error, Demon, False Prophet, etc. The Spirit of Error is the opposite of the Spirit of Truth, in I John. Likewise, False Prophets are the opposite of Prophets and Spiritual Gifts. Demons are the opposite of Angels. Using Burke's shorthand, it looks like this: Demons vs. Angels, Spirit of Error vs. Spirit of Truth, and False Prophets vs. Prophets (=Spiritual Gifts). Lest my readers misunderstand, I am not painting a picture of an actual warfare being waged between angelic beings and demonic beings; I am simply pointing out that the list of terms "Spirit=Angel=Word" stand in strict opposition to the list of terms "Spirit of Error=Demon=False Prophet." The terms in the first group are the opposite of the terms in the second group.

To the list of negative term equations, I add the term "unclean spirit," since in the synoptic Gospels, Matthew 4:23-25 uses the terminology of demons, while, in a parallel passage, Luke 6:17-19 uses the term "unclean spirit" in place of demon. In another parallel, Matthew 8:28-34 and Luke 8:26-39 use demonic terminology, while Mark 5:1-20 uses the term "unclean spirit" in place of demon. Luke 4:33 even uses the combination terminology: "spirit of an unclean demon." In Luke 8:2, the

29: Demons as the Communication of False Information 181

term "evil spirit" is used. I, therefore also add the term "evil spirit" to the list of negative term equations. Because Jesus is accused of casting out demons by the power of Beelzebub--and because Jesus responds to this charge (in Matthew 12:26 and Luke 11:18) with the rhetorical question, "If Satan casts out Satan . . . how then shall his kingdom stand?" and (in Mark 3:23-26) with the rhetorical question, "How can Satan cast out Satan?"--we might also add the terms "Beelzebub" and "Satan" to the list of negative term equations. Mark 19:17-25 refers to a "speechless spirit" and Luke 13:11 refers to a "spirit of weakness," possibly indicating the type of affliction each spirit visited upon its host. Acts 16:16 reports that a girl had a "spirit of Pytho" (meaning, I suppose, she prophesied using the Delphic oracle?). Paul "cured" her of that.

Using Burke's system of charting, then, I find the following negative list of equations:

- Spirit of Error=
- Demon=
- False Prophet=
- Unclean Spirit=
- Evil Spirit=
- Beelzebub=
- Satan.

This negative list is the opposite of (or, according to Burke, "vs.") the following positive list of equations:

- Spirit=

- Angel=

- Word=

- Bat Qol=

- Prophecy=

- Spiritual Gifts (and all of the terms that = spiritual gifts).

Beginning with I John's contrast between the Spirit of Truth and the Spirit of Error, one can easily see the primary distinction between Demons and Angels. Angels are the personification of TRUTH communication, while Demons are the personification of FALSEHOOD communication. Clearly, "error" is falsehood communication (or the communication of false information). I John links the Spirit of Error to False Prophets, the human "communicators" of FALSE INFORMATION. However, one need not have a human mediator to be given false information. A snake will do nicely. When Jesus brings the word Satan into the discussion of casting out Demons, he draws to mind the primal account of someone communicating false information—the serpent of Eden. I point out in Chapter 5:

> Johns gospel quotes Jesus (8:44): "You have the devil for your father and you wish to practice the desires of your father; . . . he could not stay in the truth, because there is no truth in him. When he tells a lie, he speaks according to his nature; for he is a liar and the father of liars." . . . Jesus is probably referring to Satan's role as a tempter. If, as the New Testament asserts, the serpent of Genesis is actually Satan, it is clear that he lies. He said, "You shall not surely die." . . . Revelation calls him the "deceiver of all humanity."

But, is a snake even necessary? James 1:13-14 seems to effectively eliminate the need for the role of a personified Satan in the temptation process. In his place, James seems to suggest that the process of temptation is conducted entirely within the mental processes of the human who is being tempted:

> Let no one who is tempted say, "I am tempted of God," for He tempts no one. But each person is tempted when he is drawn away and enticed by his own lusts. Then when the passion has conceived, it gives birth to sin, and the sin, when it reaches maturity, produces death. (Berkeley Version)

Despite what James argues, it seems easier for the human to comprehend his or her own intrapersonal struggles by personifying his or her Id, as Freud names that selfish element in the psyche. As I discuss in Chapter 7, Jewish writers name that element the YETZER HA-RA' (יצר הרע). So, who or what, in fact, induced Eve to eat from the Tree of the Knowledge of Good and Evil? Was it the Serpent? Was it Satan? Was it Eve's YETZER HA-RA'? Was it her Id? Was it primarily just Eve's own mental processes? Genesis 3:6 discusses those mental processes:

> The woman saw the tree as being good for food, delightful to the eye and a tree desirable to render one wise, so she took of its fruit and ate; she also gave to her husband, who ate with her. (Berkeley Version)

This account of Eve's thought processes does not even include the FALSEHOOD communicated by the Serpent ("You shall not surely die"). If one suggests that Eve was Demon-possessed, she is effectively let off the hook. How could God hold Eve accountable for an act that she committed while under the control of a Demon? And yet, this is precisely the type of implication that enters into scenarios in which Demon-possession is discussed. Consider, however, this possibility: the term Demon is used not only to indicate that the person is the recipient of false information, but also the term Demon represents a FALSE ENTITY itself. I will follow that thread in my next chapter.

Chapter 30
Demons as False Entities

The communication of God has elements that stand in direct opposition ("vs."--in Burke's shorthand) to elements on the false communication side:

- Prophet vs. False Prophet
- Spirit of Truth vs. Spirit of Error (or Unclean Spirit or Evil Spirit)
- Angels vs. Satan

There is no direct opposite of "God." This is uncomfortable for the human psyche that derives comfort from identifying such polar opposites. Some religionists have, therefore, attempted to present Satan as the opposite of God. The ancient Persians taught that there was a good god constantly at war with an evil god. See Chapter 4: "The Great Satan" of Iran for my discussion of why Judaism and Christianity rejected this dualism. The huge theological obstacle that blocks such dualism for Jews, Christians, and Muslims is the doctrine of Monotheism. Deuteronomy 6:4 states the doctrine: "Hear, O Israel, the Lord our God --the Lord is one." The first commandment (found in Exodus 20:3) states: "Thou shalt have no other gods before Me." Hence, the Apostle

Paul is not particularly bothered by the possibility that Christian believers might accidentally eat meat that has been sacrificed to idols. He reasons this way in I Corinthians 8:4-6:

> Relative, then, to the food that has been dedicated to idols, we know that no idol really exists; that there is no God but one. In case there are so-called gods either in heaven or on earth--such as there are gods many and lords many--yet for us there exists one God, the Father, from whom all things come and who is our goal; and one Lord, Jesus Christ, through whom all things exist and through whom we are (Berkeley).

Paul, then, regards the eating of any meat (whether or not it has been sacrificed to idols) to be innocent (not a sin). Nevertheless, he recommends not eating meat offered to an idol, if a Christian brother might mistakenly interpret the eating to indicate that we are worshipping the idol. He states in I Corinthians 8:13: "Therefore, if my eating causes my brother to stumble, I shall eat no meat forever, so that my brother shall not be tripped up" (Berkeley).

In the same epistle, I Corinthians 10:18-26, Paul returns to the issue of eating meat that has been sacrificed to idols, and introduces the way he understands and uses the term "demons":

> Observe those physically the people of Israel! Are not those who eat the sacrifices sharers of the altar? What then is my suggestion? That an idol offering amounts to anything or that the idol itself is anything? No, but that what they sacrifice, they are offering to demons and not to God, and I do not want you to fellowship with demons. You cannot drink the Lord's cup and a demon's cup. You cannot participate in the Lord's table and in a demon's table. Or shall we provoke the Lord to indignation? Are we mightier than He? Everything is allowed, but not everything is helpful. Everything is allowed, but not everything is constructive. .

30: Demons as False Entities

> . . Eat whatever is sold in the meat market, without asking questions for conscientious scruples, for the earth and its fullness are the Lord's (Berkeley).

Clearly, the question of whether one should eat meat that has been offered to idols is not a major issue in the Christian world today. I am not citing this passage in order to resolve that issue. I am writing about demons, and whether they exist, according to Paul. Paul has asked a rhetorical question: "What then is my suggestion--that an idol offering amounts to anything or that the idol itself is anything?" When asking a rhetorical question, no answer needs to be given, because the answer is obvious. Nevertheless, Paul actually answers this one—just to be sure that everyone understands: "No, but that what they sacrifice, they are offering to demons and not to God, and I do not want you to fellowship with demons." In a Burkean sense, Paul has made "idols" equal "demons." He has stated (rhetorically) that "idols" are "not anything." Earlier, in I Corinthians 8:4, he had stated, "We know that no idol really exists; that there is no God but one."

Logically, if there is no God but one, and idols do not therefore exist, and offering to idols is the same as offering to demons, we may conclude that "DEMONS DO NOT EXIST." THEY ARE FALSE ENTITIES. If Paul had thought that there really were true entities called demons, who were at war with God, could he ever have concluded that eating meat he claims is "offered" to them might be called innocent? Could he ever have suggested, "Eat whatever is sold in the meat market, without asking questions," if he thought the meat had been associated with an existing entity at war with God? The entire basis of his reasoning that allows the conclusion that it is not sinful to eat meat sacrificed to idols is that idols are nothing. They are like demons—they do not exist.

Now, of course, the carved or sculpted statues that represent the false entities do exist. Paul was not claiming that the graven images, themselves, do not exist. He was claiming that there is no personal identity in existence who is represented by the graven image. Likewise, he was not claiming that the "false communication" about the existence of a god other than the Judeo-Christian God does not exist. He is simply claiming that such an alternative god (or demon) does not exist. One might even go so far as to suggest that the "false information" itself becomes a spiritual force that affects humans. I will follow that thread in the next chapter.

Chapter 31
Demons, Voodoo, Hypnosis, Hexes, and Psychogenic Illnesses

What do demons, voodoo, hypnosis, hexes, and psychogenic illnesses have in common? They are all physical manifestations of things that do not exist in any realm other than the symbolic. They do not actually exist in the physical realm and they are not truly divine beings. Nevertheless, they do have the power to affect human beings, because humans are by nature symbol-using animals, according to Kenneth Burke. As I stated at the end of the previous chapter, one might even go so far as to suggest that the "false information" itself becomes a spiritual force that affects humans. Since the author of I John contrasts the Spirit of Truth with the Spirit of Error, we may assume that a spiritual force of false information does indeed exist, according to the Bible. And, as I have demonstrated in Chapter 23, the word "spirit" is to be equated with the word "word." A spirit is a word. Hence, the Spirit of God may be understood as God's communicative nature. Angels are also God's spirits, as Hebrews 1:7 claims: "And of the angels he says, 'Who makes his angels spirits, and his ministers a flame of fire.'" The author of Hebrews is quoting Psalm 104:4. If we stipulate that, according to the Bible, angels represent the communication of true information, demons represent the communication of false information. The huge difference for the Apostle Paul, as I discussed in my previous chapter, is that the true information emanates from an actual being—the one true God. Nevertheless, Paul disputes that there is any actual divine being from which the false information emanates. Demons are the same thing as idols—which, for Paul, are nothing/nonexistent.

Kenneth Burke attributes a good deal of power, however, to hexes and psychogenic illnesses. In *Language as Symbolic Action*, pages 6-7, Burke explains:

> In referring to the misuse of symbols, I . . . think of "psychogenic illnesses" . . . A certain kind of food may be perfectly wholesome . . . But our habits may be such that it . . . may be nauseating to us. (The most drastic instance is, of course, the ideal diets of cannibals.) . . . Instances of "hexing" are of the same sort (as when a tribesman . . . finds . . . that . . . those in authority have decreed his death, by magic, and he promptly begins to waste away and die . . .

Burke tells of the anthropologist Franz Boas. Trying to establish rapport with a tribe of Esquimaux, he ate from a pot of what he thought to be whale blubber. Overwhelmed by the disgusting nature of this thought, he rushed outside to vomit. When he found out that the food was not blubber—but dumplings—Boas was able to eat the food without vomiting.

31: Demons, Voodoo, Hypnosis, Hexes, and Psychogenic Illnesses

Similar to symbolically-induced food-based nausea, hexing, and psychogenic illness, is the practice of casting spells on voodoo dolls. According to the (voodoo-sympathetic) website, http://www.calastrology.com/voodoo.html, "Voodoo is a powerful mystical practice that can bring spectacular gifts and rewards to anyone who believes . . . ." That much is probably true: that the mystical practice brings results to anyone who BELIEVES. Even though the information is false, if someone BELIEVES it, s/he is under the power of the false information.

As a high school student, I once viewed a demonstration of hypnosis. While under hypnosis, a student was given a post-hypnotic suggestion. He was told that there was a bucket on stage in the path of his exit. He would not actually see the bucket as he exited the stage, but that upon taking three steps toward the stairs to exit, he would trip over the bucket. There was no actual bucket on stage. Yet, upon being brought out of the hypnotic state, the student walked toward the exit stairs, and (as suggested) tripped over the nonexistent bucket. The audience exploded with laughter.

Demons may often be understood to be in the same category as voodoo, hypnosis, hexes, and psychogenic illnesses. While there are a few biblical accounts of demons that are difficult to fit into this description, the vast majority of demon-possession cases fit easily. I previously mentioned Mark 19:17-25, which refers to a "speechless spirit," and Luke 13:11, which refers to a "spirit of weakness." Both terminologies possibly indicate the type of affliction each spirit visited upon its host. Both physical results—speechlessness and weakness—could be replicated by post-hypnotic suggestion, hexing, or voodoo (for the believers in those practices). David Edwin

Harrell, in his book, *Oral Roberts: An American Life*,[128] states: "Oral was keenly aware of the emotional and psychosomatic nature of much of the healing under his tent. . . . He unashamedly laid claim to psychosomatic healings." I assume that, so long as someone who believed s/he had an illness or physical condition that DID NOT ACTUALLY EXIST believed that Oral Roberts (or Jesus working through Oral Roberts) had the power to heal that nonexistent physical malady, the symbolic act of healing imposed by Roberts would effectively cure the nonexistent malady. Acts 19:13 suggests that some Jews had the power to cast out demons and Jesus seems to corroborate this fact in Matthew 12:27 and Luke 11:19. One might assume that ANYONE who is capable of persuading someone who believes in the existence of a nonexistent physical malady that the nonexistent malady does not exist might, thereby, effectively cast out a demon.

I, therefore, wonder how many "demons" exist in people as a result of the preaching and teaching of Bible-believing Christians who seek to persuade the populace that (contrary to the teaching of the Apostle Paul) DEMONS DO EXIST AS ENTITIES! How many novice Christians have been led to believe that they are under the influence of these entities (that Paul says do not exist)? Perhaps, even my writing of this book will be capable of exorcising some demons. I will address the more difficult demon-possession passages in the New Testament in future chapters, but for now, just as is the case with those who believe the "false information" communicated in voodoo,

---

[128] David Edwin Harrell, *Oral Roberts: An American Life*, Bloomington, IN: Indiana University Press, 1985.

hypnosis, hexes, and psychogenic illnesses, those who are willing to replace such false information with the true information may see their resulting physical maladies disappear.

Angels and Demons: The Personification of Communication (Logology)

Chapter 32

The Rite, the Exorcist, and Severe Demon Possession in the Bible

January 2011 brought the debut of the movie "The Rite," starring Anthony Hopkins. The film opened at number one at the box office for the week. In the film, Hopkins's character is an exorcist, in Rome. The demon-possessed characters do not levitate or spin their heads around in complete circles, as the demon-possessed Linda Blair had done in the 1973 movie "The Exorcist." Other than appearing to know things that the demon-possessed character should not have otherwise known—like, that a U.S. dollar bill was hidden in a bag and that a young priest's father would soon die—the demoniacs of "The Rite" do not seem to accomplish any super-human feats. A pregnant girl who is chained to her bed apparently loses her unborn child and fatally hemorrhages. Eyes turn red, bodies experience contortions, and fingers are cramped into claw-like configurations, but "The Rite" moves the genre of exorcism movies much closer to the believable than some of its famous predecessors.

"The Rite" even incorporates significant counterarguments to the thesis that the individuals presented as being demon-possessed are so in actuality. As I discussed in Chapter 30, the Apostle Paul suggests that "idols" and "demons" are the same thing. He also states (rhetorically) that "idols" are "not anything." In I Corinthians 8:4, he states, "We know that no idol really exists; that there is no God but one." In "The Rite," the character portrayed by Colin O'Donoghue, a skeptical American priest (presented almost as an atheist), also resists the notion that demons exist, but he does not offer any argument from scripture. Instead, his argument is presented as an atheistic argument.

The O'Donoghue character argues that, rather than being demon-possessed, the individuals so presented just believe that they are demon-possessed, and their false belief is what motivates their behavior. I also made this argument in the previous chapter, but "The Rite" offers the argument in such a way that it must be considered atheistic. Why? I guess it makes for better theater (and allows the writer/director the opportunity to place "reasonableness" on the side of atheism instead of Christianity).

The O'Donoghue character even argues that some individuals are actually psychotic—that they need psychiatric attention, rather than an exorcism. I have written an entire book on what I call "psychotic entelechy." While asserting that there are several major secular psychotic entelechies, I focus the book on the dangers of spiritual gifts theology. This is the notion that someone actually receives personal communiqués from the supernatural realm. While, similar to Kenneth Burke following John Dewey, I do not use the term "psychotic" in the psychiatric sense, I do argue that if one believes one hears voices or receives messages from the supernatural realm, the messages one receives sometimes have the capacity to induce extremely dangerous behavior on the part of the one receiving the messages. This is, in my opinion, in the realm of what the Bible might term "demon-possessed."

When I say "the Bible," I mean "only the New Testament." The Old Testament does not include a single case of demon-possession. I state in Chapter 1:

> What is significant, however, is that the discussion of the creation of angels and the Fall of the Angels did not occur until much later than the supposed event. It was not until the Hellenistic period of Jewish history (between 300 and 50 B.C.) when Jews were under the control of the Greeks (Alexander the Great and his successors) that the Fall of the Angels became a topic of much conversation. Yet, in those years following the completion of the Old Testament, there is a flood of literature containing information on the subject.

What is true of Fallen Angels is also true of Demons. Demon (δαιμόνιον) is a Greek concept, not a Jewish concept. They are not even always bad or evil, in Greek thought. Socrates, with a positive air, claims, in his Apology, to have a demon. At his trial, he says he is not an unbeliever, because he hears a voice that is a demon instructing him to be a philosopher. The Greek word for "fortunate" is EUDAIMŌN (εὐδαίμων)—meaning "(having a) good demon." That the Apostle Paul—who has received an education as a Roman citizen—would reject the existence of demons on the basis that they are the same as idols is not surprising. They are false gods who make up a part of the Greek pantheon.

Demons in the New Testament are never capable of inducing levitation or head-spinning, as with Linda Blair's character in "The Exorcist." The vast majority seem to be less remarkable in the sense that the demon-possession was exemplified by a physical malady, such as non-speaking, that was effectively cured by casting out the demon. In Chapter 31, I report:

> Acts 19:13 suggests that some Jews had the power to cast out demons and Jesus seems to corroborate this fact in Matthew 12:27 and Luke 11:19. One might assume that ANYONE who is capable of persuading someone who believes in the existence of a nonexistent physical malady that the nonexistent malady does not exist might, thereby, effectively cast out a demon.

Such is the case with the vast majority of New Testament demoniacs. However, a few do deserve closer attention. In Matthew 8:28-32, Mark 5:1-17, and Luke 8:26-33 one or two demoniacs dwelt in tombs and menaced people who traveled nearby. They wore no clothes and were very ferocious. People were fearful to travel past them. People had even attempted binding them with chains, but the chains were broken by them. When Jesus traveled there, the demoniacs called him "Son of God" and pled with him to cast them (the demons) into a herd of swine. Jesus granted the request; the swine, then, ran down the steep embankment into the lake and were drowned. The demoniac/s surely would interpret this visible development—a herd of swine racing down an embankment into a lake—as a sign that he or they were no longer demon-possessed. Apparently, the former demoniacs were freed from whatever ailed them. Luke 8:35 reports that the people came out to see what had happened. They found the formerly possessed man sitting at Jesus' feet, dressed, and sane.

So, what happened here? If we take Paul's word that demons are like idols and false gods—and, hence, do not exist—we have men who mistakenly believed they were demon-possessed. They, therefore, behaved as they assumed the demon-possessed behaved. They even believed that they were possessed of multiple demons, because, when Jesus asked, "What is your name?" the answer was "Legion," because (t)he(y) believed (t)he(y) had many demons. We have men who believed not only that they were demon-possessed, AND that Jesus was the Son of God, but ALSO that Jesus had the power to cast out demons. Hence, when Jesus granted the request they believed had come from the inner demons, they believed that he had, in fact, rid them of the demons. Except for the possible super-human act of breaking chains and for the notable occurrence of a herd of swine racing into a lake, there is no compelling evidence of the existence of a supernatural being in the form of a demon at work, here. Perhaps, Jesus granted the request to see swine run into the sea as a means of thoroughly persuading the demon-possessed that they had no demons. So long as the formerly possessed BELIEVED they were free of demons, they behaved sanely.

Another possible explanation that would be short of granting the existence of personal beings called demons would be that whatever mental problem the men were experiencing was transferred into the minds of the swine. In other words, the men may have been psychotic in the psychiatric sense and this psychosis was, then, transferred to the swine. However, the psychotic behavior of the men caused them to ferociously attack humans. The swine displayed no such antisocial behavior. Instead, they committed suicide. I am more inclined to believe that Jesus created a sense of panic in the swine, as a visual means of persuading the possessed men that the demons were gone. Incidentally, even this (counterargument) explanation of exorcism was presented in the movie, "The Rite," as Anthony Hopkins's character appeared to use a frog—pretending to extract it from a young man--to persuade the young man that he had removed the demon.

In another demon-possession case, in Matthew 17:14-20, Mark 9:14-29, and Luke 9:37-43, a boy since early childhood displays epileptic symptoms. He cannot speak, convulses, rolls on the ground, foams at the mouth, and sometimes falls into the fire and sometimes into the water. While Jesus could have simply "healed" the boy and, thus, corrected any actual physical malady he may have had, this case was diagnosed (by the boy's father?) as demon-possession, as Jesus' disciples attempted in vain to cast out the spirit. The boy's father says to Jesus, "If you can do anything, help us." Jesus calls attention to the implicit doubt in the words the father has used—"If you can do anything?" (In Luke, Jesus exclaims, "O faithless and perverse generation!") Jesus states that everything is possible for a believer. The father changes his tune: "I believe." The child throws himself into another fit, Jesus rebukes the spirit, and the boy is cured.

In this case, the child appears to believe what his father believes (something that would not be uncommon). In the field of communication, we call this a type of "altercasting." It is a sort of self-fulfilling prophecy. The father does not believe it is possible for Jesus' disciples to cast out the spirit (so, neither does the child). The father even questions Jesus' ability, but after some confrontation, he tells Jesus he believes. Then, Jesus is able to successfully cure the child. While it is true that an actual physical malady such as epilepsy exists, there is no compelling reason to believe that this child had that illness. He did, however, display such symptoms. If the symptoms were related only to a psychosomatic illness, as I discussed in the previous Chapter, just removing the belief that the boy had an incurable disease was required.

Another possibility, in this instance, is that the boy actually had epilepsy and that the father had misdiagnosed it as demon-possession. This possibility suggests the need to look at the cases of demon-possession in the New Testament to discover WHO is actually doing the diagnosing. I will follow that thread in the next chapter.

Chapter 33

Diagnosis: Demon Possession or Illness?

Jesus is presented in the gospels as one who could cure any type of malady—demon possession or illness. Nevertheless, the synoptic gospel writers (Matthew, Mark, and Luke) find it useful to distinguish between these two major types of maladies. The gospel writer John, on the other hand, only presents Jesus as curing diseases or other bodily malfunctions (not casting out demons), and Paul (as I have pointed out in past commentaries) considers demons to be the equivalent of idols: false gods, who really have no existence whatsoever. Incidentally, John the author of Revelation (in 9:20) appears to agree with Paul—that demons (like idols) are nothing. He writes of unrepentant men who worshiped the "works of their hands"—"demons and golden idols, and silver, and bronze, and wooden, which are not able to see, nor hear, nor walk."

The following list of illnesses and bodily malfunctions cured by Jesus is fairly complete:

- bent spine Lk. 13:10-21 (crippled woman)

- blind Jn. 9:1-41 (man born that way); Mk. 10:46-52; Mt. 20:29-34; Lk. 18:35-43; Mt. 11:2-19; Lk. 7:18-35

- deaf Mt. 11:2-19; Lk. 7:18-35

- diseases Mt. 11:2-19; Lk. 7:18-35

- epileptic Mt. 4:23-25

- fever Jn. 4:46-54; Mk. 1:29-34; Mt. 8:14-17; Luke 4:38-41

- lame Jn. 1:5-47; Mt. 11:2-19; Lk. 7:18-35

- leprosy Lk. 17:11-37; Mk. 1:40-45; Mt. 8:2-4; Lk. 5:12-16; Mt. 11:2-19; Lk. 7:18-35

- palsy Mk. 2:1-12; Mt. 9:1-8; Lk. 5:17-26 (paralytic?); Mt. 4:23-25; Mt. 8:5-13; Lk.7:1-10 (near death)

- plagues Mt. 11:2-19; Lk. 7:18-35

- raise dead Mt. 11:2-19; Lk. 7:18-35; Jn. 11:1-44 (Lazarus); Lk. 7:11-17

- sick on their beds Mk. 6:53-56; Mt. 14:34-36

- various illnesses Mk. 1:29-34; Mt. 8:14-17; Luke 4:38-41

- withered hand Mk. 3:1-6; Mt. 12:9-14; Lk. 6:6-11

Conspicuously absent from this list is any type of mental illness. There seems to be a strongly psychosomatic element in virtually all of the cases the synoptic gospel writers term "unclean spirit," "evil spirit," and/or "demon-possession." Even though these gospel writers use this terminology, they do not themselves appear to be diagnosing the maladies. Rather, the diagnoses seem to be generated by the culture, sometimes, even by the families of those who have the maladies (and frequently, by the "demon-possessed" individuals, themselves).

In the previous chapter, I observed that a possibility existed "that the boy [in Matthew 17:14-20, Mark 9:14-29, and Luke 9:37-43] actually had epilepsy and that the father had misdiagnosed it as demon-possession." A closer look at those accounts shows that, while Mt. 17:18 terms this demon-possession, in Mk. 9:14-29, the father diagnoses the malady as a dumb (or speechless) spirit. In Mt. 17:14-20, the father says he is epileptic; whereas, in Lk. 9:37-43, the father simply says he has a spirit. I have already offered my opinions concerning what may have transpired in this case. I mention the case here to demonstrate that the diagnosis of demon-possession was not always clear or conclusive in the various texts. Did the father believe his son was demon-possessed, truly epileptic, or just the victim of a false belief? Does the father even know? Whatever the diagnosis, the gospel accounts are in unanimous agreement that Jesus solved the problem.

The gospel writers themselves differ, even when discussing the very same cases, on whether the various cases should be termed "demon" or (unclean or evil) "spirit." What Mt. 4:23-25 calls demon, Lk. 6:17-19 calls unclean spirit. What Lk. 4:31-37 terms demon, Mk. 1:21-28 terms unclean spirit. What Mt. 8:28-34 and Lk. 8:26-39 refer to as demon, Mk. 5:1-20 refers to as unclean spirit. Lk. 8:1-3 mentions Mary Magdalene from whom seven demons had gone, but Lk. 8:1-3 also refers to evil spirits. Mk. 6:13, Mt. 10:8, and Lk. 9:1 all use the word demon, but Mk. 6:7 and Mt. 10:1 refer to the same event with the words unclean spirit. Lk. 7:18-35 describes a case referred to only as evil spirit. Mt. 12:22-32, Mk. 3:20-30, and Lk. 11:14-23 and 12:10 describe another case with all gospel writers agreeing to the demon terminology. It appears that the gospel writers, Matthew, Mark, and Luke, perceived no difficulty with substituting between the terminologies. This does not seem to support a conviction that demons in the Greek sense of the Greek word existed. I suspect that "demon" terminology had simply become a conventional way of referring to a problem with a "spirit."

As I have been demonstrating ever since Chapter 23, the word "spirit" is the equivalent of the word "word." When the New Testament contrasts the spirit of truth with a spirit of error, it is indicating that these "false words" (or spirits of error) are capable of "possessing" humans who believe them. This is especially true with highly suggestible individuals (including children). As a college professor, I have observed this phenomenon in more than one student. I know of male students who--because they speak with a lisp or have a high-pitched voice or are interested in music, dance, or theater—have been told by their contemporaries that they appear to be homosexual. Thinking logically, lisping, voice pitch, and performance aptitudes have nothing to do with one's sexual behavior. But, to the highly suggestible, the insinuation or suggestion that the male may be homosexual is enough to produce corresponding behavior. Likewise, a similar case exists with females who may have lower-pitched voices or athletic builds. Such suggestions or insinuations have the force of "spirit" for the individuals involved.

I have had students who were told they had aggressive tendencies, and they promptly lived out the implications of the terminology. I have had students who were told they were suicidal, and they succumbed to the force of this "spirit"/suggestion. Bi-polar. ADHD. Name the diagnosis, and, frequently, suggestible individuals so diagnosed will respond with the "appropriate" set of behavioral acts. I am not suggesting that there are not individuals who are truly bi-polar or who truly suffer from ADHD. I just wonder how many individuals who have received a "false diagnosis" or a "spirit of error" become somewhat "possessed" by the false word.

While it is easier to understand the terminology "spirit of error" as a "false word," allow me to unpack the terms "unclean spirit" and "evil spirit." Kosher/כשר is the Hebrew term designating proper dietary habits. Kosher is translated "clean." Whatever is not Kosher is "unclean." Hence, eating mutton, beef, or venison is Kosher or clean. Eating pork, horse meat, or dog meat, on the other hand, is unclean. Jews were promised, in the Law of Moses, that if they would eat Kosher foods, they would be afflicted with fewer diseases. We all know that anyone who eats pork that has not been thoroughly cooked, for example, may be susceptible to Trichinosis. The dietary laws were designed, primarily, to keep the population healthy. There were also Kosher laws concerning cleanliness and what one should do if one becomes ill. Those afflicted with leprosy, for example, were required to quarantine themselves from the healthy population. To warn others of their illness, they were required, even in New Testament times, to cry out "unclean." Notice that the

New Testament does not provide for anyone the diagnosis that he or she has "a demon or spirit of leprosy." That is because leprosy had quite visible and empirically-detectable physical symptoms. Likewise, while Jesus healed many with "fevers," no one had a demon or spirit of fever. If someone has no specific, empirically-verifiable physical symptoms, but still behaves as if he or she is afflicted with a disease, you could say that the person is not actually "unclean," but had a "spirit" of "uncleanness"—or, an "unclean spirit."

Similarly, the less-used terminology "evil spirit," the word "evil" as applied to a spirit is used seven times by Luke (in his two works, Luke and Acts). Other than those seven times, the term "evil" is only applied to the term "spirit" once—in Matthew 12:45, discussed in the next paragraph—and even there, Matthew did not use the phrase "evil spirit." The Greek term translated "evil" in all of these cases is the same term Jesus uses in his prayer: "Deliver us from evil." It corresponds to the Hebrew word used in the name of the Tree of Knowledge of Good and Evil, in Genesis. After Adam and Eve ate from the tree, they and all their descendants were infused with both good and evil inclinations. This is not a term that refers primarily to the spirit world; it is a term that refers primarily to HUMAN characteristics (albeit, less than desirable characteristics). The word does not conjure up for Luke super-human "evil" beings. It describes that human nature that leads one to sin. As Jesus' prayer states (in a parallelism): "Lead us not into temptation, but deliver us from evil." Whether the "evil words or thoughts" affecting the one who was afflicted were the words or thoughts of that person so afflicted, or whether they were the "evil words" inflicted upon the victims by the malicious "curses" of other humans, they could be termed "evil spirits."

Jesus himself is never specifically quoted as diagnosing a case as demon-possession, but in Mt. 12:38-45, Jesus offers a parable of someone having an "unclean spirit." I think Jesus was saying that the man in his parable believes that he has an illness and that that sheer belief is enough to produce those "unclean" (or illness-like) symptoms. If the man is cured of this false belief, but does not replace this false belief with true beliefs, he is susceptible to many other false beliefs (or spirits) more evil than the one that first afflicted him. In other words, unless he learns the truth, he remains very suggestible—very susceptible to erroneous spirits.

Many times, in the New Testament, the one doing the diagnosing of the presence of a demon or unclean spirit is the individual who is so possessed. The case of the Gadarene/Gerazene demoniacs is a case in point. They identified the name of the demon/s who possessed them: Legion (because they diagnosed themselves as having many demons). When Jesus taught in the town of Capernaum—a village very close to Jesus' home town of Nazareth—Mt. 4:23-25, 8:14-17, Mk. 1:29-39, Lk. 4:38-41 write of several unspecified cases of demon-possession. Interestingly, all demon-possessed individuals knew who Jesus was. He grew up in the region. Similarly, in Acts 19:15-16, a man possessed of an "evil spirit" knows who Jesus and Paul are, but Jesus and Paul are not the ones performing the exorcism. It seems that whenever the "demon-possessed" individual has a (self-diagnosed) self-recognition of his or her own demon-possession, and a belief in the ability of the one exorcising the demon to do so effectively, success results. In the Acts 19 case, some Jews (unknown to the demon-possessed man) tried to perform the exorcism and failed.

Before we leave the discussion of diagnosis, we should list the several clear cases of misdiagnosis of demon-possession in the New Testament. In Mt. 11:19 and Lk. 7:33-34, Jewish opponents misdiagnose John the Baptist as having a demon. In Mk. 3:19-30 and Mt. 12:22-37, scribes misdiagnose Jesus as having an unclean spirit (Mk.) and using power of Beelzebub to cast out demons. This accusation Jesus calls the unforgiveable sin. In Mt. 9:27-34, Pharisees misdiagnose Jesus as using power of Beelzebub to cast out demons. In Jn. 7:20 and 8:48-52, the crowds (Jews) misdiagnose Jesus as having a demon. In Jn. 10:20-21, Jewish opponents misdiagnose Jesus as having a demon and being insane. In Acts 17:18, Paul's Stoic and Epicurean opponents falsely accuse him of being an announcer of foreign demons. The fact that culture or society diagnoses someone as being demon-possessed does not make the diagnosis accurate.

Who is doing the diagnosing? It may be the demon-possessed person himself or herself, the demon-possessed person's parent, malicious individuals who may have cursed the individual, or the culture in general who cannot discover empirically-recognizable reasons for the unclean or illness-like symptoms. Jesus is not reported as diagnosing any specific individuals, himself—just curing them. Matthew, Mark, and Luke seem to use indiscriminate diagnosis terminology—demon, unclean spirit, evil spirit—but it is not clear whether they are attempting to diagnose or just reporting the consensus (cultural) diagnosis. John the gospel writer does not use any such terminology; he reports no case of casting out spirits or demons. John the author of Revelation sees "demons" as he sees "idols"—the works of human hands. And, Paul says that demons are like idols and false gods—they don't exist.

212   *Angels and Demons: The Personification of Communication (Logology)*

Chapter 34

Revelation and Aggadah Concerning the Origin of Demons

Bernard Bamberger[129] summarizes the story of how demons originated as that story is presented in the Ethiopic book of Enoch, a second century B.C. work:

> One passage states that the giants [who were the offspring of the fallen angels and the daughters of men] became evil spirits; another, that the fallen angels became evil spirits, leading men astray to sacrifice to demons, while the women they married became sirens. But the usual view is that when the giants were slaughtered, in accordance with the punishment decreed for them, the evil spirits emerged from their bodies. In any event, the demons, once they made their appearance, remain at large until the final judgment.

John, the author of Revelation uses this "usual view" of the origin of demons as a literary allusion, to describe the connection between the Roman Emperor Nero (the last of the Caesarean family

---

[129] Bamberger, *Fallen Angels*, 22-3.

and the three primary Roman emperors who followed him (from the Flavian Dynasty): Vespasian, Titus, and Domitian. Revelation 16:12-13 states:

> And the sixth angel poured out his bowl onto the great river Euphrates. And its water was dried up so that the way of the kings from the land of the rising sun might be prepared. And I saw out of the mouth of the dragon, and out of the mouth of the beast, and out of the mouth of the false prophet, three unclean spirits coming out as frogs. And they are spirits of demons doing signs, which go forth to the kings of the land—even of the whole inhabitable world to gather them together to the war of the great day of God Almighty.

For a thorough analysis of the identities of the dragon, the beast, and the false prophet, I refer the reader to my book, *Revelation: The Human Drama*. Nevertheless, in the interest of brevity, I will summarize:

- All scholars agree that the Dragon is Satan.
- The vast majority of scholars agree that the Beast is Nero.
- Ford and others agree that the false prophet is the Jewish High Priestly Family in Jerusalem.

In my book (pages 41-2, and others), I discuss why the Roman Emperor Vespasian and his two sons who followed him as emperors (Titus and Domitian) are the clear referents to John's literary allusion concerning the origin of demons. With G. B. Caird, I agree that Vespasian, Nero's general whom he sent to wage war on Jerusalem in 66 A.D. is the easiest and clearest understanding of the Beast (Nero) who received a death blow and then came back to life. Nero committed suicide in 68 A.D., but in 69 A.D. his Jerusalem general Vespasian became Emperor. Vespasian then promptly sent his son Titus as general to Jerusalem to finish the devastating war on the Jews. Titus became Emperor after Vespasian, and then his brother Domitian became Emperor after Titus. It was as if the Beast died, but these three "demons" came out of his mouth (and the mouth of Satan and the mouth of the anti-Christian Jewish High Priest). John is able to tie a very negative connotation to Satan, Nero, the Jewish High Priesthood, Vespasian, Titus, and Domitian by the very force of a demonic literary allusion.

While the story of the origin of demons in the Ethiopic book of Enoch is certainly Aggadah (Jewish folklore), John is not using the Aggadah as Homiletic Aggadah, as did 1 Peter, 2 Peter, and Jude (See Chapter 10). John is not preaching a sermon as Peter and Jude were doing. Neither does the fact that John is alluding to this Aggadah suggest that John believed the Aggadah to be a true account of the origin of demons. As I pointed out in my previous chapter, Revelation 9:20 appears to agree with Paul—that demons (like idols) are nothing. John writes of unrepentant men who worshiped the "works of their hands"—"demons and golden idols, and silver, and bronze, and wooden, which are not able to see, nor hear, nor walk." If demons are the works of men's hands--neither able to see, hear, nor walk—demons do not exist as super-human forces that can take over the bodies of humans.

John is also illustrating the fact that one need not believe in the historical truth of the stories from the various books of Enoch in order to use them for literary purposes. Likewise, Peter and Jude could use Fallen Angel stories from the various books of Enoch as sermon illustrations without believing them to be true historical accounts.

With this chapter, I conclude my book on angels and demons. Perhaps, owing to my own scholarship in the field of Communication, I have a perspective on the nature of angels and demons that not many other scholars have. I can see that it is sometimes necessary to "personalize" our communication. We give "names" to our books, speeches, and literary documents and endow them with powers that make them seem to stand alone as separate from those who wrote the documents or spoke the words. Hence, the U.S. Constitution and Declaration of Independence exercise authority over us as if they were actual people—even super-human people. The false teachings that are broadcast over our airwaves may have even demon-like power to possess the minds and behaviors of those who listen to and believe these falsehoods. Let listeners and readers beware! Angels and demons (in the form of godly/true and demonic/false communications) are floating in the air all around us. We must be careful about those communications that possess us!

Bibliography

WORKS BY KENNETH BURKE

Burke, Kenneth. *Attitudes toward History*. 3rd ed. Berkeley: University of California P, 1984. (Abbreviated: **ATH**)

---. *Attitudes toward History*. 2 vols. New York: New Republic, 1937.

---. *The Complete White Oxen*. Berkeley: University of California P, 1968. (Abbreviated: **CWO**)

---. *Counter-Statement*. Berkeley: University of California P, 1968. (Abbreviated: **CS**)

---. "Dramatism." In *Communication: Concepts and Perspectives*, edited by L. Thayer, 327-360. Washington, DC: Spartan, 1967. (Abbreviated: **D**)

---. *Dramatism and Development*. Barre, MA: Clark University P with Barre Publishers, 1972. (Abbreviated: **DD**)

---. "The Five Master Terms: Their Place in a 'Dramatistic' Grammar of Motives." *View* 3, no. 2 (1943), 50-52. (Abbreviated: **MT**)

---. "Freedom and Authority in the Realm of the Poetic Imagination." In *Freedom and Authority in Our Time,* edited by Lyman Bryson, Louis Finkelstein, R. M. MacIver, and Richard McKeon, 365-375. New York and London: Harper & Brothers, 1953. (Abbreviated: **F&A**)

---. *A Grammar of Motives*. Berkeley: University of California P, 1969. (Abbreviated: **GM**)

---. *Language as Symbolic Action: Essays on Life, Literature, and Method*. Berkeley: University of California P, 1966. (Abbreviated: **LSA**)

---. "On Catharsis or Resolution, with a Postscript." *Kenyon Review* 21 (1959): 337-375. (Abbreviated: **OC**)

---. "On Human Behavior Considered 'Dramatistically.'" In *Permanence and Change: An Anatomy of Purpose*. 2nd ed. Indianapolis: Bobbs-Merrill, 1975. 274-294. (Abbreviated: **OHB**)

---. *On Human Nature: A Gathering While Everything Flows 1967-1984,* edited by William H. Rueckert and Angelo Bonadonna. Berkeley: University of California P, 2003. (Abbreviated: **OHN**)

---. "On Stress, Its Seeking." In *Why Man Takes Chances: Studies in Stress-Seeking*, edited by Samuel Z. Klausner. Garden City, NY: Doubleday, 1968. 75-103. (Abbreviated: **SS**)

---. *On Symbols and Society*, edited by Joseph R. Gusfield. Chicago and London: University of Chicago P, 1989. (Abbreviated: **OSS**)

---. "Othello—An Essay to Illustrate a Method." In *Perspectives by Incongruity*, edited by Stanley Edgar Hyman. Bloomington: Indiana University P, 1964. 152-195. (Abbreviated: **O**)

---. *Permanence and Change: An Anatomy of Purpose*. 2nd ed. Indianapolis: Bobbs-Merrill., 1975. (Abbreviated: **PC**)

---. *The Philosophy of Literary Form: Studies in Symbolic Action*. 3rd ed. Berkeley: University of California P, 1973. (Abbreviated: **PLF**)

---. "Poetics and Communication." In *Perspectives in Education, Religion, and the Arts*, edited by Howard E Kiefer and Milton K. Munitz. Albany: State University of New York P, 1970. 401-418. (Abbreviated: **P&C**)

---. "Questions and Answers about the Pentad." *College Composition and Communication* 29 (1978): 330-335. (Abbreviated: **Q&A**)

---. *A Rhetoric of Motives*. Berkeley: University of California P, 1969. (Abbreviated: **RM**)

---. *The Rhetoric of Religion: Studies in Logology*. Berkeley: University of California P, 1970. (Abbreviated: **RR**)

---. "Rhetoric—Old and New." In *New Rhetorics*, edited by Martin Steinmann, Jr. New York: Scribner's Sons, 1967. 59-76. (Abbreviated: **RON**)

---. "Rhetoric, Poetics, and Philosophy." In *Rhetoric, Philosophy, and Literature,* edited by Don M. Burks. West Lafayette, IN: Purdue University P, 1978. 15-33. (Abbreviated: **RPL**)

---. "The Rhetorical Situation." In *Communication: Ethical and Moral Issues*, edited by Lee Thayer. London, New York, Paris: Gordon and Breach Science, 1973. 263-275. (Abbreviated: **RS**)

---. and Malcolm Cowley. *The Selected Correspondence of Kenneth Burke and Malcolm Cowley 1915-1981*, edited by Paul Jay. Berkeley: University of California P, 1990. (Abbreviated: **B&C**)

---. "Tactics of Motivation." *Chimera* I (1943): 27-44. (Abbreviated: **TM**)

---. "Theology and Logology." *Kenyon Review*, New Series I.1 (1979). 151-185. (Abbreviated: **T&L**)

---. *Towards a Better Life*. Berkeley: University of California P, 1982. (Abbreviated: **TBL**)

WORKS BY STAN A. LINDSAY

<u>Beginning with reference to the terms "logological" and "logology" as researched in *The Expanded Kenneth Burke Concordance* by Lindsay cited below, and referencing the abbreviations of Burke's works, cited above (plus one work by Lindsay, below). Since the term "Logology" is added to the title of this work, these references represent the entirety of Burke's use of the term he coined.</u>

Logological: P&C 409; RPL 33 (Ideal logological synonym); T&L throughout;

Logology: ATH back matter; B&C 335-337, 348-350, 390, 393, 398, 404; CG 6, 32-33; CS 220, back cover; CWO 307 (= reflexive, words about words); DD <u>throughout</u>; KB&R xiii, xix, 9, 11, 13, 17, 47, 117, 133, 173, 175, 183, 222, 225, 236, 243, 254, 259, 267-268, 277, 280, 285, 290-291, 294, 300; Lindsay, *Implicit* 1, 8, 17-20, 27-31, 41, 45, 50-51, 59, 61, 68, 70-72, 76, 87-88, 101, 107, 110, 185, 188; LSA 47 (= terministic), 50, 408, 489; OHN <u>throughout</u>; OSS 4, 23, 28, 47, 117, 118, 121, 282, back matter; PC front matter, back matter; RPL 23, 25; RR 1, 5, 8, and <u>throughout</u>; T&L <u>throughout</u>;

Lindsay, Stan A. *Anamartetous Fallen Angels.* Master's thesis. Bloomington: Indiana University, 1977.

---. *ArguMentor.* Orlando: Say Press, 2015.

---. *Basic Public Relations Documents: Implicit Rhetoric in Action.* Orlando: Say Press, 2010.

---. "Burke, Perelman, and the Transmission of Values: The Beatitudes as Epideictic Topoi." *KB Journal* 11, no. 1 (2015).

---. *A Concise Kenneth Burke Concordance.* Orlando: Say Press, 2004.

---. *Disneology: Religious Rhetoric at Walt Disney World.* Orlando: Say Press, 2010.

---. *The Expanded Kenneth Burke Concordance.* Orlando: Say Press, 2014.

---. *Hidden Mickeyisms: The Implicit Rhetoric of Disney Films.* Orlando: Say Press, 2020.

---. *Implicit Rhetoric: Kenneth Burke's Extension of Aristotle's Concept of Entelechy.* Lanham, MD: University P of America, 1998.

---. *The Logic of Christianity: A Syllogistic Chain.* (Orlando: Say Press, 2018.

---. *Making Offers They Can't Refuse: The Twenty-One Sales in a Sale.* 3rd ed. Orlando: Say Press, 2015.

---. *Persuasion, Proposals, And Public Speaking.* 2nd ed. Orlando: Say Press, 2009.

---. "Prayer as Proto-Rhetoric." *The Journal of Communication and Religion* 20, no. 2 (1997), 31-40.

---. *Psychotic Entelechy: The Dangers of "Spiritual Gift" Theology.* Lanham, MD: University P of America, 2005.

---. *Revelation: The Human Drama.* Bethlehem, PA: Lehigh University P, 2001.

---. *The Rhetoric of Disney Music.* Orlando, FL: Say Press, 2010

---. *The Seven Cs of Stress: A Burkean Approach.* Orlando: Say Press, 2004.

---. *The Twenty-One Sales in a Sale.* PSI Research/Oasis Books, 1998.

---. Waco and Andover: An Application of Kenneth Burke's Concept of Psychotic Entelechy" *Quarterly Journal of Speech* 85, no. 3 (1999), 268-284.

OTHER WORKS ABOUT KENNETH BURKE

Burks, Don M. "Dramatic Irony, Collaboration, and Kenneth Burke's Theory of Form." *Pre/Text* 6 (1985), 255-273.

---, Editor. *Rhetoric, Philosophy, and Literature.* West Lafayette, IN: Purdue University P, 1978.

Cowley, Malcolm. "Prolegomena to Kenneth Burke." In *Critical Responses to Kenneth Burke,* edited by William H. Rueckert, 247-251. Minneapolis: University of Minnesota P, 1969.

Donoghue, Denis. "American Sage." *The New York Review* 26 (September, 1985), 39-42.

Foss, S. K., Foss, K. A., & Trapp, R. *Contemporary Perspectives on Rhetoric* (30th anniv. ed.). Long Grove, IL: Waveland, 2014.

Griffin, Leland M. "A Dramatistic Theory of the Rhetoric of Movements." In *Critical Responses to Kenneth Burke,* edited by William H. Rueckert, 456-478. Minneapolis: University of Minnesota P, 1969.

Hart, Roderick P. *Modern Rhetorical Criticism.* Glenview, IL and London: Scott, Foresman/Little, Brown, 1990.

Howell, Wilbur Samuel. *Poetics, Rhetoric, and Logic.* Ithaca and London: Cornell U P, 1975.

Jennerman, Donald L. "Kenneth Burke's Poetics of Catharsis." In *Representing Kenneth Burke*, edited by Hayden White and Margaret Brose, 31-51. Baltimore and London: John Hopkins U P, 1982.

---. "The Literary Criticism and Theory of Kenneth Burke in Light of Aristotle, Freud, and Marx." Ph.D. diss. Indiana University, 1974.

Nichols, Marie Hochmuth. "Burkeian Criticism." In *Essays on Rhetorical Criticism*. Edited by Thomas R. Nilsen. New York: Random House, 1968.

---. "Kenneth Burke and the 'New Rhetoric.'" *In Contemporary Theories of Rhetoric: Selected Readings*, edited by Richard L. Johannesen. New York, Evanston, San Francisco, London: Harper and Row, 1971.

William H. Rueckert. *Critical Responses to Kenneth Burke.* Minneapolis: University of Minnesota P, 1969.

---. *Encounters with Kenneth Burke.* Urbana and Chicago: University of Illinois P, 1994

---. *Kenneth Burke and the Drama of Human Relations.* 2nd ed. Berkeley: University of California P, 1963.

---. "The Rhetoric of Rebirth: A Study of the Literary Theory and Critical Practice of Kenneth Burke." Ph.D. diss., University of Michigan, 1956.

Schiappa, Edward. "Burkean Tropes and Kuhnian Science: A Social Constructionist Perspective on Language and Reality." *Journal of Advanced Communication* 13 (1993), 401-422.

White, Hayden, and Margaret Brose *Representing Kenneth Burke.* Baltimore and London: John Hopkins University P, 1982.

Winterowd, W. Ross. "Kenneth Burke: An Annotated Glossary of His Terministic Screen and a 'Statistical' Survey of His Major Concepts." Rhetoric Society Quarterly 15 (1985): 145-177.

WORKS BY AND ABOUT ARISTOTLE

Aristotle. *De Anima,* translated by J. A. Smith. Oxford: At the Clarendon Press, 1931. Reprinted in *The Works of Aristotle Translated into English,* edited by W. D. Ross. Oxford: At the Clarendon Press, 1968

---. *On Sophistical Refutations, On Coming-to-be and Passing Away*, translated by E. S. Forster. Cambridge: Harvard University Press, 1955.

---. *Physica*, translated by R. P. Hardie and R. K. Gaye. In *The Basic Works of Aristotle,* edited by Richard McKeon. New York: Random House, 1941.

---. *Poetics,* translated by T. S. Dorsch. In *Classical Literary Criticism.* London: Penguin Books, 1965.

---. *The Rhetoric and the Poetics of Aristotle,* translated by Friedrich Solmsen. New York: Random House, 1954.

Kennedy, George A. *Aristotle on Rhetoric: A Theory of Civic Discourse*, translated with notes and commentary by G. A. Kennedy. New York & Oxford: Oxford University Press, 1991.

---. *The Art of Persuasion in Greece.* Princeton: Princeton University Press, 1963.

---. *New Testament Interpretation through Rhetorical Criticism.* Chapel Hill: University of North Carolina Press, 1984.

McKeon, Richard. *The Basic Works of Aristotle*. New York: Random House, 1941.

___. *Introduction to Aristotle*. 2nd ed. Chicago and London: University of Chicago Press, 1973.

Randall, John Herman, Jr. *Aristotle*. New York: Columbia University Press, 1960.

Ross, W. D. *Aristotle: A Complete Exposition of His Works and Thought*. New York: Meridian Books, 1960.

___. *Aristotle De Anima*. Oxford: At the Clarendon Press, 1961.

___. *Aristotle's Metaphysics*. 2 vols. Oxford: At the Clarendon Press, 1966.

___. *Aristotle's Physics*. Oxford: At the Clarendon Press, 1966.

___. *Metaphysica*. Vol. 8 of *The Works of Aristotle Translated into English*. Oxford: At the Clarendon Press, 1966

Williams, C. J. F. *Aristotle's De Generatione et Corruptione*. Oxford: At the Clarendon Press, 1982.

VARIOUS WORKS

Alinsky, Saul D. *Rules for Radicals: A Pragmatic Primer for Realistic Radicals*. New York: Random House, 1971.

Allen, James. *The First Year of Greek*. Revised ed. Toronto: MacMillan, 1931.

Beardslee, William A. *Literary Criticism of the New Testament*. Philadelphia: Fortress Press, 1970.

Best, S., and D. Kellner. *Postmodern Theory: Critical Interrogations*. New York: Guilford Press, 1991.

Cassirer, Ernst. *Language and Myth*. Translated by Susanne K. Langer. New York: Dover Publications, Inc., 1946.

Choi, C. "Why Neanderthals Likely Fathered Few Kids with Modern Humans." *Live Science.* Retrieved fro m: http://www.livescience.com/54359-neanderthal-y-chromosome-caused-miscarriages.html.

Dana, H. E., and Julius R. Mantey. *A Manual Grammar of the Greek New Testament.* Toronto: MacMillan Company, 1957.

Fisher, Walter R. "Narration as a Human Communication Paradigm: The Case of Public Moral Argument." *Communication Monographs* 51 (1984).

Harrell, David Edwin. *Oral Roberts: An American Life.* Bloomington, IN: Indiana University Press, 1985.

Higgins, Alexander G. "48 in Swiss Religious Sect Die." *Journal and Courier,* 6 October, 1994, sec. A.

Homer. *The Iliad of Homer.* Translated by R. Lattimore. Chicago: University of Chicago Press, 1961.

Junior Classic Latin Dictionary. Chicago: Follett Publishing Co., 1960.

Kirby, John T. "Classics 593R: Classical Concepts of Rhetoric and Poetics." Lecture delivered in a graduate seminar at Purdue University, West Lafayette, IN, 3 February 1994.

---. "'The Great Triangle'" in Early Greek Rhetoric and Poetics." *Rhetorica: A Journal of the History of Rhetoric* 8 (1990): 213-28.

---. "Rhetorical Theory in Bronze Age Greece?" Lecture delivered at Purdue University Colloquium for Center for Humanities Studies, West Lafayette, IN, 18 April 1994.

Krentz, Edgar. *The Historical-Critical Method.* Philadelphia: Fortress Press, 1975.

Liddell, Henry George, and Robert Scott, comps. *A Greek-English Lexicon.* Revised by Henry Stuart Jones. Oxford: At the Clarendon Press, 1968.

---. *A Lexicon Abridged from Liddell and Scott's Greek-English Lexicon.* Revised by Henry Stuart Jones. Oxford: At the Clarendon Press, 1966.

"Man of The Year: The Mystic Who Lit The Fires of Hatred," *Time*, January 7, 1980.

Ogden, C. K., and I. A. Richards. *The Meaning of Meaning: A Study of the Influence of Language upon Thought and of the Science of Symbolism.* New York: Harcourt Brace Jovanich, 1923.

Ong, Walter J. *The Presence of the Word.* New Haven and London: Yale University Press, 1967.

Perelman, Chaim. *The New Rhetoric and the Humanities*. Translated by William Kluback. Holland: D. Reidel Publishing Co., 1979.

---. and L. Olbrechts-Tyteca. *The New Rhetoric: A Treatise on Argumentation*. Translated by J. Wilkinson and P. Weaver. Notre Dame: University of Notre Dame Press, 1969.

---. *The Realm of Rhetoric.* Notre Dame: University of Notre Dame Press, 1990.

Perrin, Norman. *What is Redaction Criticism?* Philadelphia: Fortress Press, 1969.

Plato. *Gorgias*. Translated by W. Hamilton. London: Penguin, 1971.

---. *Phaedrus and the Seventh and Eighth Letters*. Translated by W. Hamilton. London: Penguin, 1973.

---. *The Republic*. Translated by B. Jowett. New York: Airmont, 1968.

Plutarch. "Life of Alexander." In *Life Stories of Men Who Shaped History from Plutarch's Lives* 163-222. Edited by E. C. Lindeman. Translated by W. Langhorne. New York: New American Library, 1950.

Robbins, Vernon K. "Structuralism in Biblical Interpretation and Theology." *The Thomist* 42 (1978): 349-71.

---. and John H. Patton. "Rhetoric and Biblical Criticism." *Quarterly Journal of Speech* 66 (1980): 327-37.

Sheler, Jeffrey L. "The Theology of Abortion." *U. S. News and World Report*, 9 March 1992, 54.

Strunk, *The Elements of Style: With Revisions, an Introduction, and a Chapter on Writing by E. B. White*, 4th ed. Boston, London, et. al.: Allyn and Bacon, 2000.

Swanson, David L. and Jesse G. Delia. "The Nature of Human Communication." In *Modcom/Modules in Speech Communication*. Chicago: Science Research Associates, Inc., 1976.

Tannehill, Robert C. The Sword of His Mouth. Philadelphia: Fortress Press, and Missoula, MT: Scholars Press, 1975.

White, Hayden. *The Content of the Form: Narrative Discourse and Historical Representation*. Baltimore and London: Johns Hopkins University Press, 1987.

226   *Angels and Demons: The Personification of Communication (Logology)*

---. "The Historical Text as Literary Artifact." In *Tropics of Discourse: Essays in Cultural Criticism*. Edited by Hayden White. Baltimore: Johns Hopkins University Press, 1987.

WORKS ON ANGELS, BIBLICAL STUDIES,

PATRISTIC STUDIES, MOHAMMEDAN STUDIES, QUMRAN,

AND RABBINIC STUDIES

For abbreviations of biblical, intertestamental, patristic, and Rabbinic sources, etc., see below (in bold):

Akiba. *Sefer Otiot de Rabbi Akiba*. ВАРШАВА, 1871.

Albeck, Chanoch, ed. *Midrash Bereshit Rabbati*. Jerusalem: Mekize Nirdamim, 1940. (Abbreviated: **BR**)

Ali, Abdullah Yusuf. *The Holy Qur-an, Text, Translation & Commentary*. 3 vols. Lahore: Shaikh Muhammad Ashraf.

"Angels and Angelology." *Encyclopaedia Judaica*. Jerusalem: The MacMillan Company, 1971.

Die Apokalypse Abrahams: Das Testament der Vierzig Märtyrer. Edited by Gottlieb Nathanael

Apocalypse of Baruch. Edited and Translated by R. H. Charles. London: Society for Promoting Christian Knowledge, 1917.

Apocalypses Apocryphae: Mosis, Esdrae, Pauli, Iohannis, item Mariae dormition, additis Evangeliorum et Apocryphorum supplementis. Edited by Konstantine von Tischendorf. Hildesheim: Georg Olms Verlagsbuchhandlung, 1966.

Apocalypsis Henochi Graece. Edited by M. Black. Vol. 3 from *Pseudepigrapha Veteris Testamenti Graece*. Edited by A. M. Denis and M. de Jonge. Leiden: E. J. Brill, 1970.

Arndt, William F., and F. Wilbur Gingrich, trans. *A Greek-English Lexicon of the New Testament and Other Early Christian Literature*. Edited by Walter Bauer. Chicago: University of Chicago Press, 1957.

The Ascension of Isaiah. Edited by R. H. Charles. London: Adam and Charles Black, 1900.

The Assumption of Moses. Edited by R. H. Charles. London: Adam and Charles Black, 1897.

Aune, David E. *Revelation 1-5*. Vol. 52 of *Word Biblical Commentary*. Edited by Bruce Metzger. Dallas: Word Books, 1997.

---. *Revelation 6-16*. Vol. 52B of *Word Biblical Commentary*. Edited by Bruce Metzger. Dallas: Word Books, 1998.

---. *Revelation 17-22*. Vol. 52C of *Word Biblical Commentary*. Edited by Bruce Metzger. Dallas: Word Books, 1998.

The Babylonian Talmud. Edited by I. Epstein. London: The Soncino Press, 1935-48.

Der Babylonische Talmud. Edited by Lazarus Goldschmidt. Haag: Martinus Nijhoff, 1906-35.

Bamberger, Bernard J. *Fallen Angels*. Philadelphia: The Jewish Publication Society of America, 5712-1952.

Barnestone, Willis. http://en.wikiquote.org/wiki/Sappho

Baron, Salo Wittmayer. *A Social and Religious History of the Jews*. Vol. II: *Christian Era: The First Five Centuries*. 2nd ed. Philadelphia: The Jewish Publication Society of America, 1952.

Barr, David. *Tales of the End: A Narrative Commentary on the Book of Revelation*. Santa Rosa, CA: Polebridge Press, 1998.

Beale, G. K. *The Book of Revelation: A Commentary on the Greek Text*. Vol. of *The New International Greek New Testament Commentary*. Edited by I. Howard Marshall and Donald A. Hagner. Grand Rapids, MI: Wm. B. Eerdmans Publishing Co., 1999.

--. *John's Use of the Old Testament in Revelation*. Sheffield: Sheffield Academic Press, 1998.

Bereschit Rabbah. 3 vols. Edited by J. Theodor and Chanoch Albeck. Jerusalem: Wahrmann, 1965 (Reprint). (Abbreviated: **BR**)

The Bible in Aramaic. Leiden: Brill, 1959.

Biblia Hebraica Stuttgartensia. Edited by Karl Elliger and Willhelm Rudollph. Peabody, MA: Deutsche Bibel Gesellschaft/Hendrickson Publishers, 2006.

Bietenhard, Hanz. *Die himmlische Welt im Urchristentum und Spätjudentum.* Vol. II of *Wissenschaftliche Untersuchungen zum Neuen Testament.* Edited by J. Jeremias and O. Michel. Tübingen: J. C. B. Mohr, 1966.

Billerbeck, Paul. *Die Briefe des Neuen Testaments und die Offenbarung Johannis*, Vol. 3 of *Kommentar zum Neuen Testament aus Talmud und Midrasch.* Edited by Hermann Strack and Paul Billerbeck. Munich: C. H. Beck'sche Verlagsbuchhandlung, 1961.

Black, Matthew. *The Scrolls and Christian Origins.* New York: Charles Scribner's Sons, 1961.

Bloom, Harold. *Fallen Angels.* New Haven and London: Yale University Press, 2007.

---. *The Western Canon: The Books and School of the Ages.* New York: Harcourt Brace, 1995.

Bonwetsch, Gottlieb Nathanael, ed. *Die Apokalypse Abrahams (Das Testament der Vierzig Märtyrer).* Leipzig: Scientia Verlag Aalen, 1897.

The Book of Jubilees. Translated by R. H. Charles. New York: The MacMillan Company & London: Society for Promoting Christian Knowledge, 1917.

The Book of Yashar. Translated by Mordecai Manuel Noah. New York: Hermon Press, 1972.

Boring, M. Eugene. *Revelation.* Vol. of *Interpretation: A Bible Commentary for Teaching and Preaching..* Edited by James Luther Mays. Louisville, John Knox Press, 1989.

Botterweck, G. Johannes., and Helmer Ringgren, eds. *Theological Dictionary of the Old Testament.* Grand Rapids, MI: William B. Eerdmans, 1975.

Bousset, Wilhelm. *Die Religion des Judentums im späthellenistischen Zeitalter.* Edited by Hugo Gressmann. Vol. XXI of *Handbuch zum Neuen Testament.* Edited by Günther Bornkamm. Tübingen: J. C. B. Mohr, 1966.

Brandon, S. G. F. *The Fall of Jerusalem and the Christian Church.* London: S.P.C.K., 1957.

---. *Religion in Ancient History.* London: George Allen & Unwin Ltd., 1973.

Braun, Herbert. *Qumran und das Neue Testament.* 2 vols. Tübingen: J. C. B. Mohr, 1966.

---. *Spätjüdisch-haretischer und Frühchristlischer Radikalismus.* Tübingen: J. C. B. Mohr, 1957.

Brown, Raymond E. *The Gospel According to John (i-xii).* Garden City, NY: Doubleday & Company, Inc., 1966.

Bruce, F. F. "The Revelation to John." In *A New Testament Commentary.* Edited by G. C. D. Howley. Grand Rapids, MI: Zondervan Publishing House, 1975.

---. *Second Thoughts on the Dead Sea Scrolls*. Grand Rapids, MI: Wm. B. Eerdmans Publishing Co., 1961.

Bryant, Beauford H. & Krause, Mark S. *The College Press NIV Commentary: John*. Joplin, MO: The College Press Publishing Company, 1998.

Buber, Solomon, ed. *Agadat Bereshit*. Reprint of Cracow ed., 1902. New York: Menorah, 1958-59.

---, ed. *Midrash Tanhuma*. (Vilna: Romm, 1913). New York, 1946.

---, ed. *Midrash Tehillim (Schocher Tob)*. Vilna: Romm, 1891.

---, ed. *Pesikta de-Rab Kahana*. Reduced photo offset of Lyck, 1868 edition, 1962. (Abbreviated: **PRK**)

Burrows, Millar. *The Dead Sea Scrolls*. New York: The Viking Press, 1955.

---. *More Light on The Dead Sea Scrolls: New Scrolls and New Interpretations*. The Viking Press, 1969.

Caird, G. B. *The Revelation of St John the Divine*, 2nd ed. London: A & C Black, 1966.

Charles, R. H., ed. and trans. *The Apocalypse of Baruch*. London: Society for Promoting Christian Knowledge, 1917.

---, ed. *The Apocrypha and Pseudepigrapha of the Old Testament*. 2 vols. Oxford: At the Clarendon Press, 1913.

---, ed. *The Ascension of Isaiah*. London: Adam and Charles Black, 1900.

---, ed. *The Assumption of Moses*. London: Adam and Charles Black, 1897.

---. *The British Academy Lectures on the Apocalypse*. London: Humphrey Milford, Oxford University Press, 1923.

---. *The Revelation of St. John*. 2 vols. of *The International Critical Commentary*. Edinburgh: T & T Clark, 1975.

---. *The Revelation of St. John*. Vol. 44 of *The International Critical Commentary*. New York: Charles Scribner's Sons, 1920.

Collins, Adela Yarbro. *Cosmology and Eschatology in Jewish and Christian Apocalyptism.* Leiden: E. J. Brill, 1996.

---. *Crisis and catharsis: The power of the Apocalypse.* Philadelphia: Westminster Press, 1984.

---. "The History of Religions Approach to Apocalyptism and the 'Angel of the Waters' (Rev 16:4-7)." *The Catholic Biblical Quarterly* 39 (1977), 367-81.

---. "The Political Perspective of the Revelation to John." *Journal of Biblical Literature* 96 (1977), 241-56.

Collins, John J. "Pseudonymity, Historical Reviews and the Genre of the Revelation of John." *The Catholic Biblical Quarterly* 39 (1977), 329-43.

Cross, Frank Moore, Jr. *Ancient Library of Qumran.* Garden City, NY: Anchor Books, 1961.

Rost, Leonhard, ed. *Die Damaskusschrift[en].* Vol 167 of *Kleine Texte für Vorlesungen und Übungen.* Edited by Kurt Aland. Berlin: Walter De Gruyter, 1933.

Daniélou, Jean. *The Dead Sea Scrolls and Primitive Christianity.* Translated by Salvator Attanasio. Baltimore: Helicon Press, Inc., 1958.

Davenport, Gene L. *The Eschatology of the Book of Jubilees.* Leiden: E. J. Brill, 1971.

Davidson, Gustav. *A Dictionary of Angels: Including the Fallen Angels.* New York: The Free Press, 1967.

"Dead Sea Scrolls Research." *A Symposium.* Jerusalem, April 21, 1965.

Di Sante, Carmine. *Jewish Prayer: The Origins of the Christian Liturgy.* Translated by Matthew J. O'Connell. New York and Mahwah, NJ: Pauline Press, 1991.

Driver, G. R. *The Judean Scrolls.* Oxford: Basil Blackwell, 1965.

Dupont-Sommer, A. *The Essene Writings from Qumran.* Translated by G. Vermes. Oxford: Basil Blackwell, 1961.

---. *The Jewish Sect of Qumran and the Essenes.* Translated by R. D. Barnett. New York: The MacMillan Company, 1956.

Eisenman, Robert H., and Michael Wise. *The Dead Sea Scrolls Uncovered.* New York: Barnes & Noble Books, 1994.

Elliott, John H. "The Rehabilitation of an Exegetical Step-Child: I Peter in Recent Research." *Journal of Biblical Literature.* Vol 95, No. 2 (June, 1976), 243-54.

Encyclopaedia Britannica online. https://www.britannica.com.

Encyclopaedia Judaica. 16 vols. Jerusalem: The MacMillan Company, 1971.

Fiorenza, Elizabeth Schüssler. "Apocalyptic and Gnosis in the Book of Revelation." *Journal of Biblical Literature.* 92 (1973), 565-81.

---. *The Book of Revelation: Justice and Judgment.* Philadelphia: Fortress Press, 1985.

---. "Composition and Structure of the Revelation of John." *The Catholic Biblical Quarterly* 39 (1977), 344-66.

---. "The Ethics of Interpretation: De-Centering Biblical Scholarship." *Journal of Biblical Literature.* 107 (1988), 3-17.

Finkelstein, Louis, ed. *The Jews: Their History.* 4th ed. New York: Schocken Books, 1970.

Fischel, Henry A. *Rabbinic Literature and Greco-Roman Philosophy.* Vol. 21 from *Studia Post-Biblica.* Edited by J. C. H. Lebram. Leiden: E. J. Brill, 1973.

Fishman, Isadore. *Gateway to the Mishnah.* Hartmore, CT: Prayer Book Press, Inc., 1970.

Fitzmyer, Joseph A. *The Genesis Apocryphon of Qumran Cave I (IQ20): A Commentary.* 3rd ed. Rome: Biblical Institute Press, 2004.

Foerster. "Δαιμων." In Vol. II of *Theological Dictionary of the New Testament.* Edited by Gerhard Kittel. Translated and Edited by G. W. Bromiley. Grand Rapids, MI: Wm. B. Eerdmans Publishing Company, 1964.

---. "Διαβολος." In Vol. II of *Theological Dictionary of the New Testament.* Edited by Gerhard Kittel. Translated and Edited by G. W. Bromiley. Grand Rapids, MI: Wm. B. Eerdmans Publishing Company, 1964.

Ford, J. Massingbyrde. *Revelation.* Vol. 38 of *The Anchor Bible.* Garden City, NY: Doubleday, 1975.

Fox, Samuel J. *Hell in Jewish Literature.* Northbrook, IL: Merimack College Press, Whitehall Company, 1972.

Fragments of a Zadokite Work. Edited by S. Schechter. Vol. 1 of *Documents of the Jewish Sectaries.* New York: KTAV Publishing House, Inc., 1970.

Freedman, H. and Maurice Simon, eds. *Midrash Rabbah*, Vol. 1: *Bereshith.* London: Soncino Press, 1939.

Friedman, M., ed. *Pesikta Rabbati*, Vol. 1: *Bereshith*. Wien: Josef Kaiser IX, 1880.

Frisk, Hjalmar. *Griechisches Etymologisches Woerterbuch*. 2 vols. Heidelberg: Carl Winter Universitatsverlag, 1960.

Gammie, John G. "Spatial and Ethical Dualism in Jewish Wisdom and Apocalyptic Literature." *Journal of Biblical Literature*. Vol 93, No. 3 (September, 1974), 365-85.

Gaster, M., tr. *The Chronicles of Jerahmeel*. New York: KTAV Publishing House, Inc., 1971.

The Genesis Apocryphon of Qumran Cave I. 2nd revised ed. Edited by Joseph A. Fitzmyer. Rome: Biblical Institute Press, 1971.

Gesenius, Wilhelm. *Hebräisches un Aramäisches Handwörterbuch über das Alte Testament*. 15th ed. Leipzig: F. C. W. Vogel, 1910.

Ghoniem, M. & M Saifullah. "The Sacrifice Of Abraham: Isaac or Ishmael?" In *Islamic awareness*. http://www.islamic-awareness.org/Quran/Contrad/MusTrad/sacrifice.html.

Ginzberg, Louis. *The Legends of the Jews*. 7 vols.; Philadelphia: The Jewish Publication Society of America, 5728-1968.

Grant, Robert M. Review of *Redating the New Testament* by John A. T. Robinson. *Journal of Biblical Literature* 97 (1978), 294-96.

The Greek Versions of the Testaments of the Twelve Patriarchs. Edited by Robert Henry Charles. Hildescheim: Georg Olms Verlagsbuchhandlung and Oxford University Press, 1960.

Greeven, Heinrich. "Εὔχομαι, Εὐχη. Πρόσευχομαι, Πρόσευχεν." In Vol. II of *Theological Dictionary of the New Testament*. Edited by Gerhard Kittel. Translated and Edited by G. W. Bromiley. Grand Rapids, MI: Wm. B. Eerdmans Publishing Company, 1964.

Grünbaum, Max. *Gesammelte Aufsätze zur Sprach- und Sagenkunde*. Edited by Felix Perles. Berlin: S. Calvary & Co., 1901.

Grundmann. "Αγγελος." In Vol. I of *Theological Dictionary of the New Testament*. Edited by Gerhard Kittel. Translated and Edited by G. W. Bromiley. Grand Rapids, MI: Wm. B. Eerdmans Publishing Company, 1964.

Haag, H. "בן(BEN) in the Semitic Languages." In *Theological Dictionary of the Old Testament*. Edited by G. Johannes Botterweck and Helmer Ringgren. Translated by John T. Willis. II, 147-59. Grand Rapids, MI: William B. Eerdmans, 1975.

"Haggadah." *New World Encyclopedia*. https://www.newworldencyclopedia.org/entry/Haggadah

Hanson, Paul D. "Rebellion in Heaven, Azazel, and Euhemeristic Heroes in I Enoch 6-11." *Journal of Biblical Literature* 96 (1977), 195-233.

Hengel, Martin. *Judentum und Hellenismus.* Vol X of *Wissenschaftliche Untersuchungen zum Neuen Testament.* Edited by J. Jeremias and O. Michel. Tübingen: J. C. B. Mohr, 1969.

Hennecke, Edgar. *New Testament Apocrypha.* Edited by Wilhelm Schneemelcher. Translated by R. McL. Wilson. Philadelphia: The Westminster Press, 1963.

Iustinus Philosophus et Martyr, 3rd ed. Edited by Otto. Vol. I of *Corpus Apologetarum Christianorum.* Ienae: Prostat in Libraria Hermanni Dufft., 1876.

Jastrow, Marcus. *Dictionary of the Targumim, the Talmud Babli and Yerushalmi, and the Midrashic Literature.* 2 vols. Brooklyn: Judaica Press, 2004.

Jellinek, A., ed. *Beth ha-Midrasch: Sammlung Kleiner Midraschim und vermischter Abhandlungen aus der alteren judischen Literatur.* Vol. V (6 vols.: Leipzig: C. W. Vollrath, 1853-77). Reprinted. Jerusalem: Wahrmann, 1967. (abbreviated: **BHM**)

Jervis, L. Ann. "'But I want You to Know…': Paul's Midrashic Intertextual Response to the Corinthian Worshipers (I Cor 11:2-16)." *Journal of Biblical Literature* 112 (1993), 231-46.

Johnson, Luke T. "The New Testament's Anti-Jewish Slander and the Conventions of Ancient Polemic." *Journal of Biblical Literature* 108 (1989), 395-418.

Josephus. *The Complete Works of Flavius Josephus: Legendary Jewish Historian and His Chronicle of Ancient History.* Translated by William Whiston. London & Ontario: Attic Books, 2008.

Jung, Leo. *Fallen Angels in Jewish, Christian, and Mohammedan Literature.* New York: KTAV Publishing House, Inc., 1974.

Justin. "Dialogue with Trypho." Dialogue 79, from *Iustinus Philosophus et Martyr*, 3rd ed. Edited by Otto. Vol. I, 284 of *Corpus Apologetarum Christianorum.* Ienae: Prostat in Libraria Hermanni Dufft., 1876.

Kahana. *Pesikta de-Rab Kahana.* Edited by Solomon Buber. Reduced photo offset of Lyck, 1868 edition, 1962. (Abbreviated: **PRK**)

Kahana, Avraham, ed. *Sefarim ha-Hizonim.* 2 vols. Tel Aviv, 1959.

Kautzsch, E., ed. *Die Apocryphen und Pseudepigraphen des Alten Testaments.* 2 vols. Tübingen: Verlag von J. C. B. Mohr (Paul Siebeck), 1900.

Kiddle, Martin. *The Revelation of St. John.* A volume of *The Moffat New Testament Commentary.* New York & London: Harper and Brothers, 1952.

Kittel, Gerhard, and Friedrich, Gerhard, eds. *Theological Dictionary of the New Testament.* 9 vols. Translated by Geoffrey W. Bromiley. Grand Rapids: Wm. G. Eerdmans, 1964-74.

Kittel, Rudolph, ed. *Biblia Hebraica 3.* Germany: Württembergische Bibelanstalt Stuttgart, 1966.

Klauser, Theodor, ed. *Reallexikon für Antike und Christentum.* Stuttgart: Anton Hiersemann, 1962.

Kohelet Rabbah. See *Midrash Rabbah.*

Koresh, David. "Letter from David Koresh to Richard DeGuerin [14 April 1993]." *Religious Studies News* 10, no. 3 (1995), 3.

The Last Chapters of Enoch in Greek. Edited by Campbell Bonner. London: Christophers, 1937.

Lardner, George, Jr. "U.S. Argues Idaho Can't Prosecute FBI Sniper: Case Stems from 1992 Ruby Ridge Siege." *Washington Post,* 14 March 1998, sec. A.

Levine, Lee I. *Caesarea under Roman Rule.* Vol. VII of *Studies in Judaism in Late Antiquity.* Edited by Jacob Neusner. Leiden: E. J. Brill, 1975.

Levy, Jacob. *Chaldäisches Wörterbuch über die Targumim und einen grossen Theil des Rabbinischen Schriftthums,* Book on Demand, 2014.

---. *Neuhebräisches und Chaldäisches Wörterbuch (über die Talmudim und Midraschim),* 4 vols. Leipzig: F. A. Brockhaus, 1867-89.

Liddell, Henry George, and Robert Scott, comps. *A Greek-English Lexicon.* Revised by Henry Stuart Jones. Oxford: At the Clarendon Press, 1968.

The Life of Enoch. Vol. IV, 129-32 of *Beth ha-Midrasch: Sammlung Kleiner Midraschim und vermischter Abhandlungen aus der älteren judischen Literatur.* Vol. V (6 vols.: Leipzig: C. W. Vollrath, 1853-77). Edited by A. Jellinek. Reprinted. Jerusalem: Wahrmann, 1967.

Lightfoot, J. B. *The Apostolic Fathers.* Edited by J. R. Harmer. Grand Rapids, MI: Baker Book House, 1976. (Reprint of 1891 MacMillan Edition).

The Literature of Formative Judaism: The Targumim & Other Jewish Writings in Late Antiquity (Origins of Judaism), 1st ed. Edited by Jacob Neusner. Routledge, 1991.

Lohse, Eduard, ed. *Die Texte aus Qumran.* München: Kosel-Verlag, 1964.

Lumpkin, Joseph. *The Books of Enoch: The Angels, The Watchers and The Nephilim: (With Extensive Commentary on the Three Books of Enoch, the Fallen Angels, the Calendar of Enoch, and Daniel's Prophecy).* 2nd ed. Fifth Estate, Incorporated, 2011.

Marmorstein, Art(h)ur, ed. "Angels and Angelology." Vol. I, 968. In *Encyclopaedia Judaica.* Jerusalem: The MacMillan Company, 1971.

McCown, Chester Charlton., ed. *The Testament of Solomon.* Leipzig: J. C. Hinrichs, 1922.

Mekilta de Rabbi Ishmael. 3 vols. Philadelphia: The Jewish Publication Society of America, 1933-35.

Michl, J. "Engel II (jüdisch)," Vol. V, 80. In *Reallexikon für Antike und Christentum.* Edited by Theodor Klauser, Stuttgart: Anton Hiersemann, 1962.

Midrash Devarim Rabbah. 2nd ed. Edited by S. Lieberman. Jerusalem: Wahrmann, 1964-65.

Midrash Ha-Gadol 'al Hamishah Humshe Torah: Sefer Bereshit. Edited by M. Margulyot (Margulies). Jerusalem: Rabbi Kook Foundation, 1946-47.

Midrash Ha-Gadol: Bereshit/Midrash Hag-Gadol Genesis. Edited by S. Schechter. Cambridge: at the University Press, 1902.

Midrash Kohelet Rabbah. See *Midrash Rabbah.*

Midrash Konen. Vol. II, 23-39 of *Beth ha-Midrasch: Sammlung Kleiner Midraschim und vermischter Abhandlungen aus der alteren judischen Literatur.* Vol. V (6 vols.: Leipzig: C. W. Vollrath, 1853-77). Edited by A. Jellinek. Reprinted. Jerusalem: Wahrmann, 1967.

Midrash Rabbah. 10 vols. Edited by H. Freedman and Maurice Simon. London: Soncino Press, 1939.

Midrash Rabbah, Vol. I: *Bereshith.* Edited by H. Freedman and Maurice Simon. London: Soncino Press, 1939.

Midrash Shir ha-Shirim Rabbah. See *Midrash Rabbah.*

Midrash Tanchuma. Mantua edition, 1563. Reprint, Jerusalem: Makor Publishing Ltd.

Midrash Tanḥuma. Edited by S. Buber. Vilna, 1913.

Midrash Tanḥuma. Edited by S. Buber. New York, 1946.

Midrash Tehillim. Edited by Aug. Wünsche. (German) Trier: Sigmund Mayer, 1892.

Midrash Tehillim (Schocher Tob). Edited by S. Buber. Vilna: Romm, 1891.

Midrash Wayyikra Rabbah, 2nd ed. 3-5 vols. Edited by Mordecai Margulies [Marguliot/Margulyot]. Jerusalem: Wahrmann, 1972. (Abbreviated: **WR**)

MIDRASH WAYYIKRA RABBAH A Critical Edition based on Manuscripts and Genizah Fragments with Variants and Notes Part Three, Chapters XXI-XXIX. Edited by Mordecai Margulies. Jerusalem: The Louis M. And Minnie Epstein Fund of The American Academy for Jewish Research, 1956.

Miller, Mark. "Secrets of the Cult." *Newsweek,* 14 April 1997, 28-37.

Moore, G. F. *Judaism: In the First Centuries of the Christian Era: The Age of the Tannaim.* Cambridge: Harvard University Press, 1932.

Moulton, W. F., and A. S. Geden, eds. *A Concordance to the Greek Testament (According to the Texts of Wescott and Hort, Tischendorf and the English Revisers).* 4th ed. Edinburgh: T. & T. Clark, 1967.

Mowry, Lucetta. *The Dead Sea Scrolls and the Early Church.* Notre Dame & London: University of Notre Dame Press, 1966.

Nestle, Eberhard and Kurt Aland, eds. *Novum Testamentum Graece.* London: United Bible Societies, 1967.

Nickelsburg, George W. E. "The Apocalyptic Message of I Enoch 92-105." *The Catholic Biblical Quarterly* 39 (1977), 309-28.

Noll, Mark. *Between Faith and Criticism: Evangelicals, Scholarship, and the Bible in America.* San Francisco: Harper & Row, Publishers, 1986.

Novum Testamentum Graece (NA28): Nestle-Aland 28th Edition (Ancient Greek Edition). Edited by Institute for NT Textual Research. Peabody, MA: Deutsche Bibel Gesellschaft/Hendrickson Publishers, 2012.

Oates, Whitney J., ed. *The Stoic and Epicurean Philosophers.* New York: Random House, 1940.

Odeberg, Hugo, ed. *3 Enoch (or) The Hebrew Book of Enoch.* A volume of *The Library of Biblical Studies.* Edited by Harry M. Orlinsky. New York: KTAV Publishing House, Inc., 1973.

Oepke, Albrecht. "παῖς, παιδίον, παιδάριον, τέκνον, τεκνίον, βρέφος." In *Theological Dictionary of the New Testament*. Edited by Gerhard Friedrich (and G. Kittel), Translated and editor G. W. Bromiley. V, 646-7. Grand Rapids, MI: Wm. B. Eerdmans, 1968.

O'Leary, Stephen D. "A Dramatistic Theory of Apocalyptic Rhetoric." *Quarterly Journal of Speech* 79 (1993), 385-426.

The Pentateuch According to Targum Onkelos. Edited by A. Sperber. Vol. I of *The Bible in Aramaic*. Leiden: Brill, 1959.

Pesikta de-Rab Kahana. Translated by William G. Braude and Israel J. Kapstein. Philadelphia: Jewish Publication Society of America, 1975.

Pesikta de-Rab Kahana. Edited by Solomon Buber. Reduced photo offset of Lyck, 1868 edition, 1962. (abbreviated: **PRK**)

Pesikta Rabbati. Edited by M. Friedmann. Wien: Josef Kaiser IX, 1880.

Philo Judaeus. *The Works of Philo Judaeus*. Translated by C. Yonge. London: George Bell & Sons, 1890.

Philonis Judaei. *Opera Omnia*. Pars II of *Patrum Ecclesiae Graecorum*. Lipsiae: Sumtibus E. B. Schwickerti, 1828.

Rahlfs, Alfred, ed. *Septuaginta (Id est Vetus Testamentum graece iuxta LXX interpretes)*. 8 ed. 2 vols. Stuttgart: Württembergische Bibelanstalt, 1935.

Roberts, Alexander, and Donaldson, James, Eds. *The Ante-Nicene Fathers*. (American Reprint of the Edinburgh Edition). Revised by A. Cleveland Coxe. Vols. I-III. Grand Rapids, MI: Wm. B. Eerdmans Publishing Co.

Schäfer, Peter. *Rivalität zwischen Engeln und Menschen*. Vol. VIII of *Studia Judaica*. Edited by E. L. Ehrlich, Basel. Berlin & New York: Walter De Gruyter, 1975.

Schechter, Solomon, ed. *Aboth de Rabbi Nathan*. New York: Philipp Feldheim, 1945.

Schürer, Emil. *The History of the Jewish People in the Age of Jesus Christ: A New English Version*. Revised and Edited by Gesa Vermes and Fergus Millar. Edinburgh: T. & T. Clark Ltd., 1973.

Seder Eliahu rabba and Seder Eliahu Zuta (Tanna d'be Eliahu): Pseudo-Seder Eliahu Zuta. Edited by M. Friedmann. Jerusalem: Bamberger & Wahrman, 1960.

Sefarim ha-Ḥiẓonim. Edited by Avraham Kahana. 2 vols. Tel Aviv, 1959.

Sefer Midrash Rabbah. Edited by I. Z. Yadler. Tel Aviv: Lipa Fridman, 1958-63.

Sefer Pirke Rabbi Eli'ezer. Edited by David Luria. Jerusalem: 1963 (Reprint).

Sefer Zohar Ḥadash. Leghorn, 1866.

Siphre ad Numeros adjecto Sifre zutta. Fasciculus primus from *Sifre de'be Rab.* Edited by H. S. Horovitz. Jerusalem: Wahrmann, 1966.

Smithsonian Institute. "Human Origins." http://humanorigins.si.edu/evidence/ humanfossils/species/homo-sapiens.

Strack, Herman L. *Introduction to the Talmud and Midrash.* Atheneum, NY: A Temple Book, 1969.

Apocalypse of Baruch: Edited from the Syriac. Edited by R. H. Charles. 1896.

Tabor, James D. "Introductory Remarks." *Religious Studies News* 10, no. 3 (1995): 3.

Tabor, James D., and Eugene B. Gallagher. *Why Waco? Cults and the Battle for Religious Freedom in America.* Berkeley: University of California Press, 1995.

Talbert, Charles. *Matthew.* Ada, MI: Baker Academic, 2010.

---. *What is a Gospel? The Genre of the Canonical Gospels.* Philadelphia: Fortress Press, 1977.

Talmud Babli. Vilna: Romm, 1886. (abbreviated: **BT**)

Tanḥuma Bereshit. See *Midrash Tanhuma.*

Targum Job. See *The Literature of Formative Judaism: The Targumim & Other Jewish Writings in Late Antiquity (Origins of Judaism).* And *The Bible in Aramaic.*

Targum Onkelos. See *The Literature of Formative Judaism: The Targumim & Other Jewish Writings in Late Antiquity (Origins of Judaism).* And *The Bible in Aramaic.*

Testament of Naphtali. See *The Testaments of the Twelve Patriots.*

Testament of Ruben. See *The Testaments of the Twelve Patriots.*

The Testament of Solomon. Edited by Chester C. McCown. Leipzig: J. C. Hinrichs, 1922.

The Testaments of the Twelve Patriots. Edited by R. H. Charles. Createspace, 2018.

Tosefta. Edited by M. S. Zuckermandel. Jerusalem: Bamberger and Wahrmann, 1937.

Toulmin, Stephen. *Knowing & Acting: An Invitation to Philosophy*. New York: Macmillan Publishing Co., 1976.

---. *The Uses of Argument*. London: Cambridge University Press, 1964.

The Treatise Ta'anit of the Babylonian Talmud. Edited by Henry Malter. Philadelphia: The Jewish Publication Society of America, 1967.

Urbach, E. E. *The Sages: Their Concepts and Beliefs*. 2 vols. Translated by Israel Abrahams. Jerusalem: Magnes Press (Hebrew University), 1975

Volz, Paul. *Die Eschatologie der Jüdischen Gemeinde im neutestamentlichen Zeitalter*. Hildescheim: Georg Olms Verlagsbuchhandlung, 1966.

Weaver, Richard M. *The Ethics of Rhetoric*. South Bend, IN: Henry Regnery, 1953.

Wells. *The Books of Adam and Eve*. In *The Apocrypha and Pseudepigrapha of the Old Testament*, Edited by R. H. Charles. Volume II: Pseudepigrapha, 137. Oxford: At the Clarendon Press, 1913.

Wikgren, Allen. *Hellenistic Greek Texts*. Chicago & London: The University of Chicago Press, 1947.

Wickham, L. R. "The Sons of God and the Daughters of Men: Genesis VI 2 in Early Christian Exegesis." In *Language and Meaning*. Edited by J. Barr, *et.al.* Oudtestamentliche Studien 19, 135-47. Leiden: E. J. Brill, 1974.

Yadin, Yigael. *The Scroll of the War of the Sons of Light Against the Sons of Darkness*. Oxford, 1962.

Yalkut Shimoni al Torah. Jerusalem.

Yalkut Shimoni. Vol. IV, 127-28 of *Beth ha-Midrasch*. Edited by A. Jellinek, (Contains Yalkut Shimoni I N. 44 only). Jerusalem. Wahrmann, 1967.

Yamauchi, Edwin M. *Pre-Christian Gnosticism*. Grand Rapids, MI: Wm. B. Eerdsmans Publishing Company, 1973.

Zeitlin, Solomon. *The Rise and Fall of the Judaean State*. 2 vols. Philadelphia: The Jewish Publication Society of America, 5728-1968.

Angels and Demons: The Personification of Communication (Logology)

Scripture Index

Genesis
- --10
- 1:3—xii, xiii, 153
- 1:26—87, 100, 143
- 3:1-8—xv
- 3:6—183
- 3:15—110
- 5—54
- 5:24—84
- 6—8, 27, 69, 73, 80-83, 86-87, 142
- 6:2—32, 34, 73, 82
- 6:4—64, 73, 82
- 6:6—64, 92
- 18:5—47-48
- 19—31
- 19:5—31
- 21:17—177
- 22:11-12—177
- 28:12—34, 126

Exodus
- 20:1-17—23-29
- 20:3—185
- 22:28—82, 85, 142

Leviticus
- --10
- 16:7-10—7

Numbers
- 13:33—86-87
- 22—177

Deuteronomy
- 6:4—185

Judges
- 13:8ff.—177
- 19:5—47

1 Samuel
- 20:19—11

1 Kings
- 19:7—177

2 Chronicles
- 32:21—177

Ezra
- --118

Nehemiah
- --118

Esther
- --118

Job
- --19, 69, 142

1:6—140

4:18—73

15:15—73

Psalms

33:9—xiii, 153

48:14—47-48

82—142-143

82:6—82-83, 85, 142

85—161

85:10-13—161

85:11-12a—xviii, 133, 145, 157

85:12a—135, 158

90:4—120

90:15—120

104:4—31, 189

104:15—47

Isaiah

--123

2:2-5—122

6:2—34

11—122

14—98

14:1-6—97

14:12—21, 141

14:12-14—4, 91-92, 94, 100

14:12-15—96

14:18-20—96-97, 141

37—177

55:11—xii, 153, 156

55:10-11—xiii

Jeremiah

30:10—127, 129, 130

Daniel

--118, 123, 177

2:31—130

7:10—151

7:13-18—122

8—161

8:12—146, 158, 161-163

10—71

Matthew

--71

1:20-23—175

3:17—170

4:23—180

4:23-25—204-205, 209

8:2-4—204

8:5-13—204

8:14-17—204, 209

8:28-32—198

8:28-34—180, 205

9:1-8—204

9:27-34—210

10:1—206

10:8—206

11:2-19—204

11:19—210

11:20-25—97-98

11:23—97

12:9-14—204

12:22-32—206

12:22-37—210

12:26—181

12:27—192, 198

12:38-45—209

12:45—208

14:34-36—204

17:5—170

17:14-20—200, 205

17:18—205

20:29-34—204

22:30—48, 69

22:36-40—41

Mark

—71

1:21-28—205

1:29-34—204

1:29-39—209

1:40-45—204

2:1-12—204

3:1-6—204

3:19-30—210

3:20-30—206

3:23-26—181

5:1-17—198

5:1-20—180, 205

6:7—206

6:13—206

6:53-56—204

9:14-29—200, 205

10:46-52—204

12:25—48, 69

19:17-25—181, 191

Luke

—71

1:11-20—176

1:13—176

1:26-38—175

2:25-38—171

2:41—43

17:18—205

4:31-37—205

4:38-41—204, 209

5:12-16—204

5:17-26—204

6:6-11—204

7:1-10—204

7:18-35—204, 206

7:33-34—210

8:1-3—206

8:2—180

8:26-33—198

8:26-39—180, 205

8:35—198

9:1—206

9:37-43—200, 205

6:17-19—180, 205

7:18-35—204

7:11-17—204

10:8-15—98

10:18—3, 22

11:14-23—206

11:18—181

11:19—192,   198

12:10—206

13:10-21—203

13:11—181, 191

17:11-37—204

18:15-43—204

18:18-21—43

20:35—69

20:36—48

22:31—20

John

1:1-3—xii, xiii

1:5-47—204

1:51—125, 145

4:46-54—204

7:20—210

8:37-44—25, 143

8:48-52—210

8:44—xviii, 28, 182

9:1-41—204

10:20-21—210

10:33-36—82-83, 142-143

11:1-44—204

14:16-17—166

14:26—166

15:26—166

16:7—166

16:13—164, 166

Acts

—55

9:5-6—170

10:31—176

12—176

16:16—181

17:18—210

19—210

19:13—192, 198

19:15-16—209

Romans

3:23—26, 144

5:11—11

6:23—26, 144

Ephesians

6:17—166

1 Corinthians

5:5—21

8:4—xix, 187, 196

8:4-6—186

8:13—186

10:18-26—186

12:7-13—100

15:45-47—102

2 Corinthians

4:4—103

Galatians

4:6-7—69

Colossians

1:15—103

1 Timothy

1:20—21, 26

Hebrews

—55

1:6—102

1:7—189

2:14—26, 144

4:15—43

11:5—54, 84

James

—55

1:13—21

1:13-14—183

1:14-15—xv

1 Peter

—55

3:17-20—58

3:18, 20—59

3:19—163

3:19-20—60, 77

5:8—109, 136

2 Peter

—53-58, 60, 68, 76, 158

2:1-9—59

2:4—51, 54, 61, 76

3:8, 10—120

1 John

—55

3:8—26, 143

4:1—xix, 166, 180

4:6—xix, 166, 180

2 John

—55

3 John

—55

Jude

—53, 55-58, 68, 76, 158

3-7—59

6—51, 54

14—83

Revelation

—55, 119, 123, 126, 147, 150

1:5—112

1:4—112

1:8—112

1:17-18—112

2—149

2:8—112

3—149

3:14—112

4:8—112

4—111, 113

5—104, 111, 113

5:1—111

5:5—112, 127

5:6, 12—112

5:9—112

5:10—127

5:13—112

5:13-14—103

7:4-8—127

9:20—214

11:17—112

12—26, 28-29, 101, 110, 145

12:7-9—103

12:7-12—22

12:7-13—100-101, 107

12:9—136, 164

12:10—109

12:12-13—101

12:9—2

13—18, 104

13:15—104

14:1—127

15:3—112

16:7, 14—112

16:12-13—214

19:12-13—xiii

19:6, 15—112

20—26

20:1-3—116

20:2-3—121

20:3—121

20:7-8—117, 121

21:2—127

21:6—112

21:22—112

22:5—127

22.13—xii, 112

Acts of John

—55

Acts of Paul

—55

Agadat Bereshit

—66

Introduction, p. 38—135

The Apocalypse of Baruch

21.6—1

Apocalypse of Peter

—55

Apocalypsis Mosis

—164

27.5—163

The Babylonian Talmud

—94

Sanhedrin 38b—136, 162

Sanhedrin 91b—41

Shabbat 88b-89a—49, 135

Yoma 82a—42

*Beres[c]hit Rabbah (Abbreviated: **BR**)*

   1.3—1
   3.8—1
   8.5—xviii, 133, 145, 157

   8.10—111

   11.9—1

   25:1—83

   26.5—82

   27:4—64, 92-93

   48.11—20, 47-48, 67

   68end—130

*Beth ha-Midrasch (abbreviated: **BHM**)*

   --20, 33, 67, 83

   V,156—74, 145

The Book of Jubilees

   2.2—1

   4.22—74

   5.1—74

   7.21—74

   10.5—74

The Books of Adam and Eve
   See: *The Life of Adam and Eve (Vita Adae et Evae)*

The Chronicles of Jerahmeel

   --67

   53—135

Damaskusschriften

   3.4—74

The Didache

   --55

I Enoch

   --10, 12, 53, 59, 68, 80, 156

   6f.—74

   6-8—94

   10.4, 6—162

   12.4, 15—74

   15:3—8

   18:15-16—94

   21—162

   21.4—162

   54:5—8, 54, 140

   65:6-7—8, 27

   69.2-4—74

   84:4—72, 74

   86.1-6—74

II Enoch

   7.1-3—74

   18—94

   18.3-5—74

   29.3—1

   29.4-5—2

3 Enoch (or) The Hebrew Book of Enoch

   --94

   88.1, 3—163

The Ethiopic Book of Enoch

   --213

Gospel of the Egyptians

   --55

Gospel of the Hebrews

   --55

Gospel of Peter

   --55

Gospel of Thomas

   --55

Hadar Zekenim

   Genesis 6:2—32

Jerusalem Talmud

   --3

Josephus, Antiquities

1:31—74

Justin. "Dialogue with Trypho."

    Dialogue 79—50, 93, 141-142

Kohelet Rabbah

    6.10—110

Koran

    --64

    Vol. I, pp.24ff. (Abdullah Usuf Ali, tr.)

Letter of Barnabas

    --55

The Life of Adam and Eve (Vita Adae et Evae)

    --99-102, 111, 143, 164

    12-17—105-107

    12.1—163

    13-14—104

    16.1—163

2 Maccabees

    8:4—43

Midrash Ha-Gadol: Bereshit/Midrash Hag-Gadol Genesis

    108-109—41

Midrash Kohelet Rabbah

    4:13—41

Midrash Konen

    25—1

Midrash Rabbah: Bereshith

    58—146

Midrash Shir ha-Shirim Rabbah

    2.1—132

    8.11—49, 135

    15.22—1

Midrash Tanhuma

    I,23f.—82

    I,30—65, 93

    Bereshit I.1&12—1

    Bereshit 4b—44

Midrash Tehillim (Schocher Tob)

    8:74—50, 75, 135

    9,82—42

    24,204, 76,373-374, and 104,442—1

    78,347—129

Midrash Wayyikra Rabbah

    23:9—82

    29:2—128-129

The Mishnah

    --3

    Yoma 8:4—38, 43-44

    Yoma 67b—11

Pesikta de-Rab Kahana (Abbreviated: **PRK**)

    Piska 23:2—126-127, 129, 145

    61b—44

Pesikta Rabbati

    16 (84a)—44

    25 (128a)—50, 135

Philo Judaeus, On the Giants

    6—74, 82

Pirke Rabbi Eliezer

    4—1

    13-14—136

Sefer Olam Rabbah

    Chapter 1, beginning—83

Septuagint

    --69

Siphre Zuta

    On Numbers, sect. 86—82

Shepherd of Hermas

Syriac Apocalypse of Baruch

    --55

    56.12—74

Targum Job

    28.7—2

Targum Neofiti

    —82

Targum Onkelos

    On Genesis 6—82

Testament of Naphtali

    3.4—74

Testament of Ruben

    5.6—74

The Testament of Solomon

    --75-76

    5:3—74

Yalkut

    I, p. 44—66, 135

Zohar Hadash
    11b and 12a—2

Index

Abraham 48, 71, 97, 124, 167-8, 177

Action xiv-xvi, 43, 126, 190

Adam xiv, 9, 11, 24, 37, 42, 54, 71, 84-5, 88, 99-107, 109-111, 113, 115, 136-7, 143, 154, 167, 208

AGGADAH 56, 58-60, 68, 158, 162, 213, 215

Altercasting 200

Anamartetous Fallen Angels xii, 13

Anecdote 19, 56

Animal xv-xvi, xx, 1, 37-9, 41, 44, 87-9, 167, 189

Animality xv, xvii, 87-9

ArguMentor 57

Aristotle xi, xviii, 56-7

Atheism/ist 196

Audience ix, 11, 57-9, 70, 76, 173-4, 191

Authority/tative 14, 44, 83, 93, 102, 190, 216

Babylon (-ian Diaspora) xiii, 17-8, 97-8, 118, 121, 127, 130, 141

Babylonian Talmud 41-2, 49, 135-6

Baptism 20

Bar[Bat]-Mitzvah 38, 43

BAT QOL 170, 180, 182

Beast 18, 84-5, 103-4, 119, 155, 214-5

Blasphemy 82, 93, 142

Burke, Kenneth xi-xvii, xx, xxii, 5-6, 20, 57, 87, 89, 153-4, 156, 179-81, 185, 187, 189-90, 196

Caesar 18, 118-9, 213

Caird, G. B. 149-50, 166, 214

Category xvii, 82, 175-6, 191

Chariot 110

Charles, R. H. 102, 104-5

Choi, Charles 89

Choice x, xiv-xvi, xviii, 4, 39, 154

Coincidence 6, 174

Consistent/inconsistent 4, 48, 109

Counterargument 196, 200

Counterpart 64, 68, 89

Create/ion 2, 9-10, 24, 39, 63, 65, 73, 84, 88, 92, 106, 110, 112, 133-7, 145-6, 149, 151, 153-60, 162, 167, 175, 197

Creed 3, 141

Culture/al ix, xiii, 3, 5, 8-12, 15, 17, 27, 32, 54, 57, 59, 70, 100, 115, 121, 124, 132, 140-1, 143, 205, 210

David, King of Israel 169-70

Debunk 18

Deductive reasoning 57

Deliberative rhetoric xviii, 56

Dialectics xvii

Disneology 153, 159

Disney 153, 159

Dragon 101-2, 107, 117, 121, 131, 214

Elijah 170, 177

Empirical 208, 210

Enoch 8, 10, 12, 27, 31, 53-54, 59-60, 65, 67-9, 72, 74-5, 77, 80, 83-5, 94, 99, 141, 156, 162-3, 213, 215

Enthymeme 57

Epideictic rhetoric 57

Evangelical 173

Faith 59, 84, 200

Fischel, Henry vii, xxi-xxii, 3, 5, 63-4, 111, 121

Force xix-xx, 20, 155-6, 159, 188-9, 207, 215

Fossil 87

Free will x, xiv-xvi, xviii, 4, 38-9, 149, 154, 159-60

Friends, friendship 9, 17, 118, 120

Ginzberg, Louis 20, 41, 67, 76, 83, 100, 102, 104, 136, 151, 155, 158

Gog and Magog 117

Guilty xviii, 22-3, 29, 32-3, 44, 55, 137

Hagar 168

Hands 107, 203, 211, 215

Hellenistic 2-3, 5, 8, 14, 18, 32, 64, 74, 82, 118, 121, 141, 197

Hierarchy 10, 39

History/ical/icity 2, 17-8, 55-8, 95, 116, 119-21, 126, 128, 132, 145, 167-9, 197, 215

Holy Spirit 113, 165-6

Hypnosis xx, 189, 191, 193

Image   24, 87-8, 100-1, 103-6, 109-10, 113, 130, 143, 159, 188

Indiana University   xxi, xxii, 3, 13, 63-4, 111, 123

Inductive   56-7

Innocent/s   33, 44, 65-8, 74-5, 135, 186-7

Internal summary   139

Isaiah   x, xii-xiii, 4, 21, 34, 91-2, 94, 96-8, 100-1, 122-3, 141, 153, 156, 170, 177

Islam   xxii, 64, 124

Ishmael   177

John the Baptist   171, 176, 210

Judicial rhetoric   xviii, 57

Jwaideh, Wadie   xxii, 64

Koran   64, 136

Lake   198-9

Lake of Fire   26, 116, 151

Lamb   110-2, 122, 145

Lincoln Christian University   xxi

Logos   xiii

Lucifer   x, 4, 21, 91-2, 94-8, 100, 141

Lutheran   44

Messiah   119, 169

Mishnah   34, 38, 43-44

Moral/morality   39, 50, 56, 73, 132, 155, 159

Moses   49, 120, 167-9, 207

Music   81, 206

Naʻarah   33, 38, 42

Narrative   43, 56-7

Neanderthal   88

Negative/s   xiv-xv, xvii-xviii, xx, 22, 154, 180-1, 215

Roberts, Oral   192

Pain principal   37

Parable   50, 58, 110, 209

Paradigm   56-7

Paris   58

Pharisees/aic   170, 210

Phenomenon/a   xi, 206

Philo   74

Philosophy   3, 89, 197

Physics   xiv, xix

Pleasure principle   37, 159

Political   xvii, 56, 97-8, 162

Postmodern/ism   165

Prayer   63, 71, 173-7, 208

Premise/s   5, 69, 83, 156, 167, 170

Priest   11, 81, 104, 166, 169, 177, 195-6, 214-5

Progressive   115, 147

Prophet/-cy   17, 22, 41, 47, 81, 118, 122, 132, 165-6, 169-71, 179-82, 185, 200, 214

Psychotic   198-9

Qur-an   136

Rabbi Simon   158, 161-3, 176

Rabbinic (Judaism) vii, ix-xii, xvi, xxi-xxii, 1, 3-5, 15, 19-20, 48, 50, 66-7, 69, 72, 82-3, 89, 92, 116, 118-9, 121, 131, 133, 135-6, 146, 163, 165, 170

Renaissance 123-4, 130

Resurrection 14, 23, 43, 48, 69-70

Revelation xii-xiii, 18-9, 22, 26, 28-9, 55, 71, 100-4, 107, 109-13, 115-6, 119, 121, 126-7, 131, 136, 143-7, 149-50, 164, 182, 203, 210, 213-16

Rite, The x, 4, 195-6, 200

River of Fire 151

Sabbath 25

Sacrifice xix, 26, 28, 161, 167, 177, 186-7, 213

Sadducees 170

Samaritans 58, 170

Sampley, Paul xxii, 64, 68-71

Saul of Tarsus 170

Saul (King) 169

Scenario 58, 88, 184

Simon Peter 20, 71, 176, 215

Son of God 82, 89, 142, 198-9

Sons of God 8, 10, 19, 25, 27, 31, 34, 69-70, 79-89, 140, 142

Spiritual gift/s 169, 171, 180, 182, 191, 196

Stoic/ism 210

Stress 20

Stream of Fire 151

Suicide 199, 207, 214

Symbol/icity, s.-using xv, xx, 87-9, 150, 153, 179-80, 189-92

Talmud 3, 11, 42, 49, 76, 83, 94, 116, 135-6

Tanach 170

Tanna/itic xxi, 3, 15, 83, 116, 128-9, 131-2

Ten Commandments xiv, 23, 29, 43, 154

Testimony 107, 110

Theory/ist 5, 63, 87, 153

Tool-using 8, 88, 140

Value/s 57

Victim/s 205, 209

Wrong, doing xvii, 58, 68-9, 71-2

Yom Kippur 43

YouTube xix

www.ingramcontent.com/pod-product-compliance
Lightning Source LLC
Chambersburg PA
CBHW081803300426
44116CB00014B/2225